Praise for
The Customer Loyalty Solution

"Arthur blows past the CRM hype and lays out the best of database marketing, presenting case study after case study of how to do it right (and sometimes not so right!). His integration of current marketing strategies, database marketing techniques, and how the Internet really helps database marketers provides new insights that everyone will learn from. Required reading!"

> —*Eric Webster, Assistant Vice President, Customer Marketing, State Farm Insurance*

"Provocative, stimulating, interesting, and loaded with case studies from dozens of companies, Arthur's book should be the bible for anyone doing cutting-edge database marketing today."

> —*Mike Brostoff, Chairman, CSC Advanced Database Solutions*

"An interesting and entertaining read which provides practical insights into the evolving world of Database Marketing/CRM. Arthur's ability to bring focus to the day-to-day challenges (and misconceptions) of the discipline makes the book a great resource for the experienced database marketer as well as the novice practitioner."

> —*Robert Burgess, Group Manager-Customer Relationship Management, Verizon Information Services*

"A lifetime's worth of experience and understanding packed into a fun and easy read for the novice and the expert. Add the excellent examples of companies that have been able to 'make it work,' and you have an invaluable resource for anyone seeking to succeed in their 1-to-1 or database marketing efforts. A must have for today's marketing manager."

> —*Kay M. Madati, Relationship Marketing Manager, BMW of North America, LLC*

Also by Arthur Middleton Hughes

The American Economy, 1968
The American Economy, 2d ed., 1969
The Complete Database Marketer, 1991
Strategic Database Marketing, 1994
The Complete Database Marketer, 2d ed., 1996
*Don't Blame Little Arthur; Blame the Damn Fool Who Entrusted Him
 with the Eggs*, 1999
Strategic Database Marketing, 2d ed., 2000

THE CUSTOMER LOYALTY SOLUTION

What Works (and What Doesn't)
in Customer Loyalty Programs

Arthur Middleton Hughes

McGraw-Hill

New York   Chicago   San Francisco   Lisbon   London
Madrid   Mexico City   Milan   New Delhi   San Juan
Seoul   Singapore   Sydney   Toronto

ISBN: 0-07-136366-1

This publication is designed to provide accurate and authoritative information in regard to the subject matter covered. It is sold with the understanding that neither the author nor the publisher is engaged in rendering legal, accounting, or other professional service. If legal advice or other expert assistance is required, the services of a competent professional person should be sought.
—From a Declaration of Principles jointly adopted by a Committee of the American Bar Association and a Committee of Publishers

All trademarked products mentioned in this book are used in an editorial fashion only, and to the benefit of the trademark owner, with no intention of infringement of the trademark. Where such designations appear in this book, they have been printed with initial caps.

McGraw-Hill books are available at special quantity discounts to use as premiums and sales promotions, or for use in corporate training programs. For more information, please write to the Director of Special Sales, Professional Publishing, McGraw-Hill, Two Penn Plaza, New York, NY 10121-2298. Or contact your local bookstore.

Library of Congress Cataloging-in-Publication Data

Hughes, Arthur Middleton.
    Winning the war for customers : what works and what doesn't in customer loyalty programs / by Arthur Middleton Hughes.
        p.   cm.
    ISBN 0-07-136366-1 (hardcover)
    1. Database marketing.   2. Customer loyalty programs.   I. Title.
HF5415.126 .H845 2003
658.8'4—dc21
                                        2002011493

This book is printed on recycled, acid-free paper containing a minimum of 50% recycled de-inked fiber.

For my wife, Helena,
and her two brothers and sisters-in-law,
Fernando Errázuriz Guzmán and María Eugenia Oyarzún
José Miguel Errázuriz Guzmán and Mónica Lopez,
who gave me the opportunity to write this book in Chile in 2002

CONTENTS

INTRODUCTION TO DATABASE MARKETING

Database marketing as we know it today began in the early 1980s. Its rise was chronicled and boosted by the National Center for Database Marketing, which was started by Skip Andrew in 1987 and has continued to hold conferences twice a year ever since. At first, many companies had heard of it, but few were actually practicing it. By 1995, however, every American company knew what it was, and most had appointed a director of database marketing. The practitioners became like religious converts. They *believed* in it.

Inside industry, some companies, including Kraft Foods, American Airlines (and many other airlines), American Express, Hallmark, JC Penney, Neiman Marcus, MCI, and scores of others, formed huge databases. The idea was that the company could reach its customers directly (instead of through mass marketing) and build their loyalty by direct communications. In most cases, it worked. Marketers soon learned how to set up control groups to prove whether what they were doing was working. They became skillful at what they were doing.

At first, these large databases were maintained on mainframes, with smaller databases kept on midrange computers. With the advent of the PC and servers, however, all large databases moved to servers, and small databases were maintained on PCs. Companies that kept their data on mainframes found that they were having considerable trouble keeping up with the twists and turns of the database marketing revolution.

One twist was the need to create a relational database, which is the optimum format for database marketing. What that means is that for each customer, we want to be able to keep all that customer's transactions and demographics available, organized in tables for easy access and use in marketing. We append external data and add surveys, profiles, and preferences. The mainframe programmers just could not keep up. Today, all large databases are maintained on servers using Oracle or SQL Server. There are also a number of good database software packages for PCs.

The advent of the Web has made the greatest change in database marketing since it began. The Web has meant that

- Marketers can access databases directly from their desktop PCs, using the Web.
- Many companies have Web sites where customers can view and order products.
- Customers can contact companies not only by calling toll-free numbers, but also through the Web, which saves companies millions of dollars.
- Companies can communicate with their customers frequently at almost no expense by using email. The result is many more communications, leading to increased loyalty and sales.
- Business-to-business use of the Web has exploded, leading in some cases to vendor-managed inventory, in which suppliers keep track of what their customers have in stock and help them to become successful.

There have been a number of wrong turns, which are described in this book:

- Selling to consumers on the Web proved to be a major disappointment, although the Web is an excellent ordering and customer contact medium.
- Customer relationship marketing (CRM) based on the idea of one-to-one marketing using a massive data warehouse, which many thought would be an advanced method of database marketing, proved to be an expensive failure.

- Packaged goods manufacturers discovered that there was no profit, and in fact considerable losses, from maintaining a database of ultimate customers. The increase in sales from personal communication did not pay for the expense of the messages and the database.
- Marketers learned that they should use their databases to create customer segments and treat each segment differently. Treating all customers alike was a loser, since customers differed markedly in their profitability.

Valuable lessons have been learned. The purpose of this book is to describe what works and what doesn't work in database marketing. Too many books describe only the success stories without talking about the failures. In each chapter of this book, you will find a list of what works and what has failed to work.

Figure I-1 What Works and What Doesn't Work

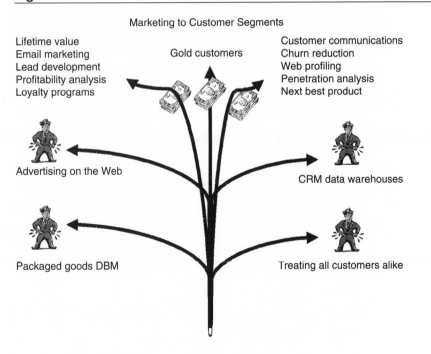

Marketing to Customer Segments

Lifetime value
Email marketing
Lead development
Profitability analysis
Loyalty programs

Gold customers

Customer communications
Churn reduction
Web profiling
Penetration analysis
Next best product

Advertising on the Web

CRM data warehouses

Packaged goods DBM

Treating all customers alike

The book contains more than 40 cases from practitioners throughout the United States, Canada, Australia, and Norway. I chose these particular cases because each of them describes the difficulties that had to be overcome and the way success was measured. Each one makes a point. Probably the key point is that success does not come from simply doing the following:

- Building a database
- Appending data
- Buying expensive software
- Running models
- Communicating with customers

Success comes from developing intelligent strategies that build customer loyalty and repeat sales. To be successful, database marketers have to think like customers and say, "Why would I want to be in that database? What is in it for me?"

Then they have to dream up strategies that they think will build customer loyalty. They have to test these strategies on a small scale, using test and control groups. They have to be constantly coming up with new ideas because they are competing with other marketers who will copy anything that works and destroy its novelty.

Database marketers constantly work with tiny response rates. Of course, everyone has heard of marketers who have gotten responses of 20 or 30 percent, but that is very rare. Instead, 2 percent is a good response rate for a direct-mail offer, and 1 percent is a good response rate for an email offer. Some marketers get up every day and go to work knowing that they will not get better than $\frac{1}{10}$ of 1 percent response on anything that they do, but they keep on going because in many cases that rate is enough for profitability.

Incrementalism

One of the first things to remember about database marketing is that its benefits are incremental. Every company that uses database marketing successfully has another profitable sales channel already working for it, such as retail stores, mass marketing, catalogs, or sales through dealers or agents. The company uses the profits made through these other channels to build the database and develop the communications that make it work. The idea in database marketing is that you can increase your profits by an incremental amount through building customer relationships and information that have the result of

- Increasing the customer retention rate or repurchase rate
- Increasing referrals
- Increasing the cross sales and up-sales
- Using the customer profile to find more loyal and responsive prospects

The database does not have to bear the full responsibility for sales—that is done by the other channels. What the database does is to increase those sales by a certain percentage. The incremental amount is seldom massive—perhaps 5 to 10 percent is all. But that 5 percent can be very profitable.

Marketers have learned how to measure profitability and lifetime value. There are many examples of this in this book. Marketers have learned to determine who their Gold customers are and how to retain them. They have learned to use recency, frequency, monetary (RFM) analysis to determine which customers are most likely to respond to offers. They have learned many rules, such as the following:

- Giving customers a choice in a direct offer *always* reduces response.
- Don't market to Gold customers, work to retain them.
- Don't treat all customers the same way—save your resources to reward your best ones.
- Always set up control groups to measure your success—if you don't, you can't prove that what you have done has really worked.
- Compute the lifetime value of your customers and put it into the customer records so that you can use it to evaluate the success of your marketing strategy.

- The more products you sell to customers, the higher their retention rate will be.
- Customers like to receive communications. Almost any communication will increase sales and retention rates.
- Referred customers have higher lifetime values and retention rates than the average customer.
- Offering discounts to attract new customers produces disloyal customers.
- Use the Web and email as a powerful two-way customer contact medium.

You will have fun with this book—reading the chapters, taking the quizzes, and using the charts. All the numerical charts in this book can be downloaded free from www.dbmarketing.com, where you will find the answers to the quizzes, more than 100 magazine articles, free software, and a lot more.

If done properly, database marketing will be fun for both the customer and the marketer. It is an intriguing game of communication and life. Enjoy it while you increase your sales and profits.

I will be glad to hear from any readers on any subject at any time. You may reach me at dbmarkets@aol.com. Point out mistakes in the book, ask for help with marketing, or send me a case study that I can use in a future book.

Arthur Middleton Hughes
Vice President for Business Development
CSC Advanced Database Solutions
2100 South Ocean Drive, Suite 16A
Fort Lauderdale, FL 33316
dbmarkets@aol.com
November 2002

ACKNOWLEDGMENTS

In addition to the many people mentioned in this book, I want to recognize the special contribution of several individuals who have been instrumental in providing me with the ideas that have shaped my knowledge of database marketing:

- Paul Wang, Associate Professor of Database Marketing at Northwestern University. Paul and I gave 28 two-day seminars together from 1994 to 2000. Paul is an outstanding teacher and a great friend.
- Bob McKim and Evelyn Schlaphoff at msdbm in Los Angeles, where I worked for 2 years. Bob and Evie taught me a great deal about the use of the Web for database marketing. Their ideas illuminate these pages.
- Fredrick Reichheld, Professor at Harvard Business School, whose book *The Loyalty Effect* completely revised my thinking in a number of crucial areas.
- Beth Clough, Director of Partner Relations at msdbm, a good friend and an expert on database marketing, who provided valuable help in the editing of this book.
- Mike Brostoff, CEO of CSC Advanced Database Solutions in Schaumburg, Illinois, who has run this highly successful database company for 20 years. Mike and Jeff Lundal of CSC invited me to work there as vice president for business development. I have been thrilled to join their team to spread the good word on database marketing throughout the world.

CHAPTER 1

HOW DATABASE MARKETING WORKS

This is my fifth book on database marketing. My first, *The Complete Database Marketer*, was published in 1991. As I write each subsequent book, I am constantly amazed at the changes that have taken place in the techniques and the uses of database marketing. Today is no exception. There is so much that is new and different that we are almost talking about an entirely new marketing method.

How It Began

I like to repeat the story of the genesis of database marketing. It got its start in a big way in the early 1980s, when mass mailers such as American Express and State Farm Insurance started using their customer lists to build ongoing relationships with their customers after the initial sale, leading to increased retention and cross sales. But the roots of database marketing go back to a period in the United States before there were supermarkets.

Back in those days, all the groceries in the United States were sold in small corner grocery stores. The proprietors knew their customers' names. They would stand at the door and greet their customers by name as they entered, asking them about their families and their concerns. They put things aside for customers, helped them carry heavy packages out to their cars, and built strong and lasting relationships. They built their businesses by developing and cultivating the loyalty of their customers.

These fellows are all gone today. They were forced out of business by the supermarkets. Mass marketing took over, along with mass production. Prices came down. Quality, quantity, and variety went up. The average corner grocer had 800 stockkeeping units (SKUs) in his store. The average supermarket today has more than 30,000 SKUs. The change affected the way Americans lived. In 1950 the average American family was spending 31 percent of its household budget on food. Today the average family is spending only 14 percent on food, and the food it is getting is better in both quantity and quality than the food it was spending 31 percent on 50 years ago. Because of the lowered cost of food, families have much more money to spend on hundreds of other products that were out of the question 50 years ago. So we have all gained.

At the same time, we as suppliers have all lost. We have thousands, hundreds of thousands, or millions of customers, but we don't know them, and they don't know us. Loyalty has gone out the window. If you talk to an employee in a supermarket, you are interrupting his regular work, which is certainly not standing by the entrance and chatting with the customers. You are loyal to that supermarket until tomorrow's newspaper, when a certificate from somewhere else leads you to drive to another store.

In the mid-1980s, computers came into wide use. This development enabled merchants to begin to bring back some of the intimacy that prevailed in the presupermarket days. The software and hardware became increasingly sophisticated, and their prices have been in a free fall for years. As a result, it is now possible to keep, economically, in a computer the kind of information on customers that the old corner grocer used to keep in his head and to use that to build lasting, profitable relationships with customers.

Many companies have collected huge amounts of data about customers and their transactions, but they have failed to make profitable use of these data. There is one principle that has remained true throughout the period since 1985: Database marketing is effective in building customer loyalty and repeat sales only if the customer benefits from it. The customer has to think, "I'm glad that I'm in that database because . . .," with the supplier filling in a meaningful end to the sentence. If the database does not touch the customer's life in some way that is satisfying to her, she will ignore the communications, leave her gold card behind when she shops, and refuse to become loyal. Too many companies have ignored that principle and, as a result, have failed to succeed in database marketing.

How to Touch a Customer's Life

How do you touch a customer's life using a database? There are many ways, some of them so simple that we overlook them. When I fly into San Francisco, check into a Hyatt hotel, and push the button for room service, the response is, "Yes, Mr. Hughes. What can I get you to eat?" I have been in this hotel for less than 20 minutes, yet down in the kitchen they already know and use my name! This is possible because Hyatt, like most other hotels today, has Caller ID on its internal hotel telephone system. When you push that button in your room, the Caller ID goes to the database that Hyatt created when you checked in and pulls up the information, "Arthur Hughes, Room 1202" on the screen so that room service can call you by name. This is database marketing. It is what the old corner grocers used to do, and it is now made possible by modern technology used in a creative way. You are 2000 miles from home, yet people know you and recognize you. It makes you feel great!

Caller ID, of course, is not just for hotels. Customer service departments throughout America are using it to recognize customers when they make repeat calls. With this technique, before a call is answered, the database showing the customer's complete purchase history, demographics, and preferences is brought up on the customer service rep's screen, so that he can respond, "Mrs. Webster. So nice to hear from you again. How did your granddaughter like that sweater you gave her last October?" This is the kind of thing the old corner grocer used to say, and we can say it today. But there is a new twist: Using cookies, we are able to personalize our Web sites so that customers get the same type of personal greeting when they return to Amazon.com, Barnes & Noble, Staples, Office Depot, and hundreds of other Web sites. Database marketing today has techniques that make its promise come alive.

How We Have Changed

There are scores of different examples in the pages of this book. The principles are the same, but the methods have changed considerably in the past 15 years:

- When database marketing began, major databases were built on a mainframe. Today they are built on a server using Oracle or SQL Server.
- In the beginning, most databases were maintained by the information technology (IT) department or a service bureau and could not be accessed directly by marketers. When access was available, it was by terminals linked to the database by telephone lines. Today, marketers using PCs access databases over the Web.
- Data used to enter the databases in batch mode as keypunchers copied customer responses received through the mail. Even telemarketers entered data onto temporary disks, which were later used to update the mainframe database in batch mode. Today customers place their orders and update their profiles on the Web, through a Web page connected with a database on a server. Many telemarketers also work directly with live data on the same server.
- Database reports used to be produced monthly by programmers and sent to the users in hard copy. Today, marketers have a menu of reports on their screens, which they can run every day and print from their desktop PC printers.
- In the past, to select customers and prospects from a database, marketers would send detailed memoranda to the programmers. Upon receipt of these memoranda, programmers would write computer programs to select the desired records and send reports on the results to the marketers by fax. The process used to take a couple of weeks. Today, using E.piphany and other advanced applications, marketers select their own records for promotions using their PCs through the Web, without the need for IT assistance. The selected records can be automatically downloaded to the marketer through the Web or saved for downloading by the mail shop or the e-blasting vendor. The process takes a few minutes.

- Data appending was rare and was done mainly by the largest companies. Today, many companies add demographic data (age, income, presence of children, credit ratings, and scores of other facts) to their customer database routinely. Business-to-business marketers add Dun & Bradstreet (D&B) data (SIC code, annual sales, number of employees) to all customer and prospect files. These data are used for segmentation and crafting of marketing communications.
- Customer segmentation was rare. Few companies had identified their Gold customers, or knew what to do with them once they were identified. Today many companies have segmented their customer base and have developed different marketing strategies for each segment.
- Communication with customers was mostly by direct mail or telephone calls. Phone calls cost several dollars each. Letters were also expensive. As a result, communications with customers were limited to monthly statements and sales calls. Today, because of the Web, scores of additional possibilities for communication with customers have opened up. Customers order on the Web, are thanked for their order, receive a confirming email, are notified by email when products are shipped, and are surveyed to determine whether the products arrived and were satisfactory. All these messages were impossible when database marketing first began. Direct-marketing promotions were sent out by third-class mail in massive batches. They still are. But to this has been added email promotions to customers who have agreed to receive them. These email promotions cost almost nothing to send, compared to the heavy costs of direct mail.Customer preferences used to be requested through direct-mail or telephone surveys. These were expensive and, consequently, rare—they were used mostly for research rather than for customized communication. Today, customers can, and do, complete their personal profiles via the Web, so that outgoing communications can reflect their preferences.
- Customers used to call toll-free numbers to get information on product shipments or technical data, and to ask for all sorts of information that was stored in a company's internal records. They still do. Increasingly, however, companies are making that information

available to customers through the Web. This saves the companies millions of dollars per year and builds customer loyalty by giving the customers direct access to company archives.

• Models were rarely understood or used. Today all companies with products that involve churn, such as credit cards and cellular or long-distance telephone service, routinely use models to predict and forestall the canceling of service.

This is an exhausting list. It shows where we were and how far we have come. Perhaps the development that has changed database marketing most profoundly in the past two decades is the advent of the Web. Today we can do things that we only dreamed about doing 10 years ago. We can truly build customer relationships with almost as many personal communications as the old corner grocers used to have with their customers.

But Does It Work?

We can do all these things, but do they really produce more profits? This is an area in which great strides have been made. Most companies are acutely aware of the need to use control groups to validate the effectiveness of every single marketing strategy and initiative. In this book you will find more than 40 case studies that were completed in the past couple of years by companies that have been able to prove that their techniques are succeeding in building loyalty, increased sales, retention, repurchase, and reactivation. Customer communications work. Personalized communications work even better. Now, with the Web, we can afford to send millions of desired and accepted messages based on data and profiles in our databases that affect customer behavior in a positive way.

Combining the Database with the Web

Perhaps the most interesting shift in database marketing has been the fact that the database and a Web microsite can be located on the same server or can be electronically connected so that they seem to be on the same server. What this means is that the database and the microsite are not two separate entities, but part of a single customer response and communication vehicle. Cookies are placed on the customer's computer so that when she comes to our site, she sees a site that is configured for her, with things that she has requested to see. This is particularly important in business-to-business marketing. For example, Dell began the process by creating Premier Pages for all customers with 400 employees or more.

Dell salespeople contact the purchasing officer at each company and make a volume pricing deal that is hard to refuse: "We will create a Premier Page for your company on the Web. If you get your employees who need Dell products to use this page with passwords controlled by you, we will give them special prices that are not available to the general public. In addition, we will send you monthly reports on what your employees are buying and how much you are saving as a result of your volume pricing deal with Dell."

Thousands of companies are copying the Dell idea, setting up special Web pages for their best customers. The system builds sales and loyalty. Of course each purchase gets an on-screen thank you and confirmation that can be printed out on the employee's PC. The employee also gets a simultaneous confirming email, plus another email when the product is shipped. She gets a final email survey a few days later asking if the product has arrived and requesting her opinion of the process. This is powerful database marketing.

Web Response

Another impact of the Web on database marketing is in the area of response to communications. Before 1996, customers responded to marketing communications by phone, mail, or fax. Now more and more, people are coming to a Web microsite to respond. Because of cookies, the Web site knows who they are and greets them by name, just as the old corner grocer used to do.

The microsite is not really a Web site, but part of the database. The customer enters an order or responds to the survey questions posed in the communication, and the data go directly into the database. The database thanks the customer for the order, which is passed directly to the Web ordering system. It then sends the customer a confirming email. A customer who has previously provided credit card information can order by one click, instead of giving a name, address, and card number over and over again.

Why do customers prefer this system of response? Because they never get put on hold. They can get an instant response in 24/7 time without getting a busy signal or the message "Your call is very important to us. Please stay on the line." Why do companies prefer this type of response? Because it saves them millions of dollars. Each call to a live operator costs a company between $3 and $7 per call. Each response to a microsite has a variable cost of less than $0.02.

Customer Service

America leads the world in telephone customer service, but we pay a high price for it. Since the beginning of the database marketing revolution, every company provides a toll-free number for customers to call with any kind of question. Operators sitting at PCs or terminals linked to the customer database and to company data and archives receive these calls through an electronic call director. As customers ask questions, the operators key in commands on their keyboards and read the answers off their screens to the waiting customers. They also note in the customer database that the customer has called, and what the customer called about.

All this expensive service is changing as a result of the Web. Customers are being given access through the Web to the same information that the customer service reps are seeing on their screens. They are able to enter the same commands and get the same information without ever being put on hold. They can search for the status of their shipment, for the price and description of obscure needed parts and supplies, for the text of previously published articles and white papers. They can see and print maps, product descriptions, specifications, illustrations, and prices. This service builds customer loyalty and saves the company millions of dollars.

Computing Lifetime Value

Until 10 years ago, few companies used their databases to compute customer lifetime value. Banks began the process. They were able to determine the profitability of every account on a monthly basis, and to roll that up to compute household profitability. The results were used to segment customers in order to learn which ones were useful to the bank and which ones were reducing the bank's profits.

I like to use the chart shown in Figure 1-1. It comes from a major bank in the South that ranked all its customers by profitability. It shows that 80 percent of the bank's profits came from the top 5 percent of its customers. The bottom 28 percent lost 22 percent of its profits. This is very powerful information that was just not available before database marketing came along. What was even more powerful was what the bank was able to do with this information. Clearly the top 5 percent of customers had to be retained. The bank's whole future rested on these people. In addition, something had to change in the bank's marketing strategy for the bottom 28 percent. Why try to retain people who are costing the bank money?

Not just banks, but insurance companies, business-to-business marketers, and scores of other enterprises began to compute numbers like these and to develop strategies that made profitable use of them. Many companies went on to determine potential lifetime value by using computer models to determine all the other products that each customer

Figure 1-1   Profits by Customer Segment

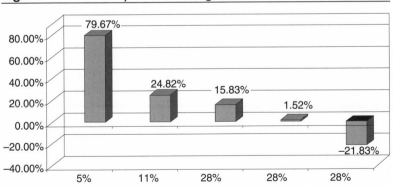

was likely to buy from the company in the future. Each such product had three attributes:

- The potential profitability to the enterprise if the customer were to buy the product (based on the customer's assets and income)
- The probability that the customer would buy the product if it were offered (based on the purchases of other customers with similar lifestyles)
- The cost to the company of selling the customer the additional product

From this analysis came the determination of the "next best product" for each customer (in terms of profit to the enterprise and likelihood of response). This product was identified in every customer's database record and shown on the screens used by all personnel who had customer contact. This has proved to be a highly successful and significant use of database marketing.

The Retention Rate

The most important number in any lifetime value table is the retention rate. This is the percentage of newly acquired customers in each segment who will still be buying from your company 1 year later. Before database marketing, few companies knew what this number was or what to do about it. I worked with an insurance company whose retention rate in the first year was only 54 percent. During this year, the company made absolutely no effort to make contact with its customers or to build a relationship with them. Lifetime value computation showed that an increase of 5 percent in this first-year retention rate would increase profits by $14 million (see Table 1-1).

The cost of getting this additional 5 percent increase was estimated at $36 per customer, or a total of $3 million, for customer communications. The beauty of using a database to do lifetime value analysis is that you focus on things that you can change by marketing strategy and that you can prove the value of each strategy in finite dollar terms.

Table 1-1 Effect of 5 Percent Increase in the Retention Rate

	New customer	Second year	Second year
Retention rate		54%	59%
Customers	130,000	70,200	76,700
Average revenue	$2,900	$2,900	$2,900
Total revenue	$377,000,000	$203,580,000	$222,430,000
Acquisition/retention	$192	$ —	$36
Commission	$959	$769	$769
Total	$1,151	$769	$805
Total cost	$149,630,000	$99,970,000	$104,650,000
Net revenue per customer	$1,749	$1,476	$1,536
Net revenue in total	$227,370,000	$103,610,000	$117,780,000

Using database marketing, the company would not have to commit the $3 million in the hope of getting this increased return. It could use the database to set up test and control groups to see if the communications would produce the desired results. It could select 5000 customers to receive the communications (at a cost of $180,000) to see if their retention rate could be increased by 5 percent. If the strategy worked, then the next year the company could apply the successful methods to all new acquisitions, spend the whole $3 million, and pocket the $14 million. (Table 1-1 and all the other tables in this book can be downloaded free from www.dbmarketing.com.)

Modeling for Churn

As the economy has grown, more companies have learned to use database marketing to retain customers. Competition in some products, particularly credit cards, cellular phones, long-distance service, and health care, has become intense. The attrition rate, or the rate at which people switch to another provider, is very high. At the same time, statistical modelers have found that regression analysis can help in predicting which customers are most likely to drop the service. The models use a combination of appended data and transaction history to pick out the variables that precede a customer's dropping the service. Then advanced database marketing techniques are used to concentrate on these potential defectors and

Table 1-2 Risk/Revenue Matrix

LTV	Probability of leaving soon		
	High	**Medium**	**Low**
High	priority A	priority B	priority C
Medium	priority B	priority B	priority C
Low	priority C	priority C	priority C

Table 1-3 Price Offers

Number tested	Number renewing	Price offer	Revenue
1000	800	$10	$8000
1000	900	$ 9	$8100
1000	950	$ 8	$7600

get them to change their minds. Defection prediction plus lifetime value analysis further concentrates the communications on those whom it is most profitable to serve. The result is risk/revenue analysis (see Table 1-2).

In this analysis, which is discussed later in this book, a concentration on those customers who are priority A or priority B reduces the task of lowering churn by 56 percent, saving resources and boosting profits.

Bruce McDoniel of Summit Marketing used this system with a large regional bank to find the right price for priority A customer renewals. The goal was to get customers to renew, but also to maximize revenue. Bruce tried three price offers that netted the bank from $8 to $10. Table 1-3 shows the result of the test.

This simple test enabled the bank to fix the offer price at $9.

Use of Database Marketing for Acquisition

Database marketing is also highly useful for acquiring new customers. The first step is to apply lifetime value analysis to existing customers to determine the characteristics of the most profitable and the least profitable customers. This analysis can be used to steer the sales force toward recruiting the right sort of people in the first place. Frederick Reichheld, in his path-breaking book *The Loyalty Effect*, showed us that some people are inherently loyal, whereas others tend to be disloyal. If companies concentrate on recruiting loyal customers to begin with, they will have a much easier time retaining their customers once they are acquired.

In business-to-business customer acquisition, customers can be scored using Dun & Bradstreet data, such as Standard Industrial Classification (SIC) codes, annual sales, number of employees, and other such data. By using this type of appended data, enterprises can learn which types of companies are most likely to buy which of their products. Their acquisitions can be accurately targeted.

In consumer acquisition, cluster coding has proved useful in many cases. Cluster coding systems, marketed by Claritas and other providers, segment the U.S. population into 62 different clusters based on lifestyle, with catchy names like Shotguns & Pickups, Money & Brains, Furs & Station Wagons, Pools & Patios, and Hard Scrabble. If you apply these clusters to your existing customer base, you may discover that your services appeal primarily to 30 percent or so of the 62 possible clusters. Marketing to the remaining 70 percent may be a losing proposition. By concentrating your acquisition resources on the prospects that are most likely to buy, you can increase your success and your profits. Cluster coding works for only a few products and services, but where it works, it is well worth the money.

Two Kinds of Databases

There are really two different kinds of databases in any company that is engaged in direct marketing of products and services. One is an *operational database*, and the other is a *marketing database* (see Figure 1-2).

An operational database is used to process transactions and get out the monthly statements.

- For a cataloger, the operational database is used to process the orders, charge the credit cards, arrange shipment, and handle returns and credits.
- For a bank, the operational database processes checks and deposits, maintains balances, and creates the monthly statements.
- For a telephone company, the operational database keeps track of the telephone calls made and arranges the billing for them.

Figure 1-2   Operational and Marketing Databases

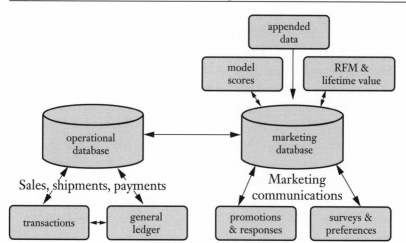

A marketing database gets data from the operational database, if there is one. These data consist of a summary of monthly transactions. But the marketing database also includes much more. It gets additional data from

- Preferences and profiles provided by the customers
- Promotion and response history from marketing campaigns
- External sources, such as Experian, Donnelly, and Claritas
- Lifetime value and RFM analysis, leading to creation of customer segments
- Modeling for churn and next best product

The marketing database passes data back to the operational database. It may advise the operational database

- The segment that each customer has been placed in, which may lead to operational decisions. Gold customers, for example, may get different operational treatment.
- Expressed customer preferences, which lead to different operational treatment; e.g., smoking or nonsmoking rooms are assigned automatically.

The operational database is run by IT. It is run on accounting principles, and it balances to the penny, since there are legal and tax aspects to its data. It is audited by external auditors. It contains only current data on customers. Old data are archived. There are no data on prospects until they make a purchase.

The marketing database is managed by the marketing department. It is usually outsourced. It is not run on accounting principles, and it does not need to balance. There are few legal or tax considerations. It contains information on current customers, prospects, and lapsed customers and communications with them. It may retain data stretching back over a period of several years.

A *data warehouse* combines all the data and functions of both an operational database and a marketing database (plus, in many cases, other functions such as employee data, payroll, product data, production data, etc.) in one huge database. The data warehouse is so big and complicated that it needs to be managed by a committee. It is often very expensive to build and maintain. It is seldom very flexible. Marketing priorities usually get short shrift in a data warehouse, as other priorities are often given preference.

Why Databases Fail

There have been many database marketing failures during the past two decades, from which companies have learned what does not work. A few of the reasons are

- *Failure to test a strategy on a small sample* before a rollout. Database marketing is particularly adapted to setting up tests, which can prove the validity of any idea before serious money is spent on it. Database marketers know this. Company management usually does not. Pushing for quick profits has led many companies to fail with ideas that could easily have been tested on a small scale first.
- *Failure to set aside control groups.* If you are going to spend a million dollars on a group of customer communications designed to boost retention or sales, you always should set aside a group that does not

get the communications in order to prove the value of the effort. Many companies still fail to do this. The result, of course, can be disaster. If the economy is going down and your sales are going down, you may assume that your methods are not working. If you set aside a control group, however, you might find that the sales of your test group went down less than those of the control group, proving that your communication program worked, even in adverse circumstances.

- *Failure to develop strategies that work.* Database marketing has often worked so well that some people have thought that it was the database and the software that were producing the miracles. It wasn't. What produced the miracles were strategies that resonated with the particular audiences represented in the databases. The scarcest commodities in any database marketing operation are imagination and leadership: the ability to think up ideas that will work and the ability to sell those ideas to management and apply them. It is a highly competitive world today. Friends and Family, created by MCI 15 years ago, was a wonderfully creative idea for acquiring new customers. It alone made MCI into a giant long-distance carrier. But once everyone else realized what it was and how it worked, it was copied by others, and it no longer had the power it once had. To succeed, you have to constantly come up with new ideas. Some people just don't understand this. They think that if they build a database and apply expensive software, profits will roll in. This is the reason for the CRM craze that hit the database marketing world in the previous decade. If you read the CRM manuals, it almost sounds as if customer acquisition and retention is a simple matter of building a data warehouse and applying expensive software to it. In general, CRM has been a gigantic failure. We shall return to this subject in the next chapter.

- *Focus on price instead of service.* The main reason why customers stop using a product or service is not the product or the price, but the way they were treated by the company providing the product or service. Management always thinks that price is the problem, hoping that through discounts, it can buy some loyal customers. Discounts do not buy loyalty. They reduce loyalty. They reduce margin. They get customers to think about how much they are paying instead of about how much they are getting. A database should not be a way to give away coupons. It should be a way to avoid having to give away coupons because the customers are so happy with the communications and services they are receiving that they will ignore the deep discounts of the competition.

- *Treating all customers alike.* Some customers are more loyal and profitable than others. Your database should identify these loyal customers, and your marketing strategy should work to retain them and to encourage others to emulate them. You should also do something to reduce the number of worthless customers on your rolls. If you treat all customers alike, you will never improve your customer mix. A retention budget of $1 million divided by 1 million customers will do very little to change anyone's behavior. Divide that $1 million among your 100,000 most valuable customers, and you have $10 per customer per year to reward loyalty and encourage retention. You may make some progress. Some company managements do not yet understand this.

Summary

Database marketing is a great success story. During the last 20 years, thousands of creative and skillful people have developed and applied new methods for using databases of customers and prospects to acquire customers, build loyalty, and increase sales. These methods are explained in detail in this book. But database marketing is more than a success story. It is a philosophy.

Looked at from the customer's point of view, database marketing is a way of making customers happy—of providing them with recognition, service, friendship, and information, for which, in return, they will reward you with loyalty, reduction in attrition, and increased sales. Generating profits by creating genuine customer satisfaction is the goal and hallmark of satisfactory database marketing. If you are doing things right, your customers will be *glad* that you have a database and that you have included them in it. They will appreciate the things that you do for them. If you can develop and carry out strategies that bring this situation about, you are a master marketer. You will keep your customers for life, and you will be happy in your work. You will have made the world a better place to live in.

What Works

- Getting customers to respond to you on the Web
- Creating premier pages for your best business customers
- Providing customer service information free on the Web
- Determining the lifetime value of your customers and using it to evaluate your marketing strategy
- Determining the next best product for each customer and putting it in the database for your employees to see and use
- Learning the retention rate for each of your customer segments and working to improve it
- Sending email communications to customers who have asked for them
- Using cookies to recognize and greet customers when they come to your Web site
- Using risk/revenue analysis to concentrate your marketing resources on customers whose behavior you need to modify

What Doesn't Work

- Building a huge data warehouse for the purpose of building profitable relationships with your customers
- Treating all customers alike
- Failing to set up control groups
- Failing to test any new idea on a small group first
- Failing to use the Web as part of your database communications program

Quiz

1. Which of the following has been a failure in database marketing since 1985?
   a. RFM
   b. The Web

    c. Treating all customers alike

    d. Email

    e. Direct mail

2. In the case given in this chapter, it was suggested that the increased retention was due to

    a. Customer communications

    b. Advanced software

    c. CRM

    d. More loyal customers

    e. Cookies on the Web

3. What is considered to be a good average response rate for email communications?

    a. 30 percent

    b. 20 percent

    c. 2 percent

    d. 1 percent

    e. 0.4 percent

4. What is the most important factor in database marketing success?

    a. Software

    b. A data warehouse

    c. The Web

    d. Marketing strategy

    e. CRM

5. In risk/revenue analysis, the marketer concentrates most on

    a. Those customers in priority A and priority B

    b. The lifetime value of priority B customers

    c. The churn model

    d. The lifetime value model

    e. The data warehouse

6. What's wrong with treating all customers alike?

    a. It's undemocratic.

    b. The resources available to devote to the best customers will be too small.

    c. Even worthless customers deserve a break.

    d. It is impossible to segment customers by behavior.

    e. Customers would not like it.

7. Where is a microsite for customer response ideally located?
    a. On the main company Web site
    b. On a PC
    c. On a mainframe
    d. On the computer holding the database
    e. In a risk/revenue matrix
8. Which is not true of the MCI Friends and Family program?
    a. It worked very well for a few years.
    b. It was copied by other companies.
    c. It made innovative use of the Web.
    d. It was a cost-effective way to add customers.
    e. It helped MCI to become a telecom giant.
9. What is a database marketing control group?
    a. Customers who get a special test group of communications
    b. Those who dictate database marketing strategy
    c. Top management
    d. Those who do not get any of the test communications
    e. A privileged customer group
10. Discount certificates are
    a. Best distributed by direct mail
    b. Used for building customer loyalty
    c. Used to boost margins
    d. Used to ward off competition
    e. Not a good way to recruit new customers who last
11. What one development has changed database marketing profoundly in the past two decades?"
    a. CRM software
    b. Data warehouses
    c. Desktop PCs
    d. the Web
    e. Customer lists

CHAPTER 2

THE MIRAGE OF CRM

Before implementing a CRM package it is necessary to understand why nearly half of U. S. implementations and more than 80% of European implementations are considered failures. It's difficult to fathom failures of such monstrous proportions, especially when complete CRM installations can cost millions of dollars and then hundreds of thousands of dollars more per annum.

John_taschek@ziffdavis.com

Customer relationship marketing (CRM) burst on the marketing world in the early 1990s. It was soon adopted by some of America's largest corporations. After working with it for several years, most analysts admit that it does not seem to deliver the benefits that it promised and that it may, after all, be a mirage. Let's see what it was supposed to do and why it failed.

The basic idea was to collect a great deal of information about customers, prospects, products, promotions, and other such things and put it into a giant in-house data warehouse. Many of these warehouses were very expensive, costing as much as $20 million. Part of the cost was that of appending external data about customers and prospects, such as age, income, presence of children, lifestyle, home value, creditworthiness, and so on. To access and manipulate the data in the warehouses, very sophisticated software, costing at least a million dollars the first year, was installed. In many companies there was a tendency to focus on information technology (IT) rather than on the business outcome. CRM was introduced by the IT unit, often without sufficiently close coordination with marketing, sales, or customer service. The result was expensive systems that did not deliver either successful campaigns or improved profits.

The National Retail Federation's annual CRM Conference survey of North American retail companies found that 69 percent of the respondents said that they had gained little or no benefit from their CRM investment. Why was this so?

What was CRM designed to do? There were really two basic goals:

- Build and maintain relationships with prospects and customers based on having lots of relevant information about them, and using that information to guide communications and contacts with the customer.
- Use that information to make the right offer to the right customer at the right time, thereby increasing sales and pleasing the customers.

The idea that these goals could be achieved was based on four assumptions, all of which proved to be invalid in practice:

1. One-to-one marketing is an achievable goal given the right information and software. Stated another way, customers' and prospects' purchasing behavior can be predicted accurately from the information that you can collect about them.
2. Customers' and prospects' behavior is heavily influenced by timely and relevant offers.
3. Companies can shift rapidly from being product-focused (with an employee's bonus being based on the number of particular products sold) to being customer-focused (with an employee's bonus being based on the amount sold to particular customer segments, regardless of what products they buy).
4. Introduction of CRM has a positive return on investment because it increases sales and profits by more than its cost.

Assumption 1: Why People Buy Things

Let's see why none of these assumptions proved to be correct. In the first place, why do customers and prospects decide to buy something? You can come up with lots of answers, but the key answer is that they decide that owning the product or service at a particular time will make them happier than not owning it. What happiness consists of is defined by the person who is trying to possess it, and it varies from person to person and from time to time.

I like Big Macs, but not all the time. Sometimes I like fish, sometimes I like chicken, and quite often I like home-cooked vegetables. There is no way that you can accurately predict what I will want to eat next unless you know what I ate last, how hungry I am, where I am at the time, whom I am with, and how much money and time I have available right now for eating. There is no way that any data warehouse could ever collect such timely and relevant information or that anyone other than the customer could accurately weigh the importance of each piece of information.

The same principle applies to predicting my interest in taking a trip, buying clothing, buying a car or an appliance, or taking a college course. You can collect some relevant information, but you cannot collect enough to make accurate predictions concerning what Arthur Hughes will do today. What you can say with some accuracy is that people in Arthur Hughes's age and income group who have similar purchasing habits are more likely to buy a certain type of clothing or insurance policy than the average person picked out at random. But of course, that is not CRM or one-to-one marketing. That is regular database marketing, where you are targeting segments. You don't need a data warehouse for that. You need only a database (which can be built for a fraction of the cost of a data warehouse) that permits dividing the customer and prospect base into purchasing segments.

What is the difference between database marketing and CRM? They are both based on databases of prospects and customers that are used to guide marketing and sales strategy. CRM requires a large data warehouse with costly software, aimed at determining and influencing the behavior of *individuals* through one-to-one marketing. Database marketing is based on a data mart, which costs about 10 percent of the amount required for a CRM warehouse. Database marketing is usually aimed at identifying *customer segments* and marketing to them, and also building one-to-one relationships with existing customers through loyalty-building communications.

To see the difference, think of 100,000 customers on whom you have data. With database marketing, it might be possible to predict with 75 percent certainty that 40 percent of a certain segment of those customers will buy product X within the next month. But you cannot be 75 percent certain that Arthur Hughes (a member of the segment) will buy the product next month—or ever, for that matter. The first conclusion comes from segment analysis using database marketing. The second conclusion would come from CRM if it could be made to work. Unfortunately, it cannot.

We should note here that there has been a corruption in terminology. Many companies are practicing database marketing, but are calling it CRM because that sounds more modern and up to date. They don't have a data warehouse. They don't have million-dollar software. They don't really even attempt one-to-one marketing. They have just built a modest data mart and are creating marketing segments and marketing to them. They call what they are doing CRM, but it is really plain old database marketing, which works wonderfully in the right situation.

Assumption 2: Timely and Relevant Offers

The second assumption is wrong for a similar reason. Do you eat because you are hungry, or because you received a timely communication telling you that a particular restaurant was having a special on lobster dinners? Of course, if you are hungry, you enjoy lobster, and you have the time and money to go to that restaurant right now, the offer would be a delightful blessing. But the warehouse cannot contain that information. Mass marketing on TV showing people eating delicious lobster dinners at a low price can work wonderfully. The image sticks in people's minds and will be recalled the next time they are hungry. You don't need a warehouse to design and place such ads. Mass marketing works very well and is a lot cheaper in terms of sales per dollar spent.

Of course, there are situations in which a timely and relevant offer can make the difference in a sale. Banks know a lot about people's demographics and behavior. They can predict the probability of a particular customer's buying a particular product and the lifetime value that the customer would produce for the bank if it were to offer the product and the customer were to accept the offer. This also applies to automobile companies that have customers on 3-year leases, and to scores of other situations. But for most of these situations, good old database marketing will work just fine. We can pick out all the people who have lived in their homes for 5 years or more and do not have a home equity loan, and send them an offer. It works. We are marketing to segments. We don't need a warehouse or one-to-one marketing to be successful.

Assumption 3: Becoming Customer-Centric

The third assumption, that companies can rapidly move from being product-focused to being customer-focused, is the weakest of all. After working with dozens of large American corporations, I can report that it is almost impossible for most companies to become customer-focused. Why is this so? Because of the way business is developed. You create a new camera, a new computer, a new automobile, or a new hotel. The company that develops the product wants to realize a return on its investment. It puts a product manager in charge of marketing the product and tells her to get busy.

The product manager does everything she can think of: mass marketing, point-of-purchase displays, retailer subsidies, direct marketing. Of course, if you have a list of prospects in your warehouse, she may try a promotion to that list to see if it works. But her goal is to sell hotel space in this new hotel, and only secondarily to increase overall customer lifetime value to the company.

Could you replace all the product managers with customer segment managers and have no product managers at all? Not likely. No company has ever done that, and none ever will. Once you have developed a product, you can't leave the promotion of that product to chance. You simply won't say, "We will be nice to our customers and hope that they notice our new hotel. We won't specifically promote this new hotel, because one of our older hotels may suit some customers better."

Assumption 4: CRM Mathematics

To understand the return on investment from CRM, let's do a little math. We have to start with some basic principles. Customers do respond to communications, offers, and promotions. For the communication to work, however, the seller has to have some sort of established business. He has a product or service to sell and a working distribution channel. In order to use CRM, he has to have a revenue stream (otherwise, where would he get the money to build his warehouse?).

The reason for using CRM is to make *incremental increases* in the level of sales that is currently being made through mass marketing, retail stores, catalogs, and database marketing. The marketer assumes that if there were just more information about the customer's decision-making process, it would be possible to increase the sales level (of customers and prospects) by as much as 5 or 10 percent. Let's say that the marketer is selling some product or service for $150. It could be rental cars, small appliances, or carpets. The marketer contacts 20 million customers per year and has sales of $900 million. The current marketing methods involve mass marketing and direct marketing to customer segments, including a loyalty program. We will assume that of the $150, net profits per sale are 10 percent after deducting all costs, including marketing.

Pricing the CRM Program

We will assume a modest CRM warehouse containing data on 14 million prospects and past customers and 6 million current customers. Let us assume that we can build it for $10 million, including the software for access, with annual maintenance costs of $1.5 million, which include the costs for the staff, NCOA (National Change of Address), and appended external data. Amortized over 3 years, the warehouse will cost us $5.5 million per year, as shown in Table 2-1.

Let's compare this to the cost of database marketing in the same situation, shown in Table 2-2. It costs far less. We are assuming a cost of $1.5 million to build the database. Many databases are built for far less, such as $500,000, and some, of course, cost more. The number $1.5 million is a good number for a large corporate marketing database.

Cost of Communications

To these CRM or database costs, we must add the cost of communications with customers and prospects. After all, if we are going to make the right offer to the right customer at the right time, we have to communicate the offer to customers personally, or what is the warehouse for? Let's assume that our firm has been collecting email names to keep the cost of communications down. It has email names for half of its customers. Table 2-3 shows the total CRM and database cost, assuming an average of only three communications per customer per year. Note that when CRM or database marketing is used properly, some likely customers may get more than four communications a year, and some will get only one.

Table 2-1 Warehouse Cost

	Cost
Cost to build warehouse	$10,000,000
Amortize over 3 years	$ 4,000,000
Annual maintenance	$ 1,500,000
Annual cost	$ 5,500,000

Table 2-2 Database Cost

	Cost
Cost to build database	$1,500,000
Amortize over 3 years	$ 600,000
Annual maintenance	$1,000,000
Annual cost	$1,600,000

Table 2-3 Comparison

	Communications		Per	CRM	Database
	Quantity	Rate	year	annual cost	annual cost
DB/warehouse				$5,500,000	$1,600,000
Mail communications	3,000,000	$0.60	2	$3,600,000	$3,600,000
Email communications	3,000,000	$0.04	4	$ 480,000	$ 480,000
CRM/database costs				$9,580,000	$5,680,000

Table 2-4 Net Profit

	Without CRM or database marketing	With CRM	With database marketing
Customers	6,000,000	6,000,000	6,000,000
Annual sales per customer	$150	$165	$165
Sales	$900,000,000	$990,000,000	$990,000,000
Profit per sale	10%	10%	10%
Gross profit	$90,000,000	$99,000,000	$99,000,000
CRM/database cost	$0	$ 9,580,000	$ 5,680,000
Net profit	$90,000,000	$89,420,000	$93,320,000

So with these costs in hand, what will be the result of using CRM or database marketing? See Table 2-4.

Using either CRM or database marketing, we have managed to increase the average sales per customer by 10 percent, to $165. We may have done this by getting some customers to place larger orders, by getting some to place more orders, by reducing the attrition rate, or by a combination of these and other methods. Sales have increased by $90 million, with increased gross profits of $9 million. Unfortunately, when we factor in the cost of CRM, net profits have gone down by $580,000. That is what virtually all companies that installed CRM have discovered. Note that these figures assume that CRM is working—that it is in fact increasing sales by 10 percent. But in many cases, for the reasons given earlier, CRM has no such valuable benefit. In the majority of companies, it does not affect the sales rate at all. Much of the money spent on CRM is wasted. That is the reason for the Gartner Group's pessimistic conclusion on CRM.

The methods whereby database marketing produces the gains in profit shown in this section are explained in the remaining chapters and case studies in this book. A further discussion of the benefits of a data warehouse is given in Chapter 10, "Customer Management."

The Loyalty Effect

CRM is often justified by citing references to reports like those of Bain & Company, which maintain that companies can boost customer net present value by as much as 95 percent if they can retain only 5 percent more of their customers. Numbers like these have often been used to persuade management that a CRM package could pay for itself very rapidly. The assertion that growth in net present value results from increased retention is central to Frederick Reichheld's excellent book *The Loyalty Effect*. Figure 2-1 shows Reichheld's increases in customer net present value in various industries as a result of a 5 percent increase in the retention rate.

These numbers seem too good to be true. In fact, they *are* too good to be true. Let's see what the real numbers might actually be. Let's take one industry from the list as representative of the problem: life insurance. We will take a typical term life insurance policy of $500,000 for a 45-year-old nonsmoker that costs $1000 per year. For such policies,

Figure 2-1   Reichheld 5 Percent Retention Gains

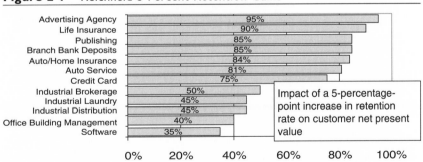

Source: Frederick Reichheld, *The Loyalty Effect* (Boston: Harvard Business School Press, 1996), p. 36.

Table 2-5 Life Insurance Net Present Value

	Year 1	Year 2	Year 3	Year 4	Year 5
Retention rate	50%	60%	65%	70%	75%
Customers	100,000	50,000	30,000	19,500	13,650
Payments	$1,000	$1,000	$1,000	$1,000	$1,000
Revenue	$100,000,000	$50,000,000	$30,000,000	$19,500,000	$13,650,000
Commissions	$ 20,000,000	$ 250,000	$ 150,000	$ 97,500	$ 68,250
Claims	$ 75,000,000	$37,500,000	$22,500,000	$14,625,000	$10,237,500
Total costs	$ 95,000,000	$37,750,000	$22,650,000	$14,722,500	$10,305,750
Profit	$ 5,000,000	$12,250,000	$ 7,350,000	$ 4,777,500	$ 3,344,250
Discount rate	1.00	1.07	1.14	1.21	1.29
Net present value	$ 5,000,000	$11,491,557	$ 6,468,043	$ 3,943,929	$ 2,589,822
Cumulative NPV	$ 5,000,000	$16,491,557	$22,959,601	$26,903,530	$29,493,352

the first-year retention rates are very low. Subsequent rates are much higher. Table 2-5 shows the net present value for such policyholders for the first 5 years.

This chart shows that the cumulative net present value (the present value of the profits) from 100,000 new policyholders will be $29.5 million over 5 years. Note that we are assuming that 50 percent of the policyholders drop their policies during the first year. After that year, the retention rate increases. Of particular importance is the discount rate. This is the rate used to discount future profits and convert them into net present value profits. The formula for the discount rate is

$$D = (1 + i * \text{rf})^{\text{years to wait}}$$

In the third year (2 years to wait), for example, the formula is

$$D = (1 + 0.06 * 1.1)^2$$

This becomes

$$D = 1.14$$

In this formula, i is the market rate of interest, figured at 6 percent, and rf is the risk factor, which is determined to be 1.2 for the first year and 1.1 for subsequent years. The risk factor is a number that represents the risk that you won't generate the sales and profits at all. A perfectly safe business has a risk factor of 1. The risk can come about because customers don't pay, because of heavy competition, because of product obsolescence, etc. Years to wait is the amount of time that the insurance company has to wait before the profits materialize. The first year, we are assuming that the waiting time is zero, because we are asking the policyholders to pay in advance. The chart could be made more complicated by adding administrative costs, medical examinations, etc. Leaving these out, we have a relatively clear picture of the marginal profits that a life insurance company can expect to realize over 5 years from 100,000 policyholders.

Using the Bain & Company figures, we should expect to see this $29.5 million 5-year profit go up by 90 percent, to $56 million, if we were to increase the retention rate by 5 percent. But that is not what happens. Table 2-6 gives the profits over 5 years assuming that the retention rate is somehow increased by 5 percent.

The cumulative net present value does go up, but only by about 15 percent, as Table 2-7 shows.

Now, 15 percent is a good solid number, but it is not 90 percent. Unfortunately, the rate is probably much less than 15 percent, because we have not figured in the costs of getting the 5 percent increase in retention. Here is where CRM really has trouble.

Table 2-6 New NPV

	Year 1	Year 2	Year 3	Year 4	Year 5
Retention rate	55%	65%	70%	75%	80%
Customers	100,000	55,000	35,750	25,025	18,769
Payments	$1,000	$1,000	$1,000	$1,000	$1,000
Revenue	$100,000,000	$55,000,000	$35,750,000	$25,025,000	$18,768,750
Commissions	$20,000,000	$ 275,000	$ 178,750	$ 125,125	$ 93,844
Claims	$75,000,000	$41,250,000	$26,812,500	$18,768,750	$14,076,563
Total costs	$95,000,000	$41,525,000	$26,991,250	$18,893,875	$14,170,406
Profit	$5,000,000	$13,475,000	$ 8,758,750	$ 6,131,125	$ 4,598,344
Discount rate	1.00	1.07	1.14	1.21	1.29
Net present value	$5,000,000	$12,640,713	$ 7,707,752	$ 5,061,375	$ 3,561,005
Cumulative NPV	$5,000,000	$17,640,713	$25,348,465	$30,409,840	$33,970,846

**Table 2-7 Gains from 5
Percent Increase**

Present 5-year NPV	$29,493,352
New 5-year NPV	$33,970,846
Increase	$ 4,477,494
Percent increase	15%

How does Reichheld suggest that the 5 percent increase be brought about? He has some very ingenious and valid ideas. The book is filled with excellent suggestions. Here are only a few of them:

- Improve employee loyalty by increasing the employee retention rate (since retained employees help to retain customers).
- Recruit the right sort of customers to begin with (some customers are inherently loyal, and others are inherently disloyal).
- Change the commission system to reward retention as much as or more than acquisition.

Nowhere in Reichheld's book does he suggest building a huge data warehouse and purchasing CRM software to go with it. If we had done this, we would have had to factor into Tables 2-6 and 2-7 the cost of the CRM needed to produce the 5 percent increase in the retention rate. The 15 percent growth in net present value might disappear or even become negative if we were to do so.

So, unfortunately, CRM proponents have been using numbers from Reichheld's book to justify their programs without any solid justification in the book whatsoever.

What to Do with the Data

There is a fundamental disconnection between the goals of CRM and the results. If you have invested millions of dollars and you have a wonderful data warehouse and analytic software, then what? How do the data warehouse and software increase the retention rate? Somehow, you are supposed to take the software and change customers' behavior. The CRM Forum (www.crm-forum.com) lists three reasons why CRM usually fails:

1. Problems with organizational change and internal politics
2. Lack of the right skills and enterprisewide understanding of the initiatives
3. Poor initiative planning

Unfortunately, many CRM analysts write a type of dense prose that is almost impossible for normal people to understand. Take this example from a Gartner Group report on the CRM Forum:

> *Enterprises struggling with lack of coordination across departments should consider the needs of individual groups and work on a top-down/bottom-up strategy. Because department-level CRM deployments may be more cost-effectively supported by a Tier 2 system integrator with domain-specific skill sets and software relationships, the enterprise should identify a master list of approved smaller service providers to work on individual projects.*

It really should not be so complicated. The goal of CRM is to select the right prospects and to get customers to be more loyal and buy more. Software is of only marginal help in doing this. The goals can be achieved only by coming up with products, services, tactics, strategies, and communications that the customers will like and respond to. The CRM warehouse and software do none of these things. The goal can be realized, however, in many other ways, which are outlined in this book.

So, what should you do? Sungmi Chung and Mike Sherman suggested in the *McKinsey Quarterly* that the two most essential resources in any CRM program are a wealth of hypotheses about the composition of possible target segments and a variety of offers to test these hypotheses. They point out that

> *Less is more if it makes it possible for the process of testing and refining offers to start sooner rather than later. It will be more than enough to begin with some demographic details about customers and information about the products they currently own, such as their account balances, and the kinds of transactions they have undertaken during the course of the previous 12 months.*

Summary

CRM is, in general, a mirage, an illusion based on a nice idea (the right offer to the right customer at the right time) that does not work out in practice:

- One-to-one marketing, which sounds wonderful, may in fact not be possible in most product and service situations. We lack the information. The data about any individual that are available may not be sufficient to predict that individual's behavior, although it may be sufficiently accurate to predict the behavior of the customer segment of which he or she is a part.
- Making the right offer to the right customer at the right time may be impossible. People make decisions based on personal factors that cannot be captured in a database. We can, however, profitably target segments.
- Companies cannot easily shift from being product-focused to being customer-focused. It sounds great, but few have actually done it. Most never will.
- Even if CRM were to work in theory, it does not work in practice because the increased profits are swamped by the increased costs.
- We must keep in mind that customer communications, which are triggered by CRM or a database, produce only incremental results. You are already selling something. You hope to sell more and keep customers longer by using the database and communications. The incremental sales are usually only slightly more than the sales you would have gotten without the database and the communications. You have to justify your CRM not on the basis of total sales, but on the basis of these incremental sales.
- Many marketers are doing database marketing and calling it CRM. They don't have a warehouse or million-dollar software. They are marketing to segments and making money doing it. That is great. But it is not CRM.
- NCR, which sells the TeraData computer, has developed some very sucessful data warehouse applications for very large banks,

insurance companies, and others; two of these are described in detail in this book. These applications are an exception to the general rule about data warehouses. NCR has succeeded where most other CRM developers have failed.

What Works

- Mass marketing for certain products and services
- Building a customer and prospect database and using it to market to customer segments for certain products and services
- Having your products available in retail locations that are convenient for your customers
- Communicating with customers to maintain their loyalty; sending them emails, thanking them for their patronage, and getting them to fill out customer preference profiles

What Doesn't Work

- Giant CRM multimillion-dollar data warehouses designed to produce one-to-one marketing.
- Million-dollar software that is designed to make the right offer to the right customer at the right time.
- One-to-one marketing, except in certain limited situations.
- Changing a company so that it is customer-focused instead of product-focused. It's a nice idea, but no one has ever done it, and no one ever will.

Quiz

1. Which is not a basic assumption of CRM?
   a. A warehouse permits a firm to make the right offer to the right customer at the right time.
   b. A data warehouse is essential to marketing success.

    c. One-to-one marketing is achievable.

    d. Companies can become customer-focused.

    e. Increased employee loyalty is essential to increased customer retention.

2. The formula for the discount rate includes all but which of the following:

    a. The waiting time

    b. The market rate of interest

    c. The marketing costs

    d. The risk factor

    e. The years to wait

3. Which of the following is not given in the chapter as a reason why CRM is a failure?

    a. CRM software is not available today.

    b. The data to predict customers purchasing behavior are lacking.

    c. Data warehouses are very expensive.

    d. Companies cannot become customer-focused.

    e. *The Loyalty Effect* does not support CRM.

4. Turn the following paragraph into English:

> *Enterprises struggling with lack of coordination across departments should consider the needs of individual groups and work on a top-down/bottom-up strategy. Because department-level CRM deployments may be more cost-effectively supported by a Tier 2 system integrator with domain-specific skill sets and software relationships, the enterprise should identify a master list of approved smaller service providers to work on individual projects.*

5. What does the National Retail Federation's CRM Conference survey of North American retail companies estimate the CRM failure rate to be? Nearly

    a. 80 percent

    b. 70 percent

    c. 60 percent

    d. 50 percent

    e. 40 percent

6. Which of the following was not listed in the chapter as a recommendation by Frederick Reichheld in *The Loyalty Effect*?
   a. Improve employee loyalty
   b. Build a data warehouse
   c. Recruit the right sort of customers to begin with
   d. Change the commission system
   e. Increase the customer retention rate

7. What does NPV stand for?
   a. Not previously viewed
   b. Net present value
   c. The rate of profits from an enterprise
   d. The cumulative profits expected in the future
   e. The discount rate

8. What does it mean to say that database marketing and CRM produce only incremental results?
   a. They don't work.
   b. They don't work very well.
   c. The basic product sales are produced by other channels.
   d. A 5 percent increase in the retention rate produces a 95 percent increase in profits.
   e. None of the above.

9. Why will most companies never become customer-focused?
   a. Because companies are designed for customer acquisition
   b. Because Reichheld said it cannot work
   c. Because companies want to see that individual products succeed
   d. Because the compensation system cannot be changed
   e. Because of test and control groups

10. What does the book suggest as the best way to attract customers to Red Lobster?
    a. Database marketing
    b. CRM
    c. Mass marketing
    d. Certificates
    e. None of the above

CHAPTER 3

SELLING ON THE WEB

The number of online 13- to 22-year-olds will grow from 17 million to 22 million by 2004. How can your company target a group that, unlike adults, internalizes the Internet? What do you need to do to attract and keep them as customers? How should you alter your marketing and product development strategies? Forrester's Wired Youth Summit will help you understand this sought-after group and give you new ideas you can use today to develop these critical relationships.

W hen the Web arrived in the mid-1990s, just about everyone in marketing thought it would be a great sales medium to consumers—something like TV, radio, or direct mail. Billions and billions of dollars were invested with that idea in mind. Thousands of new companies sprang up to sell on the Web or to provide services to those who would be selling there. Every major corporation in America produced a Web site, most of which involved the marketing of some product or service. Hundreds of sites planned to make money from advertising placed on their sites by others. Spending on the Web was a big part of the boom times of the nineties.

In fact, between 1995 and 2002, very few companies were selling very much to consumers on the Web. With the exception of travel, music, pornography, and books, the sales were very, very small. Why were they so small? At first, people said it was because half the nation was still not on the Web (hence millions of dollars were spent to equip schools for the Web). Then the argument ran that even those who were on the Web were hesitant to buy because of the possibility of credit card fraud. No one was saying that the Web was not a great sales medium. Everyone just said, "These things take time." Amazon.com, the leader that showed everyone how Web sales should be done, didn't make a profit until 2001. But Amazon's failure was said to be due to its overextension into too many products. If it had just stuck to books, it could have been profitable, everyone agreed.

The quote at the beginning of this chapter is really a joke. Here is a "wired youth summit" that teaches you how to sell to young people who have "internalized" the Web. I could be wrong, but my experience tells me that in most cases these consumer sales will not materialize for the reasons given in this chapter. Teaching retailers how to reach these "wired youths" through the Web is a futile exercise. Amazon was the first Web bookstore. Within 3 years of its debut, almost everyone in the middle class in America had heard of it and had used it. It was impossible for any "pure-play" Web bookstore to start up and succeed in competition with Amazon. Established booksellers such as Barnes & Noble and Borders opened up competing Web sites. In other fields, retailers rushed to become the first mover. More than a dozen online supermarkets were started, such as Peapod, Web Van, and Web Grocer. Many travel sites opened up: Travelocity, Expedia, Priceline. Banks, insurance companies, discount brokers, department stores—every type of business rushed to be the first and the best on the Web.

As people began to see that the sales just weren't materializing, they began to try to understand why. There was the debate between the "pure-play" and the "bricks and clicks" merchants. Pure-play referred to Web sellers who had no retail stores. At first, Amazon was pure-play, as were E*TRADE and Priceline.com. Some said that success at Web selling would more likely come to established chains that had bricks-and-mortar enterprises, could offer local delivery, were used to filling orders in quantities of one, and understood retailing. Barnes & Noble, by this reasoning, should be much more successful than Amazon because Barnes & Noble had thousands of retail stores. But, despite the debate, only AOL, eBay, and a few others, whether pure-play or bricks and clicks, were making a profit. Everyone knew that it would all work out some day, but when?

Part of what was pushing everyone to spend like mad on the Web was the idea of the "first mover advantage." America Online gave away six diskettes to every man woman and child in America and soon not only became number one, but absorbed most of its rivals and then took over the giant Time Warner conglomerate. AOL was always profitable. But several unprofitable dot coms had successful IPOs, making their backers very wealthy. After that, investors went absolutely crazy over the Web.

Many of these Web companies focused on the "new economics." Profits were unimportant to the new economics. The important things were hits and clicks. How many people visit your Web site? How long do they stay there? What do they look at? What do they click on? Those who pointed out that the Web sites did not show any profits were considered "old-fashioned" people who "just didn't get it." Many of the Web firms were run by young people, many of them technically inclined, who had never run a business of any kind before. They wore jeans and ponytails and shopped for organic foods. It was a weird, wonderful world, and it lasted about 5 years.

It all came to a halt in May 2000 when the judge's decision in the Microsoft case came down. While Microsoft was the biggest software company in the world, it was not a dominant presence on the Web. But Microsoft, in everyone's mind, was at the heart of the boom of the 1990s. Most people felt that the boom was due to the PC revolution, which Microsoft was given credit for starting and servicing. The Web was the second step in the PC revolution. If the government was going to break up Microsoft, what was next? Perhaps the whole boom was on shaky ground. Venture capitalists began to wonder if they would ever get back the hundreds of billions of dollars that they had invested in Web companies—99 percent of which had yet to show a return, or a hope of a return.

That was when hundreds, then thousands, then millions of people began to realize and admit that the emperor had no clothes. Investors began to look more closely at their Web investments, and they did not like what they saw. Microsoft, after all, was one of the most profitable companies in the history of the world. But only a handful of the hundreds of thousands of Web sites were profitable at all. And, worse, few of them had any hope of profitability in the near future. Most of them even lacked a long-term profit forecast. Selling on the Web to consumers turned out to be a gigantic failure. Let's see why that was.

The Web Is a Passive Medium

You listen to radio, watch TV, or read newspapers and magazines because of the content. Nearly everyone in the United States uses one or more of these media every single day. While you are doing so, the media blast ads at you. You can try to ignore those ads, but you cannot be totally unaware of them. The Web, on the other hand, is not nearly as essential to daily life, and probably never will be. There is content there, but most of it duplicates content that can be found in other media. Furthermore, it is easier to get the content from those other media. If you turn on the TV or the radio, or pick up your newspaper from your front door stoop in the morning, there is the content ready for you. You can read or listen while you eat breakfast or while you are getting dressed. You can listen in your car on your way to work. To access the Web, you have to sit down at your computer. You cannot do this while you are dressing, eating, or driving.

Once you get to work, however, the Web is available. Most employees do not have TV or radio at work, but nearly every office worker today has a PC, many of them with Web access. Office workers can, and do, read and write email all day long. It has become essential to modern office work. But email is not the same thing as the Internet. Employees are supposed to be working while they are at work, not surfing the Net. Some employees do listen to the radio while they work, but no one can work while surfing the Net (unless they are in search of business information). So the Web is basically off limits for most people for most of the working day. The same thing is true in the evening. You can sit down at your computer in the evening, and millions do just that. But what most people are doing is reading their email or playing computer games. Only a few spend much time surfing commercial Web sites. It is an exhausting and boring experience after the first week or so.

So the Web cannot be an active medium, blasting ads at people. The people are not watching. Web sites are passive; they are active only when people decide to look at them for a particular reason, which does not happen as often as people had at first assumed it would. What do people do on the Web? Some do personal (or professional) research. The Web is the greatest research tool ever invented. You can find information on just about anything. Some visit chat rooms. Some get details on news or events that go beyond what can be found in the mass media. Some buy products that they cannot easily find in stores. Some listen to or download music.

My vacuum cleaner story, I believe, is typical of consumer Web use. I bought a Hoover with a microfiltration system that needed special bags. When my bags ran out, I went to several supermarkets and department stores in search of more microfiltration bags. None of them stocked the bags. So in desperation I looked up Hoover on the Web. Sure enough, the company had a Web site that offered the right bags. I purchased several. I am sure that Hoover does not make a profit by selling small parts like this on the Web. What the Web site does for Hoover is make its microfiltration vacuum cleaner a viable product. Without the Web, few would ever be able to find the replacement bags.

The Web Is an Ordering Tool, Not a Selling Tool

In addition to vacuum cleaner bags, I have bought scores of books and movies on the Web. I have bought vitamins and hard-to-get replacement light bulbs and electronic parts. I would never buy clothing, an automobile, a TV, a house, a computer, or a microwave on the Web. Why not? Because when I buy most things, I want to see and feel the product, or talk to someone about it before I buy it.

Sears reports that many customers who are buying major appliances have already done their research on the Web. When they come to the store, they know what they want. But before they plunk down $1000, they want to see the product and talk to a salesperson. I researched Dell, Compaq, IBM, and Gateway on the Web before I bought the computer I am using to write this book. I finally settled on Gateway. But when I actually bought the computer, I called Gateway on the phone and talked to a sales rep, who put the package together for me with an Iomega Zip drive. This was a $1500 purchase. The sales rep talked me into a 1300-megahertz model that was on sale, rather than the 1500-megahertz that I had selected on the Web. I saved $300.

Web Advertising Was Highly Overrated

Since everyone assumed that consumers would flock to the Web and spend hours every day looking at Web sites, it made sense to clutter their computer screens with advertisements. A large percentage of the dot com business plans included advertising as an important revenue source. This was significant not only for the "portal" sites, such as Yahoo! and America Online, but also for thousands of other sites, such as those of the *New York Times* and the *Washington Post* and Women.com. Most of these sites had no other source of revenue. At first, advertising agencies placed substantial amounts of their clients' ads on the Web, hoping for success. When few people seemed to be responding to the ads, the idea was, "It is early yet. As people get used to the Web, the sales will follow." The sales did follow in a few areas (books, travel, and financial services), but even there, the profits were meager. The response rates to banner ads dropped from 2 percent to tiny fractions of 1 percent.

After the crash, most major corporations drastically reduced their advertising on the Web. The banners tended to be quick-decision, low-budget operations. Gone were the shopping arcades and many consumer product ads. Why? Because they didn't work as well as mass media ads.

Why Web Supermarkets Failed

Web supermarkets were featured in Don Peppers and Martha Rogers' first book, *The One to One Future*. Peapod, a Web supermarket, was used to explain how one-to-one marketing was the wave of the future. Unfortunately, Peapod is in trouble today, and most of its competitors have failed. Why? The reason is not difficult to discover. Supermarkets have become so competitive that their profit margin is only about 1 percent. That means that out of every dollar you spend there, the store gets only a penny in profit.

A Web supermarket has to operate in that environment. It has to take that penny and use it to pack customers' orders in boxes (using either low-cost workers or high-cost technology), put the boxes in refrigerated trucks, and deliver them to houses scattered all over a metropolitan area. No one can make any money doing that, and no one did. The Web supermarkets had to charge more than bricks-and-mortar supermarkets, but even the extra charge did not pay for the service they were providing.

Furthermore, most Web supermarkets failed to achieve the profits from the impulse buying that takes over when people visit a real supermarket. No one goes to a supermarket to buy a quart of milk and comes home with just a quart of milk. But if you are ordering on the Web, you haven't made the investment to get into your car and drive to a supermarket, park, find a cart, wander down the aisles, and then wait in line at the checkout counter. Everyone wants to make that investment worthwhile, so people pick up a few more items while they are there. A buyer on the Web who needs only a quart of milk doesn't see all the colorful vegetables piled up at the entrance. She doesn't see the ladies handing out samples to eat. She doesn't see the magazines at the checkout line. Her only investment is the $10 delivery charge. To avoid that delivery charge, she decides to pick up the milk at the 7-11 on her way home from work.

So, What Is Left? A Huge Research and Transaction Tool

Consumers buy books, credit cards, travel, pornography, and financial services on the Web. A much smaller number of people than had been anticipated in the 1990s look at or respond to ads. What they often do is research. Ordinary households use the Web as a combination of Yellow Pages and *Consumer Reports*. They look up maps, cars, appliances, real estate, and interest rates, and they use this information when they buy. Because of the Web, consumers are far better informed today than they were 5 years ago. It is not unusual to see a consumer going to a dealer carrying a PC printout that has all the background on what she plans to buy.

Dealers have to be more informed about their competition (and they find it easier to be thus informed) because their customers are better informed as a result of the Web.

My wife, Helena, and I were confronted with a problem. We had bought a condo in Fort Lauderdale, but our two cars were in Arlington, Virginia. We wanted to move one car to Florida and keep it there. I am not up to driving to Florida, and neither is Helena. So what could we do? We used www.Google.com and entered "Automobile Transportation." The first name on the list was www.intercitylines.com, which specializes in moving cars in closed vans. The price was right, and we made a deal then and there on the Web. How could we have found such a firm without the Web? The company is in Massachusetts, and it does not advertise in our Yellow Pages. This is what the Web is all about.

So what does this mean for those who want to use the Web to sell to consumers today? Manufacturers and catalogers need to have a really good site that has pictures and images of all their products and those products' features. They need to:

- Make it easy for customers to look up their products.
- Have a guide to local dealers by Zip code.
- Use the Web to sell spare parts that dealers cannot or will not stock.
- Make it easy to print on a PC what the consumer sees on the Web.

Premium Distribution

The Web has become a super method of distributing premiums or certificates. Here is how this works: Consumers arrive at commercial Web sites to do their research. Many of them will print out a page containing the information about your products. Since this is so, why not give them a reason to purchase the product right away by giving them a certificate (see Figure 3-1)? The certificate serves two purposes:

1. It drives traffic to the retailer.
2. The process of delivering it to the customer provides you with a customer's email name and address for further marketing efforts.

Here's how to do this. When a consumer is looking at your product on your Web site, there should always be a "Receive a valuable additional premium" button on the site next to the item. When consumers click on that button, they see a panel where they enter their name, address, and email address. If they have already printed a certificate from your site on this or a previous visit, the panel is automatically filled in, and all they need to do is to click on the "Send Certificate" button. When they click on this button, they will be sent an email containing the certificate as an attachment, which they can print on their PC printer. Are you afraid that some customers will abuse the certificates? No problem. You maintain a database, and if you allow only one certificate per product per email address, your Web site can easily control that.

What the certificate contains are two bar codes. There is a bar code for the product to be purchased and a bar code that has been created for the customer. To use the certificate for a mail-in rebate, the customer takes it to a retailer, buys the product, and receives a purchase receipt. He mails the certificate with the purchase receipt to the address shown on the certificate. At the fulfillment center, the certificate is scanned, capturing the product and customer data. There is no need for

Figure 3-1 Use of Web Certificates

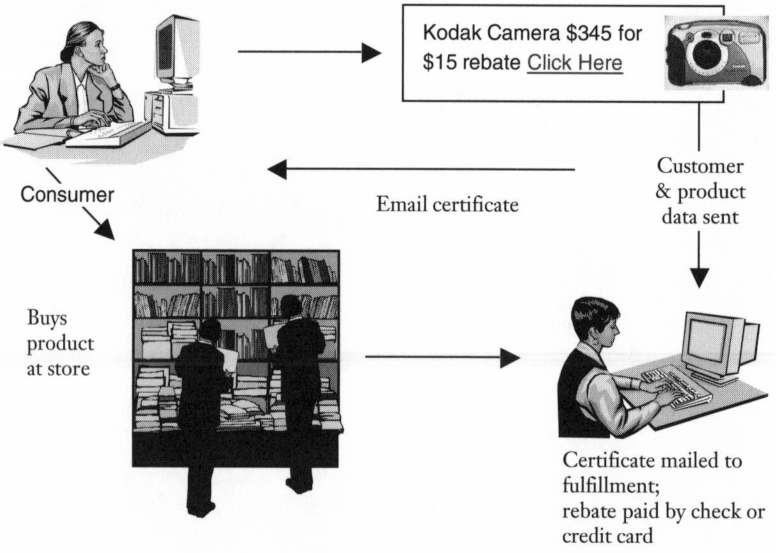

data entry at the fulfillment center, since your Web application automatically transmits all customer names to the center along with their bar codes at the time they are sent the emailed certificate. The fulfillment center simply checks the purchase receipt against the database created by the Web site and clicks OK. If a rebate is involved, a check is issued and mailed automatically.

A variation of this method, which can save the manufacturer money, is to have the customer provide his credit card data, which can also be converted to a bar code lookup table (not the actual credit card number) by the Web site software. At the fulfillment center, the scanning process can credit the rebate to the customer's credit card account, thus saving the cost of mailing a check. The customer receives an email from the fulfillment house simultaneously with the mailing of a check or the crediting of the credit card.

There are several important elements in this process:

- The customer cannot provide a fake email address, since a valid email address is required in order to get the certificate. She can't provide a fake name or address, or she will not get a cashable check. She can't provide a fake credit card number, or she won't get a refund.
- In applying for the rebate, the customer gives permission for the use of her email address for future promotions. If she does not want to receive information, the rebate could be smaller or not available.
- The manufacturer gains a database of customers and email addresses, which can be used for promotion.
- If the customer does buy the product, that fact is stored in the database and makes the database more valuable.
- The fulfillment house process is fully automated and therefore is cheaper and faster.
- The manufacturer can get daily reports on the success of the rebate program by product, state, region, and type of consumer.
- When registering for the certificate, the consumer can be asked for more information, such as income, age, and so on.

The certificates should not offer discounts. Discounts erode value. A better offer would be a premium, such as training or software that would go with the camera, or a rebate.

Pure-Play Selling on the Web

Less than 5 percent of the people who visit an online retail site actually buy something. Compare this with the performance of someone who drives up and parks at Wal-Mart or a supermarket. No one walks away from this trip empty-handed. Why don't people buy on the Web? Many sites are still too difficult to navigate. Flashy graphics that take minutes to download turn people off. The rigidity of shopping online is frustrating. My experience is typical.

When Orbitz.com opened its travel site, I was one of the first to use it. I ordered a cheap Thanksgiving flight to Manchester, New Hampshire, for Helena and me. Then I called my son David, who said that the timing was wrong. Orbitz.com would not let me change my flight times, despite several emails. I ended up wasting $400. My travel agent has always been able to make changes in nonrefundable flights. The irony of the situation is that when Thanksgiving rolled around, I received a maddening email from Orbitz.com telling me to get ready for my wonderful trip to Manchester. I will never again use Orbitz.com for anything. Its inflexible method of operation turned me off permanently. Its customer service was totally unresponsive. This is not what the Web should be.

Brooks: Clever Efforts to Promote Web Sales

To keep more customers, Web retailers have had to change their ways. To attract and hold customers, Brooks used a service called the Angara Reporter that collected demographic information, such as age, gender, and location, from At Home Corp.'s MatchLogic.com and Engage Inc. visitor profiles to create a rough idea of the kinds of customers who visit particular types of sites. Brooks used this information to personalize the content that visitors saw and to tailor offers on the basis of the profiles. Angara's profile was based on a database of 100 million Web visitors.

Visitors to Brooks's site were sorted by the site's best guess as to gender, marital status, and geography. Different visitors saw different home pages. A woman visitor would see a different page from that shown to a man. An unmarried younger man might see a different page from that shown to an older male. Brooks expected that this feature would offer a level of personalization that its regular stores could not match. Yet, as of this writing, Brooks has yet to make a profit. What can we learn from this?

- There are many very sophisticated and clever things that you can do using a database to create sales to consumers on the Web that you could not possibly do in regular merchandising.
- These things all cost money.
- Total Web sales are very tiny in comparison to retail sales.
- These clever things have yet to produce a lasting profit for anyone.
- Anyone trying to sell consumer products on the Web (with a few exceptions, such as Amazon and eBay) is going to lose money for the foreseeable future.

Dealer Locator

Commercial Web sites should make it very easy for customers to find dealers. This sounds like an obvious suggestion, but in fact it is often very difficult for manufacturers to provide a dealer locator. Most goods are sold through wholesalers or distributors. These folks keep the dealers' names to themselves. Yet providing information to the ultimate consumer is a very efficient way of delivering customers to dealers and building total market share.

How can you find dealers? Follow the money trail. Make it easy and profitable for dealers to be identified. To do this, have a Web microsite where dealers can provide their location, phone number, directions, store hours, and other such information (Figure 3-2). When dealers come to your microsite to register, have them provide the name of the wholesaler or distributor that supplies your products to them. Once your Web site has captured the dealers' name, the Web site can automatically send the information to the appropriate wholesaler or distributor for verification before it becomes a part of your consumer Web site dealer locator. Some wholesalers or distributors will help you in this process; others will not.

Figure 3-2 Finding a Dealer

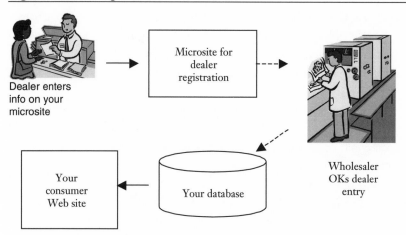

The dealers provide you with their information plus their email address. Then, when customers come to your Web site and ask for a local dealer, if the customers give you permission, you can send their names to the dealer for follow-up.

Citigroup Strikes Out

In 1997, Citigroup, the parent company of Citibank, launched e-Citi, a Web bank that was designed to compete with Citibank itself and other parts of the $230 billion company. Citigroup put a lot of resources into the venture. Within 3 years the Web bank had 1600 employees and 100 different Web sites. Between 1998 and 2000, Citigroup spent $1.1 billion on the effort. It was a gigantic failure. By March of 2000, when Citigroup called it to a halt, the venture had only 30,000 accounts, compared to the 146 million accounts in Citibank.

What went wrong? For one thing, e-Citi was set up as an independent venture. Customers could not use Citibank branches. This was a fundamental mistake. People using a Web bank have a large number of questions to start with:

- How do I deposit money?
- What ATMs can I use?

- Whom do I talk to when I have a problem or need a loan?
- Whom can I relate to?

Since, on top of all that, there was no institution to identify with, it is amazing that Citigroup was able to find 30,000 people who were willing to open accounts.

No Web bank has ever made a profit, and none ever will. What can be profitable is for an existing bank with lots of branches to persuade some of its customers to use the Web for some of their transactions. Web transactions cost about one penny each. Branch visits cost at least $2. The cost savings to the bank can be very substantial. But customers will use the Web only if they have confidence in the institution and if there is someone whom they can go to see when they need help.

After Citibank folded the e-Citi operation, the company formed an Internet Operating Group to see which Citibank services could be profitably shifted to the Web. The company created an online-payments business called C2It that let customers email money to one another for a 1 percent fee. Individual Citibank units were encouraged to shift functions to the Web. Eighteen months later, Citigroup was serving 10 million customers online with a variety of services. Looking forward, Citigroup expects to cut $1 billion off its annual costs through using the Web.

eToys Strikes Out

When eToys went public in 1999, its market value reached $7.7 billion. The company was backed by Intel, Sequoia Capital, and Idealab. What a great beginning! Its Web site included a sophisticated search engine that let parents look for toys appropriate for a child of a particular age, or for toys of a particular brand or theme. It created "wish lists" that let children choose gifts and email their lists to family members. Once the firm's Web site was out there for everyone to see, however, competitors like Amazon and Wal-Mart were in a position to copy the firm's ideas and beat its prices, and they did. Soon competitors began to sprout up everywhere: KBKids, Smarterkids, Toysmart, ZanyBrainy, NuttyPutty, JC Penney, Target, and FAO Schwarz joined Amazon and Wal-Mart in selling toys on the Web. Many of them spent lavishly on advertising.

eToys assumed that loyal customers would come back once they had been acquired. On the Web, customers soon learn that it is very easy to shop around—and they do. Proximity works with bricks-and-mortar stores. You can drive to them, park in their parking lots, and go inside. The Web is very different. It is very hard to create and maintain customer loyalty on the Web. eToys could not count on its customers coming back, and they didn't.

Even given the competition, eToys assumed that the growth of the Web would provide enough buyers for everyone. The company planned to double its sales every year. That was achievable only when sales were very small. In fact, competitors multiplied and national sales grew only modestly, and so eToys' forecasts were worthless.

Perhaps eToys' biggest mistake was spending too much to create a distribution network. The company's investment in property and equipment amounted to more than $120 million. This meant that property investment equaled about 95 percent of the year's revenue. A similar figure for retailers was 20 percent, and one for catalogers was 13 percent. Faced with these investments, eToys could not make a profit without a massive sales increase. That increase did not occur.

Business-to-Business Web Transactions

The Web has proved to be an excellent transaction medium for business-to-business dealings. Some companies selling memory chips for computers, for example, have registered sales of several hundred million dollars per year. For a few, these transactions represent more than 85 percent of their total revenue. Their sales are to companies that buy computer components to install in units for sale or to upgrade their own equipment. This type of Web transaction will continue to grow in the years ahead.

How do customers find out about these transaction sites? About a third of them comes from advertisements placed in print magazines, a third comes from Web ads on technical sites, and the remainder comes from search engines. Many have established premier pages for their best customers. On these pages, their best customers have established accounts, so that their employees can order the units charged directly to their company accounts.

Business-to-business Web transactions continue to register success in a wide variety of fields. Why are they more successful than consumer Web sales? There are several reasons:

- The average order size of business transactions is much greater than the average consumer order size.
- The universe of business customers is much smaller. It is less expensive to reach them through direct mail or print or Web advertising than to reach average consumers.
- Premier pages work well here. They don't work at all with consumers.
- Business customers have a continuing and predictable need for most of the business products sold through the Web. Consumer purchases cannot be predicted as easily.
- Business-to-business transactions on the Web are conducted during the day, when buyers and sellers are in their offices working at their company PCs. Consumers, on the other hand, if they are employed, have to do their Web shopping after they get home at night. There are competing demands on their time. It is more fun to go to the mall with their families or to watch television. That is why about 80 percent of all sales on the Web are business to business.

Selling on the Web: What We Have Learned

- *Business-to-business e-commerce transactions can be highly successful.*
- *Pure-play Web e-commerce seldom works.* Success comes to established businesses that add a Web presence. To make the Web work, you have to build a very expensive distribution system. Once you have built such a system, you are not a pure-play operation anymore.
- *Barriers to entry on the Web are very low.* It is very easy and inexpensive to start a new Web site in any category. It is very hard and expensive to build a chain of stores and warehouses. That

means that if you are successful on the Web, you will very soon have many Web competitors.

- *People like to hold something in their hands before they buy it.* What about catalogs? A catalog is something you can hold in your hands, pass around, and scribble on; you can tear out pages and stick them on your refrigerator. You can't do any of this easily on the Web.
- *There is precious little loyalty on the Web.* To keep people coming back, you have to personalize your Web site and communicate often. Mass advertising is too expensive for most Web sites. Loyalty is very difficult to generate and maintain on the Web.

So if you have an established land-based business and want to benefit from the Web, what should you do?

- *Look on the Web as more of an ordering medium than a selling medium.* Put your Web URL on all your catalogs, brochures, and direct mail pieces. Provide one-click ordering to make it super fast.
- *Provide a dealer locator.*
- *Create a profile of every customer.* Give all your customers, whether business-to-business or business-to-consumer, a personal PIN, and invite them to come to your Web site to update their profile. Give them a gift for doing so. What is a profile? It contains not just the customer's name and address, but the customer's email address (with permission to use it), demographics, family composition, preferences, and purchasing history. Get the customer's permission for you to remember his or her ID and password—that is, permission to put a cookie on his or her PC. If the customer is a business, use the profile to find out what it does, how it uses your products, and how often it buys. Use the profile to populate your database that is used for regular offline sales.
- *Use the profile to personalize your site.* As Amazon or Staples does, say, "Welcome back, Susan" (using a cookie). Then vary the site content based on the profile. If Susan has children under the age of 4, your site will look different from the way it will look if she has children in college. This is not expensive to do. Most sites that have customer profiles developed can become fully personalized for a hundred thousand dollars—not millions.

- *Communicate often.* When customers hit the one-click order button, thank them then and there for the order and reiterate what it was for. While they are reading this, send them an email repeating your thanks. Then send an email saying, "Your order will be shipped on . . ." Then another email: "Your order was shipped by UPS with this tracking number . . ." And another email a week later: "Did your order arrive on time? Were you satisfied with it? <u>Click Here</u> to let us know your reaction."

Success on the Web

If you can't make money selling on the Web, what should you do? Measure your success in other ways. This should not be total sales. Total Web sales are still a small fraction of all sales. For most catalogers, Web sales seldom exceed 15 percent of total sales. What the Web does is permit you to save some money, if you do it right. You have to have a Web site today. It is how companies are judged by customers, suppliers, and investors. You can't hide your head in the sand just because you cannot make money from your site. So build it, and keep the costs down. Then do the following things:

- *Put lots of free information on the Web.* Every company has information lying around that could be made available to customers. Magazines and newspapers have archives. Technical companies have lots of technical reference data. Travel services (hotels, resorts, airlines, travel agencies, cruise lines) have massive amounts of information about destinations: maps, weather, activities, amenities, local lore and history, tours, and so on. Put all that on the Web for free. Why? Because it will save you lots of money. Encourage travelers to find out what it is like to go to Italy by reading your Web site and looking at pictures rather than by talking to your customer service reps all day. Once they have made up their minds, they can then call a CSR to book their trip.
- *Measure your success by reduction in calls to CSRs.* Begin the year by estimating the number of incoming and outgoing calls that you expect to field during the year. Analyze those calls. How much will they cost? Why are they made? Which types of call could be

handled on the Web? Then set up your Web site to answer the questions most likely to be asked of a CSR. "Where is my order?" "How do I get replacement parts?" "What is the weather going to be like in Prague?" If you do this right, you will be able to save millions of dollars by shifting these calls to the Web. I worked with a travel-related firm that received more than 7 million telephone calls a year, costing it more than $48 million. This company measured its Web success by the number of these inquiries that it could get its customers to make on the Web. Each CSR call cost the company $6.50. Each Web visit cost less than $0.10. If even 10 percent of these calls could be shifted to the Web, the company could easily save millions of dollars. Some companies that have done this find that CSR calls do not decrease, but that customers use the Web to get the information and call the CSR to close the deal. This is wonderful!

- *Sell parts and replacements.* Any established business can profitably provide replacement parts through the Web. Look at Hoover.com, where you can find replacement parts that are not carried in any retail store. Go to GEAppliances.com, where you can find 50,000 parts that you can buy on the Web.
- *Travel sites can help your travel business.* Travel-related businesses can profit from being on the Web even if they don't sell anything directly. Hotels, car rental agencies, airlines, and amusement and theme parks can benefit. I am writing this from Fort Lauderdale, Florida, where I am spending some time with my children and grandchildren. We needed a six-passenger minivan, but Hertz, Avis, Budget, National, etc. were sold out. I found a brand new minivan from Payless Auto Rental (who ever heard of that firm?) on the Web. How else would I have been able to locate such a company?
- *Publicity.* Every rock star today has a personal Web site. Why? Vanity? Not at all. If you register at a Web site for Sheryl Crow or Madonna, you will be added to a list. When the singer's next album is released, you will probably get an email. Experts in the industry can demonstrate a relationship between emails to fans and retail store sales. Publicity on the Web can be made to pay.
- *Sell to business customers.* This is a major growth area.

Why Selling on the Web Cannot Be Easy

Using the Web to compete with established businesses was a pipe dream. It could never work. Why not?

- Established businesses spent millions to get where they are, and they will not fall down and play dead just because some Web site comes along.
- If it were easy, you would have lots of Web competitors, and you would soon find it difficult.
- Furthermore, if it were easy, the established businesses could always beat you by doing exactly what you are trying to do, because they know a lot more about it than you do.

Measuring the Value of a Site

From the previous discussion, it is obvious that for most companies, Web sites cannot be successful sales channels to consumers for most of their products. They are primarily ordering vehicles and information providers. They may be excellent sales channels for spare parts and supplies and for obscure and slow-moving items that dealers will not stock. To think properly about the role of the Web site, we must begin to think of it as a cross between mass media ads, spare parts distributors, and customer service. The value of a manufacturer's consumer Web site today is estimated in Table 3-1.

Table 3-1 Monthly Value of a Commercial Consumer Web Site

	Customers	Rate	Value
Visits per month	500,000	$ 0.02	$ 10,000
Customers registered	20,000	$ 1.00	$ 20,000
CSR time saved	50,000	$ 4.00	$ 200,000
Data printed	40,000	$ 2.00	$ 80,000
Rebate certificates printed	25,000	$ 2.00	$ 50,000
Certificates redeemed	15,000	$64.00	$ 960,000
Parts sold	8,000	$12.00	$ 96,000
Total value			$1,416,000

Let's start one step up from the bottom:

- *Parts sold.* Every Web site should sell spare parts and replacement items that dealers will not or cannot stock. These parts are not a profit center. They are a reason for consumers to visit the site. They can be the most important draw on any site and can turn existing customers into advocates. To determine the value of parts sold, we have to consider three factors:
    - The profit made on the parts themselves, which may be quite low, depending on how you want to price them
    - The acquisition of a customer name and email address, which can be valuable for marketing
    - The goodwill and brand name publicity value of the site
- *Certificates redeemed.* To determine the value of these certificates, we need to consider the profit from the sale of the item less the rebate and fulfillment costs. If the profit, for example, is $80, we must subtract $15 for the certificate and $2 for the fulfillment cost, giving us $63 net profit. To be totally accurate, you can make the assumption that some of your products might have been sold to these same people without the certificate, so that the profit from the sale that is attributable to the Web would be less than the full profit. You can experiment and test to get the right answer.
- *Certificates printed (whether redeemed or not).* There are two benefits of having a certificate printed. First, of course, is the fact that some of the certificates will be redeemed, which has already been discussed. But whether a Web certificate is redeemed or not, it has value to the issuer, because before the certificate is printed, we require a valid name, address, and email name. To determine the value of a name, we can use the method described in Chapter 5, "The Value of a Name." Here we are assuming that it is $2.
- *Data printed.* When people go to your Web site, you make it easy for them to find information and print it out on their PC printers. Make sure your name and identification is on everything that they print. People who are looking for a refrigerator may print out information from your site and take it with them when they visit a store. They will print out the specifications of your automobiles,

your swimming pools, and your condominiums. This is wonderful! It's great advertising to have detailed information on your products in the hands of people who are about to make a purchase. This is worth a lot of money to you, and it is much cheaper than mass marketing, where you pay for ads that millions will not read or listen to.

- *CSR time saved.* One important function of your Web site must be to reduce the time that your customer service reps spend explaining things that are more easily read and printed by customers. Put thousands of pages of information on your site free. Provide a super search engine so that anyone can find anything in three clicks. Measure your success by hours of time saved by customer service reps at $4 per telephone call. Encourage your CSRs to get customers to do the research themselves.
- *Customers registered.* Of course you want customers to register if they come to the site. Most of them won't, of course, but many will. You can follow up with an email thanking them for the site visit and answering any questions that they posed when they registered. Why is registration worth money? Because you will use the email names that they give you to send marketing messages to in the future.
- *Web visits.* There is value to a Web visit, whether or not the consumers who visit print data or certificates. Your Web page is, after all, an advertisement. We can assign a value to this, just as we do to TV, radio, or print ads. We are assuming that a Web visit is worth $0.02.
- *Total value.* Assigning a total value to a Web site is important. It permits you to decide how much to spend on the Web site, and it lets you budget for the staff that is maintaining it.

If you do a good job of designing your Web site, it will capture many customer names every month. These names may be used for marketing programs. In this example, the total value is $1.4 million per month. Your site may not be as valuable as this, but you can use this table to estimate the benefit of your site to your company. It is probably worth more to you than you thought.

What Works

- Business-to-business Web transactions.
- Using the Web as an ordering site to support paper catalogs.
- Using the Web to sell spare parts and replacements for products sold in retail stores.
- Using the Web as a dealer locator.
- Using the Web to capture information about customers that can be used to create emails that will drive those customers to your site to make a purchase.
- Providing free information and pictures on your Web site to save the time of customer service reps.
- Using the Web to replace customer service time.
- Distributing certificates through the Web.
- Registering customers on the Web.

What Doesn't Work

- Thinking of the Web as a sales medium. It isn't. It is an ordering medium.
- A pure-play, stand-alone, consumer selling Web site (with limited exceptions for travel and pornography) without a catalog or retail stores.
- Assuming that advertising on the Web will be the main source of revenue.
- Catalogs on the Web without paper catalogs to drive people to the site.
- Web supermarkets.

Quiz

1. Why did the judge's decision in the Microsoft case lead to the dot com crash?
   a. Microsoft was the heart of the Web.

    b. The public feared that the government was going to go after the Web next.

    c. Profits on the Web were very high.

    d. The Web was a major sales medium.

    e. None of the above.

2. Why did Web advertising fail?

    a. Ad prices were too high.

    b. There were too many ads on the Web.

    c. The Web is a passive medium.

    d. Competing media combined to kill it.

    e. Few Web sites depended on ads for their revenue.

3. Why did all Web supermarkets fail?

    a. Because no one wanted to have groceries delivered

    b. Because of the economics of the supermarket industry

    c. Because major chains fought them

    d. Because investors could not be found to start such enterprises

    e. Because selling groceries on the Web was a crazy idea

4. What are the flaws in the Web certificate idea?

    a. There are none. It is a wonderful idea.

    b. Customers will give fake email names.

    c. Customers will give fake addresses.

    d. Customers will abuse the system by sending in for too many refund checks.

    e. Customers hate certificates and will not use them.

5. Why did e-Citi fail?

    a. Citibank did not give it adequate funding or time.

    b. The e-Citi customers could not use Citibank branches.

    c. Citibank was not very well known.

    d. Citibank did not devote enough employees to the project.

    e. The reason is unknown, since most Web banks are highly successful.

6. Why did eToys fail?

    a. It had inadequate market capitalization.

    b. Its site was not very sophisticated.

    c. Many competitors copied its ideas and stole its customers.

   d. It did not spend enough on its distribution network.
   e. The answer is unknown, since most Web-only merchants have been successful.

7. Which was not suggested as a way for land-based businesses to be successful on the Web?
   a. Provide a dealer locator.
   b. Get customers to provide profiles.
   c. Keep customer communications to a minimum.
   d. Provide free information on your site.
   e. Personalize your site using cookies and customer profiles.

8. Which was not suggested as a way to succeed on the Web?
   a. Provide free information.
   b. Eliminate telephone customer service.
   c. Sell replacements and parts.
   d. Have a Web site.
   e. Encourage publicity.

9. Which does the chapter suggest is the most profitable single activity on the Web for a typical company?
   a. Selling replacement parts
   b. Advertising on the site
   c. Customer visits
   d. Certificates
   e. Customer service

10. Which is the one reason not given for significant success from a Web site?
   a. Customer visits
   b. Advertising
   c. Publicity
   d. Customer service
   e. Consumer product sales

CHAPTER 4

COMPUTING LIFETIME VALUE

I think that without numbers there is no future. You cannot measure your progress unless you've got benchmarks against which to evaluate costs and profits. So ROI, RFM, and lifetime value are the minimal critical benchmarks you must now establish if you want to measure the profitability of your business today. Those same benchmarks then become the standards by which you measure your business's future growth and the justification for the database tools you must have to get that growth. Without the numbers, you don't have a future.

—John Travis, Manager, Business Development, Hudson's Bay Company

There are really only three marketing functions:

1. Acquiring customers
2. Retaining or reactivating them
3. Selling them more products

Everything else is a modification of one of these three functions. Measuring customer lifetime value is central to all three functions, as we will see in this chapter. Lifetime value tells you how much you should be spending on each function, and it measures whether your marketing efforts are doing any good.

Lifetime value is a measure of the net profit that you will receive from a given customer during his or her future lifetime as your customer.

I have computed the lifetime value of customers for a great many different companies, including banks, credit card issuers, insurance companies, packaged goods companies, software companies, hardware companies, and automobile companies. The case study given in this chapter deals with a fictitious automobile company. It is interesting because it illustrates how to compute the automobile repurchase cycle over a 9-year period, which is what automobile companies have to deal with. The case illustrates the methods used. The numbers have been modified so that they are not derived from any particular automobile company—the case does not disclose any proprietary information, but rather is a summary of my experience with three very different automobile companies over several years.

Asian Automobiles

In this chapter, we will take you through the computation of lifetime value for an automobile company, which we call Asian. Then we will show you the strategies that arise as a result.

Asian sells automobiles and arranges car leases and loans. The company had 2 million customers on its database. These customers included current owners of new Asian cars, owners of used Asian cars, and Asian leaseholders. The first and most important part of the lifetime value project was determining the repurchase rate of Asian's customers.

The repurchase rate for automobiles is very complicated. Some people buy a new car every year. Others buy them only every 2, 3, 4, 5, 6, 7, or even more years. Some buy two or more cars. Others buy used cars. Still others buy an Asian, drive it for a while, then sell it and buy some other brand. Then they come back to Asian after a few years. In all of this buying and selling, what is the repurchase rate?

The repurchase rate for automobiles is the percentage of the average group of customers who will buy a new car from the same manufacturer when they turn in their existing vehicle.

The repurchase rate is further complicated by the fact that Asian has many different models of cars, and each model has its own unique repurchase rate.

The goal for any automobile company is to have a repurchase rate of more than 100 percent. How would that be possible? It would occur if customers never died, if they always bought the same brand when they turned in their existing vehicle, and if many of them bought two or more cars. For the automobile industry as a whole, the repurchase rate is about 35 percent. The goal is to determine the repurchase rate for every Asian model and for owners of used Asian cars as well.

To accomplish this, it is necessary to develop some tables from the database that illustrate the situation. Such tables should begin with a particular year, such as 1997. You can then determine what Asian cars the owners of 1997 models owned in the summer of 2002. Next, you create the same tables for the owners of 1998, 1999, 2000, and 2001 models. Finally, you have to create similar tables for Certified Previously Owned (CPO) Asian cars—Asian cars that were bought used. These data are usually available because manufacturers require their dealers to report the owners of each new and each used Asian. This information is stored in Asian's database. Table 4-1 shows what the 1997 Asian owners owned in the year 2002.

From these data, one would assume that the repurchase rate varied from 22 to 38 percent, but that is not the case. To get the real repurchase rates, you have to figure in the Asian owners who bought cars every year, every 2 years, and so on. The numbers shown in Table 4-1 mask the fact that in the 5 years between 1997 and 2002, a significant

Table 4-1 Changes in Ownership over the Years

Chart A	Totals	A Model	B Model	C Model	D Model	E Model
Owned 1997	120,409	17,472	53,259	26,784	17,646	452
Owned 2002	91,875	14,133	38,950	19,585	14,111	339
Bought new	30,295	4,003	11,666	7,861	6,619	146
A Model	9,491	980	6,221	1,464	802	24
B Model	3,735	1,729	1,040	565	382	20
C Model	8,491	651	3,047	3,924	844	26
D Model	6,684	396	838	1,267	4,126	57
E Model	1,893	247	521	641	466	19
Repurchase rate	25%	23%	22%	29%	38%	32%

number of people bought two, three, or more new cars from the company and resold them, and many purchased multiple vehicles and kept them. Dozens of charts are needed to measure and account for the varying behavior of customers. Overall, the picture that emerged was of the average Asian customer buying a new car every 3 years because of the expiration of the lease and loan arrangements. The raw numbers have to be converted into adjusted numbers as shown in Table 4-2.

Putting the numbers from all years together gives us the results shown in Table 4-3. From Table 4-3, we are able to go on to compute the automobile owners' lifetime value. The lifetime value chart for the B Model is shown in Table 4-4.

Table 4-4 needs some explanation. In the first place, the data showed that the repurchase rate tended to go up for long-term Asian car owners. Long-term owners tend to be more loyal than newer owners. The $4000 profit per car is the profit to Asian, not the profit to the Asian dealer. Asian is actually selling cars to dealers, not to the general public. The acquisition cost per car was the amount per car that Asian spent on co-op ads and other promotions. Each dealer, of course, had its own

Table 4-2 Adjusted Repurchase Rates

		Totals	A Model	B Model	C Model	D Model	E Model
			Raw Totals				
1997		25.16%	22.91%	21.90%	29.35%	37.51%	32.28%
1998		24.00%	16.00%	23.00%	26.00%	35.00%	17.00%
1999		16.00%	11.00%	16.00%	14.00%	23.00%	20.00%
2000		7.00%	5.00%	6.00%	6.00%	8.00%	20.00%
2001		4.00%	4.00%	3.00%	4.00%	5.00%	20.00%
			Adjusted Totals				
1997	0.33	7.90%	7.40%	6.00%	11.00%	12.70%	10.90%
1998	0.5	11.50%	8.20%	11.30%	13.10%	17.40%	8.50%
1999	1	15.80%	10.90%	16.10%	14.10%	22.60%	20.00%
2000	1	7.00%	5.20%	5.60%	6.40%	8.00%	20.00%
2001	2	7.90%	7.20%	6.10%	7.10%	9.90%	40.00%
Total	5	0.10%	39.00%	45.20%	51.60%	70.60%	71.00%

Table 4-3 Final Repurchase Rates

	Totals	A Model	B Model	C Model	D Model	E Model
Repurchase rates	50.10%	39.00%	45.20%	51.60%	70.60%	71.00%

Table 4-4 Lifetime Value

B Model cars	Years 1–3	Years 4–6	Years 7–9
Revenue			
Repurchase rate	45.20%	47.40%	51.20%
Customers	264,124	119,384.	56,588
Net profit per car	$4,000	$4,000	$4,000
Net revenue	$1,056,496,000	$477,536,192	$226,352,155
Costs			
Acquisition cost per car	$400	$300	$275
Acquisition cost	$105,649,600	$ 35,815,214	$ 15,561,711
Marketing costs ($20/yr)	$ 5,282,480	$ 2,387,681	$ 1,131,761
Total marketing and sales	$110,932,080	$ 38,202,895	$ 16,693,471
Profit	$945,563,920	$ 439,333,297	$ 209,658,684
Discount rate	1.11	1.31	1.54
NPV of profit	$851,859,387	$ 335,368,929	$ 136,142,002
Cumulative NPV of profit	$851,859,387	$1,187,228,316	$1,323,370,318
Lifetime value	$3,225.23	$44,94.97	$50,10.41

advertising and promotion costs, which are not reflected in these numbers. The marketing costs ($20 per customer per year) are the amounts that Asian spent annually on the database and on communications with customers. This is a high number. Many car companies spend only a fraction of this amount on marketing to existing customers.

The profit is equal to the revenue less the costs. This profit has to be discounted to reflect the net present value of the funds involved.

The net present value is the current (today's) value of money that you are going to receive in the future, as $1000 to be received a year from now is not worth as much as $1000 received today. To compute the value of $1000 to be received a year from now, you have to discount it by an amount that reflects the cost of waiting. Waiting has a cost, because if you had the $1000 now, you could invest it and receive a return. By waiting, you forgo that return. We discount all future profits in a lifetime value chart to produce net present value. The numbers behind Table 4-4 are shown in Table 4-5.

The discount rate reflects the fact that for Asian, automobile sales are a business-to-business transaction between Asian and its dealers. See Chapter 2 for the formula for the discount rates.

Finally, of course, the lifetime value of a customer is derived by dividing the cumulative net present value number in each of the three

Table 4-5 Discount Rate Conversions

Factor	Rate
Time delay 1–3 years	2.0
Time delay 4–6 years	5.0
Time delay 7–9 years	8.0
Risk factor	1.20
Cost of capital	4.6%

time periods by the original 264,124 customers. What we are computing is the lifetime value of these 264,124 customers. Table 4-4 tells us that the value of a newly acquired customer to Asian is $5010 in the ninth year.

What You Can Do with the Numbers

Knowing what the lifetime value of a customer will be 9 years from now is not very valuable unless you can use that number to drive marketing strategy in some way that will increase company profits. That is exactly what we are going to do. Let's look again at the repurchase rate by model (see Table 4-3).

The average Asian repurchase rate is about 50 percent, but the repurchase rate for B Model cars is only 45.2 percent. The B Model is Asian's most popular car. Suppose the repurchase rate for this car could be raised so that it was equal to the average repurchase rate for all Asian cars, namely 50 percent. This is certainly an achievable goal. If it were to be reached, what would it do for Asian's profits? We can calculate that by making two assumptions:

1. We can come up with strategies that raise the repurchase rate of this model of car.
2. The strategies will succeed in bringing the repurchase rate up to 50 percent, or about even with the repurchase rate for the average Asian car.

What might these strategies be? There are many things that Asian might offer its customers:

- A welcome kit inviting new owners to come to a Web site to update their profile and to provide an email address for future correspondence
- Regular communications about the car, including service requirements
- A car birthday card
- An Asian magazine for new-car owners only
- Invitations to events sponsored by Asian, including skiing and yachting excursions, golf tournaments, and fashion shows
- Special preview information for owners on new Asian models and features
- A customer service call twice a year:

  "Welcome, Arthur. I am Jennifer, your personal Asian customer service representative. I am here to make your B Model ownership a wonderful experience. Here is my personal phone number. Call me whenever you need assistance of any kind. You can reach me at any time. I am here to help."

  What could Jennifer do?
  - She could provide the owner with the distance and directions to the nearest gasoline station, hotel, restaurant, or hospital.
  - She could call the police, when needed, or provide emergency road service.
  - She could help to locate cars that have been stolen or that have been lost in a vast airport parking lot.
  - She could locate the nearest Asian dealer and schedule service.
  - She could communicate with the owner by email, sending birthday cards and service reminders.

In other words, it is possible to make owning an Asian B Model so attractive that enough owners will want the same model next time to make the repurchase rate climb from 45 percent to 50 percent. Let's say that the cost of these additional services would be $30 per car per year. Putting that increase into the calculations, Table 4-6 shows what would happen to B Model lifetime value. Comparing before and after, we have increased Asian's profits by $56 million over 9 years, as shown in Table 4-7.

Table 4-6 Lifetime Value after Retention Programs

New LTV	Years 1–3	Years 4–6	Years 7–9
Revenue			
Repurchase rate	50.00%	53.00%	56.00%
Customers	264,124	132,062	69,993
Net profit per car	$4,000	$4,000	$4,000
Net revenue	$1,056,496,000	$528,248,000	$279,971,440
Costs			
Acquisition cost per car	$400	$300	$275
Acquisition cost	$105,649,600	$39,618,600	$19,248,037
Marketing costs ($50/yr)	$ 13,206,200	$6,603,100	$3,499,643
Total marketing & sales	$118,855,800	$46,221,700	$22,747,680
Profit	$937,640,200	$482,026,300	$257,223,761
Discount rate	1.11	1.31	1.54
NPV of profit	$844,720,901	$367,959,008	$167,028,416
Cumulative NPV of profit	$844,720,901	$1,212,679,909	$1,379,708,324
Lifetime value	$3,198.20	$4,591.33	$5,223.71

Table 4-7 LTV Gain

	Years 1–3	Years 4–6	Years 7–9
New lifetime value	$3,198.20	$4,591.33	$5,223.71
Previous lifetime value	$3,225.23	$4,494.97	$5,010.41
Difference	($27.03)	$96.36	$213.30
Times 264,124 customers	($7,138,486)	$25,451,592	$56,338,006

Let's see just what this $56 million profit means. If you look at years 1 through 3, you will see a loss of $7 million. The loss comes about, of course, because we are spending $30 more per customer per year to build and maintain a profitable relationship with Asian's customers. These improved relationships will not show up until the 3 years are over and Asian's customers make a decision on their next new car. Without a long-range plan, few car companies would be willing to stand for a $7 million loss in the first 3 years. Numbers like this are the reason why database marketing is such a hard sell for all but the most established and forward-thinking companies. But the $56 million profit is real. It includes all costs, and it absorbs the $7 million loss in the first 3 years. As we shall see later, this $7 million loss is not real. It is offset by gains from buyers who get a new car every 1 or 2 years.

Buying a Car Every Year

Relationship building does not need to stop with moving the B Model repurchase rate up to 50 percent. In fact, there is much more that you could do with the lifetime value analysis in this situation.

The tables given so far have assumed that the average Asian customer buys or leases a new car every 3 years—and, in fact, that is the case. What it ignores, however, is the fact that there are a substantial number of Asian customers who buy new cars every year or every 2 years. What will be the impact of the retention-building programs on these people? Detailed studies of the Asian database showed the following:

- Six percent of Asian B Model owners bought a new car every year.
- Six percent of Asian B Model owners bought a new car every 2 years.
- The overall increase in sales due to the new program will affect not just the third-year totals, but the interim-year totals as well, because your communication strategies will affect these 1- and 2-year buyers and get them to improve their repurchase rates.

There is an extra 1.2 percent increase in sales in addition to the overall 5 percent increase (from 45 to 50 percent), for a total increase of 6.2 percent. Plugging that 6.2 percent increase into the tables raises the $56 million to $73 million. But that's not all.

Automobile Financing

In the LTV analysis, it is also necessary to consider automobile financing. Like most car companies, Asian runs an automobile leasing and finance business as well. This is a profitable business for Asian. If we are going to increase the repurchase rate of Asian automobiles, we will also automatically increase the profits from leases and financing. To see how this is calculated, let's look at a baseline automobile leasing lifetime value table (see Table 4-8).

There are some interesting new rows on this table. Asian does not get to finance every Asian car that is sold, of course. The financing really depends on the market at the particular dealership. There are

Table 4-8 Car Leasing LTV

Revenue	Years 1–3	Years 4–6	Years 7–9
Repurchase rate	45.20%	47.90%	49.90%
Refinance rate	62.00%	64.00%	66.00%
Retention rate	28.00%	30.70%	32.90%
Customers	100,000	28,000	8,596
Amount financed by lease	$30,000	$32,000	$34,000
Total amount financed	$3,000,000,000	$896,000,000	$292,264,000
Income before taxes	$1,452.22	$1,582.92	$1,725.38
Total income before taxes	$145,222,000	$44,321,754	$14,831,389
Costs			
Acquisition cost	$ 6,000,000	$ 1,680,000	$ 515,760
Marketing costs ($12)	$ 1,200,000	$ 336,000	$ 103,152
Total marketing & sales	$ 7,200,000	$ 2,016,000	$ 618,912
Profit	$138,022,000	$ 42,305,754	$ 14,212,477
Discount rate	1	1.33	1.64
NPV of profit	$138,022,000	$ 31,808,838	$ 8,666,144
Cumulative NPV of profit	$138,022,000	$169,830,838	$178,496,982
Lifetime value	$1,380.22	$1,698.31	$1,784.97

hundreds of banks and finance companies in the auto leasing and loan business. Asian will get the financing only if it has a good offer and the dealer pushes the sale. Asian has determined that it gets the financing in only 62 percent of the new car purchases. For that reason, a repurchase rate of 45.2 percent of cars translates into a 28 percent retention rate for leases or loans.

To get the dealers to insist on Asian financing, Asian has to make it worth their while. It does this by paying the dealer a premium of $60 per lease or loan as a commission. That is shown here as the lease acquisition cost. In addition, Asian contacts its customers with a welcome kit and other communications to ensure that customers appreciate the value of Asian financing and will use Asian again when the time comes. Asian spends $12 per customer every 3 years on communications to improve the customer retention rate.

The discount rate for automobile financing is different from that for automobile sales. With automobile sales, the discount rate is based on a business-to-business sale of cars to dealers, in which the manufacturer sometimes has to wait for the dealer to pay. With automobile financing, the discount rate is based on business-to-consumer financing. The payments by the consumers are immediate (unless some promotion is involved), so the waiting period is less, but the risk factor is slightly higher.

The final result is that each new customer who buys an Asian automobile and finances it with Asian returns about $1785 to Asian over 9 years in the form of profit from financing. What will happen to that financing profit if Asian does boost the repurchase rate of B Model cars from 45.2 percent to 51.2 percent (adding the growth from sales during the 3-year period to the growth to 50 percent)? The results are shown in Table 4-9. The net increase in long-term profit to Asian is almost $7 million over 9 years (see Table 4-10). And Asian did not have to do anything unusual to get this increase.

Adding the profits from the sales of new cars to the profits from the financing, the total profit from the relationship-building program

Table 4-9 Improved Lease LTV

Revenue	Years 1–3	Years 4–6	Years 7–9
Repurchase rate	51.20%	54.20%	57.20%
Refinance rate	62.00%	64.00%	66.00%
Retention rate	31.74%	34.69%	37.75%
Customers	100,000	31,744	11,011
Amount financed by lease	$30,000	$32,000	$34,000
Total amount financed	$3,000,000,000	$1,015,808,000	$374,386,196
Income before taxes	$1,452.22	$1,582.92	$1,725.38
Total income before taxes	$145,222,000	$50,248,206	$18,998,807
Costs			
Acquisition cost	$ 6,000,000	$ 1,904,640	$ 660,682
Marketing costs ($12)	$ 1,200,000	$ 380,928	$ 132,136
Total marketing & sales	$ 7,200,000	$ 2,285,568	$ 792,818
Profit	$138,022,000	$ 47,962,638	$ 18,205,989
Discount rate	1	1.33	1.64
NPV of profit	$138,022,000	$ 36,062,134	$ 11,101,213
Cumulative NPV of profit	$138,022,000	$174,084,134	$185,185,347
Lifetime value	$1,380.22	$1,740.84	$1,851.85

Table 4-10 Lease LTV Gain

Improvement in LTV	Years 1–3	Years 4–6	Years 7–9
New LTV	$1,380.22	$1,740.84	$1,851.85
Previous LTV	$1,380.22	$1,698.31	$1,784.97
Difference	$0.00	$42.53	$66.88
Times 100,000 customers	$0.00	$4,253,296	$6,688,364

should come to approximately $80 million ($73 million plus $7 million) over 9 years. This is the way lifetime value is used to determine the value of relationship-building programs.

That is not the end of the lifetime value story for Asian, however.

Used-Car Owners Buy New Cars

The repurchase data developed for Asian produced some unanticipated results concerning Asian used-car owners. Many car companies do not consider the LTV of used-car owners in their marketing programs. The conventional wisdom concerning used-car owners is that they do not represent a value to the manufacturer. After all, the manufacturer made its profit when the car was originally sold to the dealer. When the car returns to the dealer as a trade-in, the dealer makes the profit on the resale of the vehicle. When you look at the performance of owners of used Asian cars, however, you find something very interesting (see Table 4-11).

This table shows just one year. As you can see, 6275 of the owners of used Asian cars in 1997 bought new Asian cars by 2002. Similar charts were developed for each year. Putting them together, the final result was that in the average year, 6400 owners of Asian used cars purchased a brand new Asian. The owners of Asian used cars were, in fact, the greatest single prospect group for the purchase of new vehicles other than new Asian car owners.

Lifetime value is forward-looking. It does not deal with the past. We are asking, "How much profit will you make from these people over a

Table 4-11 New-Car Purchases by Used-Car Owners

	Used Asian Owned in 1997					
	Totals	A Model	B Model	C Model	D Model	E Model
Owned in 1997	63,761	32,777	3,691	16,065	10,545	684
Asian bought by 2002	6,275	2,558	828	1,759	1,111	19
New A Model	2,467	1,670	173	372	236	16
New B Model	801	242	295	149	107	9
New C Model	1,642	583	73	692	265	29
New D Model	1,094	132	53	166	705	39
New E Model	475	147	41	147	120	19

Table 4-12 LTV of Used-Car Owners

	Years 1–3	Years 4–6	Years 7–9
Revenue			
Repurchase rate	51.20%	54.20%	57.20%
Customers	6400	3277	1776
Net profit per car	$4000	$4000	$4000
Net revenue	$25,600,000	$13,107,200	$7,104,102
Costs			
Acquisition cost per car	$200	$200	$200
Acquisition cost	$1,280,000	$655,360	$355,205
Marketing costs ($50/yr)	$ 320,000	$163,840	$ 88,801
Total marketing & sales	$1,600,000	$819,200	$444,006
Profit	$24,000,000	$12,288,000	$ 6,660,096
Discount rate	1.11	1.31	1.54
NPV of profit	$21,621,622	$ 9,380,153	$ 4,324,738
Cumulative NPV of profit	$21,621,622	$31,001,774	$35,326,512
Lifetime value	$3378.38	$4844.03	$8831.63

period of time?" When you ask the question this way, it is clear that used-car owners have a lifetime value for Asian. We calculated the number of Asian cars that typical Asian car owners were buying each year. By knowing the profit to Asian from the cars they were buying, it was possible to calculate the lifetime value to Asian of owners of used Asian cars, which is shown in Table 4-12.

This shows that the owner of a used Asian car has a lifetime value to Asian of $8832 over 9 years. What can you do with this information? You can use it to calculate the value to Asian of programs designed to increase purchases of used Asian vehicles by members of the general public. A program that was previously considered to be something that would help the Asian dealers is actually profitable for the manufacturer and probably deserves more effort than has previously been expended on it.

Use of Lifetime Value Data

Lifetime value has been adopted by companies of every type throughout the developed world as a means of valuing their customers and directing their marketing programs. It is not that difficult to compute if you have a database that contains transaction history, and if you can determine the revenue and costs involved in those transactions. The real value of lifetime value is not in the numbers, but in the use that is made of the numbers. Without imaginative strategies, the LTV numbers are useless.

Throughout this book, we will be using lifetime value tables to evaluate the effectiveness of various relationship-building strategies. Most lifetime value tables cover only 3 or 4 years. It is only in the automobile and similar industries (farm vehicles, trucks, capital equipment), where there is a lease or loan arrangement that typically lasts 3 or 4 years, that we have 9-year tables like those shown in this chapter.

Once lifetime value has been calculated, it can be put into every customer's database record. The numbers will be different for each individual. Here is how they are calculated.

Owners of 2002 B Model cars will have one value. Owners of 2003 B Model cars will have another value. This reasoning applies to the owners of every Asian model in every year, and to every used Asian model. It applies to Asian lease and loan holders. People who own two or more cars have the values of these cars added together. The final result is a unique LTV number for every customer based on everything that customer owns.

None of this takes into account the demographics of the customers. Is the LTV of a 50-year-old customer different from the LTV of a 30-year-old customer? How would you discover that? The answer lies in the different repurchase rates for different age groups. Instead of looking at only the LTV by model, we can look at it both by model and by age group. We can look at the LTV of women versus the LTV of men. We can look at the LTV of people living in the Northeast versus those living on the West Coast. We can look at the differing LTVs of white, black, and Hispanic owners. Where do we stop in our calculations?

We have to consider two things:

1. Do the demographics result in significant differences?
2. If so, can we use these differences to craft different relationship-building strategies that will improve the repurchase rate?

The first question can be answered in short order by an analysis of the database going back 6 years. We can tell pretty rapidly whether older people have a higher repurchase rate than younger people, whether there are differences between whites and blacks, whether there are differences between East and West, and so on. In most cases, there will be only marginal differences, so we forget about those factors. You will have to look at the numbers to decide whether you can create a marketing program that recognizes and uses the differences.

For each possible program, we have to decide whether the cost of the program will be sufficiently low and the benefits sufficiently high for the resulting LTV to actually go up when the programs are put into place. In many cases there is little we can do. There are more possible database marketing programs that drive LTV down than there are that drive LTV up. That is part of the reason why CRM has been such a failure in so many industries.

Creating LTV Segments

Once we have LTV in everyone's database record, we can begin to think about segmentation. We have already segmented customers by model and year, and we may also have segmented them by demographics. One important segmentation method is by total value to the company. We can arrange all customers by LTV from top to bottom and create segments that we call Gold, Silver, Bronze, Steel, and Lead. Our Gold customers are the most valuable ones. They have the highest lifetime value. They probably own more of the company's products, and they have a higher spending rate and retention (or repurchase) rate. They are cheaper to serve, and they tend to buy higher-priced options. They are less price-sensitive than other segments. We really want to retain these Gold customers. We must devise programs to keep them coming back for more. We will add their segment designation to their database record so that we can recall them easily when we want to communicate with them.

Multiple Product Ownership

Most companies have more than one product that they can sell to their customers. Statistics from a variety of industries, such as banks, insurance, and travel, show that the retention rate is often a function of the number of products owned. The more of a bank's products you own, for example, the less likely you are to drop the bank's credit card when you receive a competing offer. Because of the importance of multiple product ownership, many companies have put major resources into selling their customers a second product—not only for the profit they make from the second product, but also because the second product shores up the retention rate for the first product. Since multiple product ownership is important, when you create a LTV table, you can segment customers by the number of products owned and create separate retention rates, and hence LTVs, for owners of multiple products. The chart that a bank developed is shown in Figure 4-1.

Potential Lifetime Value

As stated earlier, lifetime value is a forward-looking concept. We don't care about the past. What we want to know is, how much profit will we make from this customer in the future? The number of years is important, of course. If you knew that Arthur Hughes would be a customer for the next 40 years, whereas Bill Anderson would be a customer for only 5 years, you might treat Arthur Hughes and Bill Anderson differently, and perhaps treat Arthur Hughes better. *But you cannot know that.* Neither Arthur nor Bill knows it either. What you can know is that Arthur Hughes is a member of a segment that has a retention rate of 60 percent. You know his lifetime value after 3 or 4 years based on his

Figure 4-1   Gain in Retention Rate

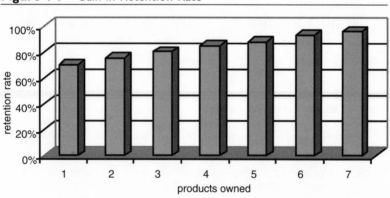

current rate of spending, the number of products that he owns, and the retention rate of his segment.

There is something else that you can predict, however. You can look at all the additional products that you can sell to Arthur Hughes and estimate the increase in his lifetime value that would occur if you were to sell him each of several possible products. You can also predict the likelihood of his buying each of these products, based on the response rate of members of his segment when they are offered the products. You can draw up a table for each customer like that in Table 4-13.

The most profitable product you could sell this customer would be product B, with a potential LTV of $1200. But the product he would be most likely to buy would be product C, with a potential LTV of only $300. Potential value is computed by multiplying the 3-year LTV by the probability of the customer's buying each product. Putting both together, it looks as if the next best product for Arthur Hughes right now is product C. If you can sell him that, then go for product E, which has the next highest total value to your company. Banks do this analysis today. The next best product is put into every customer's database record. Bank employees are asked to look at these records when they are communicating with customers so that they can discuss the next best product. This is using a lifetime value table to increase bank profits.

Prospect LTV

Thus far, we have discussed the lifetime value of customers only. We have not discussed prospects. Of course, prospects have a potential lifetime value. How to go about determining this is covered in Chapter 13, "Finding Loyal Customers."

Table 4-13 Next Best Product

Possible Product	Probability of Buying	3-Year LTV	Potential Value
A	45%	$ 400	$180
B	5%	$1200	$ 60
C	85%	$ 300	$255
D	35%	$ 200	$ 70
E	20%	$1000	$200

Using LTV to Sell Your Marketing Program

One of the most powerful uses of LTV is internal to the company. Every marketing organization in every corporation has to come up before a flinty-eyed chief financial officer every year to get a budget for its next year's activities. Before LTV analysis, this was not a very easy sell. Advertising can point to the colorful TV ads that it produces. Sales can point to the number of customers that were signed up last year and the number that are projected to be signed up in the year to come. What can marketing point to?

Here is where LTV comes into its own. In the Asian automobile case, the database marketing manager can come to the CFO and say, "I can bring in $56 million more profits during the next 9 years if I can have a budget for a welcome kit and a series of strategic customer communications." When asked to prove this statement, the marketer can trot out the projections shown in Table 4-7 and back them up with detailed tables like the ones shown in this chapter. Assuming that the presentation goes well, the CFO will retain these charts and refer to them in future budget sessions. She is likely to ask, "What was your actual repurchase rate? What were your actual marketing costs?"

The great thing about LTV is that these numbers are all actual projections that can be audited by PricewaterhouseCoopers or Deloitte & Touche. They are not smoke and mirrors, but projections of real events that will actually occur and can be verified. Database marketing, therefore, becomes a combination of science and art. The art, of course, is thinking up the strategies that will produce the improved customer relationships, and hence the improved repurchase rate. The science is putting all these projections together in an LTV chart that makes sense and proves the value of your efforts.

What Works

- To compute lifetime value, you need a customer database that includes transactions. You need to be able to estimate the revenue and the costs in order to compute the profit from each transaction.
- You use past history to determine the retention (or repurchase) rate.

- Lifetime value can at first be computed for all customers as a group, but once it has been developed, it should be determined for customer segments.
- The LTV of an individual customer is derived from the LTV of the segment that includes that customer, adjusted for the products the customer owns and other factors that seem to determine the customer's particular LTV.
- Lifetime value produces numbers that can eventually be audited after the fact. A year later, you can go back and see what the retention (repurchase) rate was; what the spending rate was; what the marketing expenditures, the profits, and the discount rate were. It is not smoke and mirrors.

What Doesn't Work

- Computing LTV using complex formulas that your top management does not understand. If your management doesn't understand exactly how you developed it, it will have no confidence in it and will not use it profitably.
- Looking at LTV numbers by themselves. An LTV number by itself is meaningless. Its most important use is in calculating whether proposed marketing programs will increase or decrease lifetime value.
- Spending resources on getting an exact lifetime value number. LTV is a future number. The future has so many unknown factors that you should use LTV as a rough guide: Do this, and don't do that. That is all it is good for.

Quiz

1. Compute the discount rate in the third year. Interest rate = 6 percent. Risk factor = 1.4.
2. Use this number to compute the net present value of profits in the third year, if the profits are $45,447,221.

3. Compute the retention rate for years 1 and 2 in the following table, given the number of customers shown.

	Year 1	Year 2	Year 3
Customers	312,886	219,445	188,994
Retention rate			

4. If a company has a retention rate in the second year of 60 percent, what will selling an additional product to the customer in that year do to the retention rate in the third year compared to what it would have been?
    a. Make it go up.
    b. Make it go down.
    c. Not enough information is given to know one way or the other.
    d. It depends on the discount rate.
    e. It depends on the lifetime value.
5. Which is more important in determining potential lifetime value?
    a. The probability of the customer's buying an additional product
    b. The profitability of the customer's buying that product
    c. Current lifetime value
    d. Both a and b
    e. None, since potential lifetime value cannot be predicted
6. What is the best way for marketing to justify its annual budget?
    a. Movement in the discount rate
    b. Movement in the lifetime value in future years
    c. Movement in the potential lifetime value of prospects
    d. Reduction in the retention rate
    e. None of the above
7. What is the next best product for a customer?
    a. The one with the most margin for the seller.
    b. The one with the highest probability of a sale.
    c. This cannot be known in advance.
    d. The one with the highest value to the company, which is determined by multiplying the probability of purchase and the profitability if purchased.
    e. The one with the highest lifetime value if purchased.

8. If analysis shows that LTV will go down in future years, what should you do?
   a. Revise your marketing program.
   b. Redo your LTV tables, since future LTV always goes up.
   c. Revise the discount rate.
   d. Add more marketing dollars.
   e. Reduce the retention rate.
9. Suppose you have two segments. Segment A has an LTV of $150 in 3 years, and segment B has an LTV of $200 in 3 years. What should your strategy be?
   a. Work to retain segment B and increase the LTV of segment A.
   b. Get rid of segment A and find more people that fit into segment B.
   c. You can't decide based on what we know at present.
   d. Retain both, since the LTV is positive.
   e. None of the above.

CHAPTER 5

THE VALUE OF A NAME

The names and addresses of ultimate consumers have always been valuable in direct marketing, if you know how to use them. But not all names are valuable.

In the last 20 years, we have discovered that the names and addresses of purchasers of packaged goods sold in retail stores have almost no value. This is because you can't profitably use direct mail to get people to buy packaged goods in retail stores.

What could I do with a clean, household database of all the families in the United States that use Ivory Soap? I could lose a lot of money. Database marketing is incremental. You are already selling Ivory Soap in retail stores. Your assumption is that, by sending direct-mail messages, you might sell a little bit more Ivory or a little bit more of another P&G product, perhaps 10 percent more. When you look at the cost of direct mail, you will soon learn that you are dead wrong. Ivory Soap is selling in some supermarkets at $1.29 for four bars. The profit on those four bars is obviously tiny. A 10 percent increase would be even tinier. A good response to direct mail is 2 percent. There is no way that direct mail could possibly increase sales sufficiently to pay for itself when promoting most packaged goods.

This is true not only for Ivory Soap but for almost everything sold in a supermarket, office supplies store, hardware store, or department store. Manufacturer after manufacturer has tried promotions with rebates by direct mail. They have collected thousands of consumer names and addresses in this way. None of them has figured out a way to make money from those names.

That does not mean that consumer names are worthless for direct mail. Catalogs obviously work extremely well. Supermarkets profitably send circulars that get customers to come back, or to shop on Tuesday night. Names of parents of new babies are very valuable indeed. What does not work well is the two-step *direct-mail process* for regular packaged goods: Send consumers a direct-mail letter inviting them to go to a retail store to buy the product. If you use TV, radio, or print to do this, it works like gangbusters.

Why are the names of packaged goods purchasers worthless? There are several reasons:

- The margins on these products are low.
- Certificate redemption is very slow—it takes up to 6 months to find out what is happening.
- To make a profit, you need repeat sales (low margin). You can't redeem a certificate for every sale, or you would go broke. So you never find out about the subsequent sales.
- There is no way to figure out if you are succeeding. When people buy packaged goods at a retail store, their purchase may be captured by the store when the product is scanned. If the store has a proprietary card, it may know that Helena Hughes bought a tube of Crest toothpaste on August 17. But the store won't tell Crest about it because of privacy considerations. The small amount that Crest might pay for the information would not compensate for the bad public relations if Helena found out that her name was being used and complained about it publicly. Retail stores simply will not sell this information. They have been burned, and they know better.
- Crest doesn't want the information, anyway, because it can't figure out how to use it to make a profit.

The Phone Call

A year after the dot com crash, I had a telephone call from the CEO of a dot com start-up (yes, they were still starting them up, despite the carnage). He told me that his new venture would generate thousands of satisfied Web consumers who would gladly provide permission for resale of their contact information. He asked me what the value of these names would be, so that he could plug this number into the business plan required by his investors. He called me because he had been told that I had written several books and articles on the subject and could probably provide the answers he sought, over the phone.

The question had me stammering. I had never thought about the value of a name in the abstract like this. There are many things that have to be pinned down before the value can be determined. In the first place, the questions are, "Of value to whom? What are these names, and who would want to buy them? What can these names do for a potential buyer?" The CEO did not have the answers to these questions, but he assumed that I did.

So I started to examine the question in detail. Let's visualize an ideal situation. Suppose you had the names of 500 Boeing executives earning $100,000 a year or more who have to relocate from Seattle to Chicago within the next 60 days. What is the value of these names? To a large real estate chain in Chicago, these names could be very valuable indeed, as Table 5-1 shows.

Assuming that the Chicago real estate chain can sell homes to 5 percent of these executives (a not unreasonable assumption), then each of the 500 names is worth $900. The Chicago chain might be induced to offer as much as $450 per name and could still make $450.

But this is assuming that the names can be sold only to a real estate dealer. The executives will be buying many new services in Chicago after they move, including

- Moving services
- Doctor and dentist

Table 5-1 Chicago Home Buyers

	Amounts
Names	500
Home value	$300,000
Commission rate	6%
Commission revenue	$9,000,000
Success rate	5%
Net profit	$450,000
Name value	$900
Name offering price	$450

- Bank and insurance services
- Automobiles and furniture

These names are valuable to many different businesses. Their value certainly exceeds $450 when all these potential buyers are factored in. Clever and aggressive marketing could yield a substantial profit from selling the names.

Is such a list of names of executives who are moving unique to the Boeing situation? Not at all. Companies shift their executives around all the time. But my dot com CEO's list of names was not a list of high-income executives. It was a list of young people between the ages of 15 and 35 who had purchased music over the Web. What would be the value of these names? This is a different proposition altogether. We have to ask ourselves, "Who will want to buy these names?" The Chicago buyers that we mentioned before would probably not be interested. Perhaps the names could be sold to other e-commerce sites. Amazon or CDNow might buy them. Some retailer or cataloger might want them. Here the value would be much lower. Let's see how the marketer could go about calculating the value of a rented name.

We can begin with the lifetime value of the acquired customers. Table 5-2 computes the lifetime value to a retailer selling music CDs where the average sale is $20.00.

Table 5-2 CD Buyers

	Year 1	Year 2	Year 3
Retention rate	40%	50%	60%
Customers	200,000	80,000	40,000
Average sale	$20.00	$30.00	$40.00
Sales per year	3	4	5
Revenue	$12,000,000	$9,600,000	$8,000,000
Cost %	80%	75%	70%
Costs	$ 9,600,000	$7,200,000	$5,600,000
Marketing ($10/yr)	$ 2,000,000	$ 800,000	$ 400,000
Total cost	$11,600,000	$8,000,000	$6,000,000
Profit	$400,000	$1,600,000	$2,000,000
Discount rate	1	1.08	1.16
NPV of profit	$400,000	$1,485,608	$1,724,243
Cumulative NPV of profit	$400,000	$1,885,608	$3,609,852
Lifetime value	$2.00	$9.43	$18.05

What Table 5-2 tells us is that the average newly acquired customer of this company is worth $18 in the third year. The details of this chart are explained in Chapter 4, "Computing Lifetime Value." For now, let's just concentrate on what it tells us. The retention rate of customers tends to go up after the first year, as does the average order size. Of the 200,000 customers who might make a purchase, the average person might buy three times a year. Forty percent of these purchasers would still be customers in Year 2, making four larger purchases per year. Fifty percent of those would last to a third year, buying even more.

The costs of servicing customers typically tend to go down each year, as shown here. The discount rate is needed to convert future profits into net present value of profit so that these profits can be added together to get the cumulative profit. The lifetime value is determined by dividing the cumulative NPV of profit by the original 200,000 customers to determine the value of a newly acquired customer. In this case, the newly acquired customers are worth $18 in the third year. This is the value to a company selling CDs that has already acquired these customers.

So to the dot com the names are worth $18 to their owner. What would they be worth to a potential buyer? Let us assume that the potential buyer is selling a product of similar value, so that the buyer's customer lifetime value once it has acquired the customers would be identical—$18. What is the value of these names to a new company that wants to sell products to these customers? The value of a name has to be related to the cost of acquiring the customer by using various media (see Table 5-3).

An outside buyer renting the name from the original company has to consider the costs of acquiring these customers on its own. There are two methods the buyer could use: direct mail or email. Let's consider both possibilities; the costs are given in Table 5-4.

Table 5-3 Sales by Medium

	Budget	Reached	CPM	Sales rate	Sales	Cost per sale
TV	$400,000	74,074,074	$5.40	0.04%	29,630	$13.50
Radio	$400,000	71,428,571	$5.60	0.03%	21,429	$18.67
Print	$400,000	25,000,000	$16.00	0.07%	17,500	$22.86
Direct mail	$400,000	1,086,957	$368.00	1.80%	19,565	$20.44

Table 5-4 Two Methods of Contact

	Direct mail	Email
Names	200,000	200,000
Cost of message	$0.37	$0.04
Sending cost	$74,000	$8,000
Response rate	1.8%	1.0%
Responses	3,600	2,000
Customer lifetime value	$18.05	$18.05
Value of customers acquired	$64,977	$36,099
Value after sending cost	($9,023)	$28,099
Prospect lifetime value	($0.05)	$0.14
Offering price	0	$0.07

If the response rate for direct mail is 1.8 percent, any direct-mail offer would be a loser. This is proof of the assertion that database marketing does not work with packaged goods. But with email, profitable database marketing becomes a possibility. The response rate will be lower, at 1 percent, but the marketing costs are far lower. The value of a prospect's name is 14 cents. A marketer might be willing to offer half that for a name.

The lifetime value sets an upper boundary for the offering price. Anyone who offers to pay the full lifetime value for a prospect's name will never make a profit. As a rule of thumb, we can assume that buyers will never offer more than half the projected lifetime value to acquire a name. So the offering price of a name with a projected LTV of $0.14 could not be higher than $0.07.

So, if the offering price of a prospect name to an e-commerce consumer name buyer is $0.07, what is the name worth to the seller? Here we have to consider marketing costs. Buyers do not materialize from nowhere once names are acquired. To sell names, most companies need the services of list managers and brokers who must advertise and get fees. The list owner will be lucky to get 75 percent of the offering price from any one buyer. With luck, the names can be sold several times per year. So we end up with the value of a name looking something like Table 5-5.

So we have an answer for the CEO of the new dot com. His names are worth $0.16 each if he finds a good list manager and promotes the names, and if everything goes well.

Table 5-5 Value of a Name

	Amounts
Offering price	$0.07
Marketing costs	25%
Net revenue	$0.053
Sales per year	3
Value of a name	$0.158

As you can see, this type of analysis is not difficult to do. It should be done before any business is created. If it had been done by the thousands of dot coms that were set up during the boom, we might not have had the dot com wipeout and the stock market crash. Let's hope we see some sharp-pencil accounting in the future when "cool ideas" are floated to venture capitalists.

Using LTV to Compute a Name Value

The lifetime value chart shown in Table 5-2 is typical of standard lifetime value charts. The details of such charts are spelled out in Chapter 4. A lifetime value chart has many uses. It can be used to determine

- How much to spend on acquisition of customers
- How much to spend on retention programs
- How much to spend on referral programs
- The payoff from particular marketing strategies
- The rental value of a name
- The value of a company, based on its acquired customer base
- Which groups of customers you should try to retain, acquire, or discard
- And many other things

Let's try to determine the value of a name in a business-to-business setting. Assume we have a company that sells chemicals to industrial users. Let's call our company WardChem. We have about 45,000 customers who spend from $5000 to $500,000 per year on chemicals. The average order is $2500, and the average customer buys from us eight times a year. Later we will break our customers down into segments (low-volume, medium-volume, high-volume, etc.), but for now, we will lump them all together into a single lifetime value table (Table 5-6), so that we can understand the principles involved.

We are assuming newly acquired customers in year 1 and examining their performance over the next 3 years.

- The retention rate is the percentage of customers that remain from year to year. As we can see, WardChem loses 30 percent of its newly acquired customers after the first year. It does better in subsequent years, with the retention rate rising to 80 percent in the third year.
- Retained customers are those same customers in their first, second, and third years with WardChem. New customers who arrive in year 2 or year 3 are not shown here. The year they arrive is their year 1. Let us assume that WardChem retains a base of about 45,000 customers. It does this by losing 9000 customers and gaining 9000 new ones every year. We are studying the history of the retained customers.
- The average order size tends to grow every year. This is typical of all corporations.
- The number of orders per year also tends to grow.
- The cost percent is a rough number that estimates the average

Table 5-6 Lifetime Value for Wardchem

	Year 1	Year 2	Year 3
Retention rate	70%	75%	80%
Retained customers	45,000	31,500	23,625
Average order	$2,500	$2,700	$2,900
Orders per year	8	9	10
Total revenue	$900,000,000	$765,450,000	$685,125,000
Cost rate	75%	71%	69%
Variable costs	$675,000,000	$543,469,500	$472,736,250
Acquisition cost ($1,400)	$ 63,000,000	0	0
Retention costs ($90/yr)	$ 4,050,000	$ 2,835,000	$ 2,126,250
Total costs	$742,050,000	$546,304,500	$474,862,500
Gross profit	$157,950,000	$219,145,500	$210,262,500
Discount rate	1.01	1.09	1.17
Net present value of profit	$155,779,959	$200,894,344	$179,159,636
Cumulative NPV of profit	$155,779,959	$356,674,303	$535,833,940
Lifetime value	$3,462	$7,926	$11,907

percentage of the selling price of company products that goes for manufacturing, distribution, and other costs. The balance is profit or marketing costs.

- The acquisition cost is computed by adding together all the expenses involved in acquiring new customers during a given year—advertising on TV, radio, print, and direct mail; sales force salaries, commissions, and bonuses—and dividing that total by the number of customers actually acquired during that year.
- The retention costs are those costs spent to keep customers happy and buying. This could include an annual retreat, customer communications, or customer services.
- The discount rate is used to compute the net present value of the profits received. Money that will arrive in 1 year or 2 years is obviously not as valuable today as money that arrives today. The discount rate is a number that puts all these amounts on the same basis so that they can be added together. As discussed in earlier chapters, the formula for the discount rate is

$$D = (1 + i * \text{rf})^{\text{waiting time}}$$

In this formula,
   i is the interest rate that the company pays for money
   rf is the risk factor (the risk that the money will not materialize at all)

- The waiting time is the length of time you have to wait before the money arrives. With consumers, this is usually 0 for the first year, 1 year for the second year, and so on. With business-to-business selling, the picture is different. Most business-to-business customers pay in 30, 60, or 90 days. So the waiting time is determined by adding these periods to the years.

   Table 5-7 is a simple chart that is used for calculating the discount rate of a business-to-business situation.

- The net present value of profits is the gross profits divided by the discount rate.
- The cumulative NPV of profits is calculated by adding the profits from previous years to this year's profits.

Table 5-7 Discount Rate Calculation

	Year 1	Year 2	Year 3
Years to wait	0	1	2
Interest rate	6.80%	6.80%	6.80%
Risk factor	1.1	1.1	1.1
Accounts receivable days	70	75	80
Discount rate	1.01	1.09	1.17

- The customer lifetime value is calculated by dividing the cumulative NPV of profits in each year by the total number of newly acquired customers—in this case, 45,000. In this example, newly acquired customers are worth $11,907 in their third year with WardChem.

Calculating LTV by Segments

Calculating LTV for customers as a whole is useful. Calculating the LTV of customer segments is even more useful. An automobile company may find that the LTV of various models may be quite different, as shown in Chapter 4. Two factors, in general, are responsible for the difference:

1. The manufacturer's profit per car
2. The repurchase rate

With that knowledge, it is possible to determine the additional total profit that a company would earn if the repurchase rate could be modified by changing the behavior of customers. This knowledge can lead to the development of marketing programs aimed at particular customer segments.

Increasing the Retention Rate

All the factors in a lifetime value table can be influenced by marketing programs: the average order size, the number of orders per year, and the retention rate. To see the way this works, let's focus on only one factor, the retention rate, and see what would happen if WardChem could increase that rate by 5 percent—an achievable goal for most companies. Let's see how WardChem could go about it.

- It could set up a relationship-building team for its top customers.
- It could provide a much higher level of customer service.
- It could set up a super-customized Web page for each customer.
- It could put thousands of pages of technical information about its chemicals on the Web for its customers (only) to use.

Let's assume that the cost of all these additional relationship-building activities is about $110 per customer per year, or about $5 million. There could be two results: The retention rate might go up by 5 percent, and the number of orders might go up by one-half order per year. Table 5-8 shows what could happen.

Lifetime value in the third year has gone up from $11,907 to $13,362. What does that mean for WardChem in terms of profits? As Table 5-9 shows, it means more than $65 million more profits—after taking into account the extra $5 million per year spent on relationship-building activities.

Table 5-8 Revised Lifetime Value

	Year 1	Year 2	Year 3
Retention rate	75%	80%	85%
Retained customers	45,000	33,750	27,000
Average order	$2,500	$2,700	$2,900
Orders per year	8.5	9.5	10.5
Total revenue	$956,250,000	$865,687,500	$822,150,000
Cost rate	75%	71%	69%
Variable costs	$717,187,500	$614,638,125	$567,283,500
Acquisition cost ($1,400)	$ 63,000,000	0	0
Retention costs ($200/yr)	$ 9,000,000	$ 6,750,000	$ 5,400,000
Total costs	$789,187,500	$621,388,125	$572,683,500
Gross profit	$167,062,500	$244,299,375	$249,466,500
Discount rate	1.01	1.09	1.17
Net present value of profit	$164,767,265	$223,953,322	$212,564,425
Cumulative NPV of profit	$164,767,265	$388,720,586	$601,285,011
Lifetime value	$3,661	$8,638	$13,362

THE VALUE OF A NAME

Table 5-9 Gains through Retention-Building Activities

	Year 1	Year 2	Year 3
New LTV	$3,661	$8,638	$13,362
Old LTV	$3,462	$7,926	$11,907
Difference	$200	$712	$1,454
Times 45,000 customers	$8,987,305	$32,046,283	$65,451,072

Lifetime value charts like these are used in calculating the value of a name. They are very powerful predictors of success in database marketing.

The Value of an Email Name

A name and address with the matching email name and permission to use it can be a very valuable commodity—much more valuable than a simple name and address. There are many reasons why this is so:

- It is far cheaper to send email communications than direct-mail communications, so you save money on each communication.
- Since emails are so cheap and so fast, you can undertake many communications that you simply could not do at all with direct mail.
- Using emails, you can build close relationships that you could not build if you were limited to direct mail or phone. As a result, the email will increase the retention rate of certain customers, which adds directly to their lifetime value.
- Emails can be used in viral marketing. What this means is that you can get customers to write to one another and pass your message to other people whom you don't know.
- The speed of emails permits you to send types of messages that could not be sent by any other medium. Airlines, for example, send weekly messages about the availability of unsold seats at rock-bottom prices. These messages could not be sent by mail because of the time issue, or by phone because of the cost and the annoyance factor.

Let's put all these factors together as shown in Table 5-10 to begin to estimate the value of an email name.

Table 5-10 Annual Email Name Value

	Direct mail value	Email value
Regular promotion	$0.80	$1.28
Low-cost item promotion	NA	$0.32
Last-minute special	NA	$2.48
Retention messages	$2.40	$3.68
Follow-up messages	$1.20	$9.12
Viral marketing	NA	$0.24
Newsletter	$1.20	$2.24
Rental value	$0.42	$4.20
Total annual value	$6.02	$23.56

These numbers are very important, as they lie at the heart of the relationship between modern database marketing and the Web. Let's discuss each type of promotion in turn.

Regular Promotions

Message for message, email is cheaper to send. Victoria's Secret has used email marketing for several years. It has more than 4.5 million customer email names in its database. It outsources its email to Digital Impact. The emails are timed to coincide with Victoria's Secret catalog distribution. This type of email generates a purchase rate of about 6 percent, according to Shar Van Boskirk of Forrester Research.

Suppose you send regular promotions eight times per year to your customer base. Your response rate might look like Table 5-11. As you can see, the response rate for direct mail is higher than that for email. This will normally, although not always, be true. However, the higher cost of direct mail swamps the improved response rate, giving the profit per name from email a 60 percent lift.

If you do eight promotions per year, your email addresses are worth $1.28 per year, or $0.48 more than a simple name and address.

Low-Cost Item Promotion

There are many items that you simply cannot profitably promote by direct mail. One example is the Universal Music promotion of music

Table 5-11 Profit per Name from Regular Promotions

	Direct mail	Email
Sent	200,000	200,000
Cost for each	$0.50	$0.04
Promotion cost	$100,000	$8000
Response rate	3.0%	1.0%
Responses	6,000	2,000
Profit per response	$20.00	$20.00
Profits	$120,000	$40,000
Net profits	$20,000	$32,000
Eight promotions per year	$160,000	$256,000
Annual profit per name	$0.80	$1.28

Table 5-12 Profit per Name from Low-Cost Item Promotion

	Direct mail	Email
Sent	200,000	200,000
Cost for each	$0.50	$0.04
Promotion cost	$100,000	$8000
Response rate	3.0%	1.0%
Responses	6,000	2,000
Profit per response	$8.00	$8.00
Profits	$48,000	$16,000
Net profits	−$52,000	$8000
Eight promotions per year	NA	$64,000
Annual profit per name	NA	$0.32

CDs, which sell for about $20 each. The profit to a company selling a $20 item directly is probably on the order of $8 per item. Table 5-12 shows the way the promotion could work out.

Using direct mail for this type of promotion is a loser, so no one would attempt it. Each email name, on the other hand, earns a healthy $0.32 per year. This is found money that comes from having email names.

Last-Minute Special

Only certain types of companies have last-minute specials. These include airlines, railroads, hotels, rental car companies, cruise lines, and producers of live theater, sporting events, and concerts—any company that sells something that disappears if it is not used. Last-minute specials also

Table 5-13 Profit per Name from Last-Minute Special

	Direct mail	Email
Sent	NA	200,000
Cost for each	NA	$0.04
Promotion cost	NA	$8,000
Response rate	NA	0.5%
Responses	NA	1,000
Profit per response	NA	$70.00
Profits	NA	$70,000
Net profits	NA	$62,000
Profit per name	NA	$0.31
Fifty promotions per year	NA	$2.48

apply to retail stores that are having a special sale that comes to an end in a very few days. These promotions cannot be sent by regular mail because it is too slow. Table 5-13 shows what the value looks like.

The profit from a last-minute special is pure profit. The seats are going empty. It costs very little to let people sit in them. Even at a very low response rate, the profits are substantial, and the annual value of a name is considerable.

Retention Messages

Every database marketer likes to think up retention messages. What are retention messages? They are such things as birthday cards, anniversary cards, season's greetings, thank-you messages, customer surveys, service reminders, quarterly savings summaries, etc. The value of these messages is not in the response, since none is requested or expected. Their value is derived from the fact that they keep customers from defecting by building profitable relationships with them. The profit comes from the increased retention rate and the consequent increased lifetime value.

To understand this, let's set up a control group that does not get the retention messages. Table 5-14 shows the lifetime value of this group.

This represents customers of a women's dress chain that has several stores. It costs the chain $170 to acquire women who make two visits to the chain per year, spending an average of $160 per visit. The chain retains only 40 percent of these women into the second year. Of those retained, 50 percent remain to the third year. For the loyalists who are

Table 5-14 Control LTV for Women's Dress Chain Customers

	Year 1	Year 2	Year 3
Customers	200,000	80,000	40,000
Retention rate	40%	50%	60%
Visits per year	2	3	4
Amount spent per visit	$160	$200	$220
Revenue	$64,000,000	$48,000,000	$35,200,000
Cost rate	60%	58%	56%
Cost	$38,400,000	$27,840,000	$19,712,000
Acquisition cost ($170)	$34,000,000		
Direct mail marketing messages @ $0.50	6	6	6
Marketing costs	$ 600,000	$ 6 00,000	$ 600,000
Total cost	$73,000,000	$28,440,000	$20,312,000
Profit	−$9,000,000	$19,560,000	$14,888,000
Discount rate	1	1.07	1.15
NPV of profit	−$9,000,000	$18,246,269	$12,955,280
Cumulative NPV of profit	−$9,000,000	$9,246,269	$22,201,548
Lifetime value	-$45.00	$46.23	$111.01

still shopping at the chain, the number of visits and spending per visit tend to grow. The chain spends $4.00 per year on direct-mail marketing messages, including seasonal specials. It loses money on women in the first year, but overall it earns a good profit from those who remain, so that the lifetime value of a newly acquired customer after 3 years is $111. The chain is doing well.

Now we will determine the effect of additional email retention messages on a similar group of women, which we will call the test group. These women get 36 personalized email retention messages per year from the store, in addition to the regular direct mail. These messages cost $0.04 per message. They have the effect of increasing the retention rate by 5 percent, the number of visits per year by 0.2 visit, and the spending rate per visit by $5. Table 5-15 shows the results.

As you can see, these retention messages have a dramatic effect on the women's behavior. Note that we could not have had this effect by simply increasing the number of direct-mail messages, which were costing us about $0.50 per message. Had we tried that, 36 messages per year would have cost us $18 per customer, or $3.6 million per year, which would have seriously eaten into profits. In addition, many of these email messages were quite timely and could not have been sent at all by direct

Table 5-15 Improved LTV through Retention Messages

	Year 1	Year 2	Year 3
Customers	200,000	88,000	47,520
Retention rate	44%	54%	64%
Visits per year	2.2	3.2	4.2
Amount spent per visit	$165	$210	$240
Revenue	$72,600,000	$59,136,000	$47,900,160
Cost rate	60%	58%	56%
Cost	$43,560,000	$34,298,880	$26,824,090
Acquisition cost ($170)	$34,000,000		
Direct mail marketing messages @ $0.50	6	6	6
Marketing costs	$ 600,000	$ 600,000	$ 600,000
Email messages @ $0.04	36	36	36
Email total	$ 288,000	$ 126,720	$ 68,429
Total cost	$78,448,000	$35,025,600	$27,492,518
Profit	−$5,848,000	$24,110,400	$20,407,642
Discount rate	1.00	1.07	1.15
NPV of profit	−$5,848,000	$22,491,045	$17,758,376
Cumulative NPV of profit	−$5,848,000	$16,643,045	$34,401,421
Lifetime value	−$29.24	$83.22	$172.01

Table 5-16 Gains through Retention

	Year 1	Year 2	Year 3
Control	−$45.00	$46.23	$111.01
Test	−$29.24	$83.22	$172.01
Gain from use of email	$15.76	$36.98	$61.00
With 200,000 customers	$3,152,000	$7,396,776	$12,199,873

mail. The effect of the email can be seen in Table 5-16. The gain to the chain is $12 million in pure profit in the third year.

Now we can evaluate the retention messages as shown in Table 5-17. As you can see, increases in retention and lifetime value are much more difficult to measure than other direct marketing factors. You have to set up control groups that do not get the retention messages and then see, after a year or so, whether there is a difference in the retention rate and the lifetime value. The only difference between email and direct mail here is that direct mail is probably more effective in building retention than email. A thank-you letter that is printed and mailed means more than a thank-you email. The same might be true of birthday cards and other retention messages. On the face of it, however, it is a lot easier to get management to spring for $8000 for email birthday cards than for $100,000 for direct-mail ones. The probability is that emails will be much more widely used as people come to see their value. So the email will probably be the clear winner in retention messages.

Follow-Up Messages

Here is an area where email wins in a walk. When people order something, you follow up with an email confirmation (or a mailed confirmation). When the product is about to be shipped, you email a notice with the tracking number (it is too late to do this by mail). When the product arrives, you send an email survey: Did it arrive OK, and was it to your liking? Here, again, the email wins. The value is measured in customer retention and increased lifetime value, as shown in Table 5-18.

Table 5-17 Name Value from Retention Messages

	Direct mail	Email
Sent	200,000	200,000
Cost for each	$0.50	$0.04
Promotion cost	$100,000	$8,000
Increased retention	0.080%	0.050%
Current LTV	$111.01	$111.01
Increased LTV	$0.80	$0.50
Total LTV increase	$160,000	$100,000
Net profits	$60,000	$92,000
Eight messages per year	$480,000	$736,000
Annual name value	$2.40	$3.68

Table 5-18 Name Value from Follow-Up

	Direct mail	Email
Sent	200,000	200,000
Cost for each	$0.50	$0.04
Promotion cost	$100,000	$8,000
Increased retention	0.01%	0.01%
Current LTV	$111.01	$111.01
Increased LTV	$0.80	$0.80
Total LTV increase	$160,000	$160,000
Net profits	$60,000	$152,000
4/12 per year	$240,000	$1,824,000
Annual name value	$1.20	$9.12

You may be able to send only 4 direct-mail follow-up messages per year, but you can send 12 or more emails, depending on the number of transactions. The effect on retention and LTV from each message would be the same to the customer.

Because of the cost of sending follow-up messages by direct mail, very few companies send such messages. A better comparison than email versus direct mail for follow-up messages would be to test email versus no follow-up at all. The boost in retention can be measured over a period of a year and can be quite substantial.

Viral Marketing

This is an interesting concept that works only in certain product situations. You can get some customers so excited about some product that they will write to their friends about it. For what kinds of products or situations does viral marketing work?

- Concerts
- Firearms
- Automobiles
- Travel destinations
- Books
- Political candidates
- Health foods

As you can see, the list is long. How does viral marketing work?

As shown in Figure 5-1, you send an email to customers inviting them to invite other customers by entering their names on a microsite (shown in Figure 5-2). This site, which is connected to your database, records the names and suggests messages to be sent to the names. When the customer clicks OK, the messages are sent, and if the recipients of the message click here, they see a microsite inviting them to accept the offer, thus helping both the customer and themselves.

In this case, one email results in the capture of more names and ultimately thousands of other emails, all promoting your product. Viral

Figure 5-1   Viral Marketing

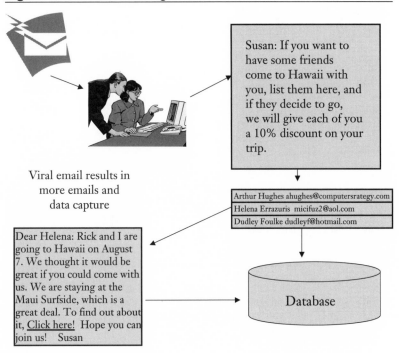

Susan: If you want to have some friends come to Hawaii with you, list them here, and if they decide to go, we will give each of you a 10% discount on your trip.

Viral email results in more emails and data capture

Arthur Hughes ahughes@computersrategy.com
Helena Errazuris micifuz2@aol.com
Dudley Foulke dudleyf@hotmail.com

Dear Helena: Rick and I are going to Hawaii on August 7. We thought it would be great if you could come with us. We are staying at the Maui Surfside, which is a great deal. To find out about it, Click here! Hope you can join us!   Susan

Database

Figure 5-2   Viral Email Dispatch

Name	Email	Click Here to see Message
		Send
		Send
		Send
		Send
		Send
		Send

marketing is unique to email marketing. It cannot be effectively done by direct mail or phone. The name value is shown in Table 5-19.

Viral marketing can be used for very inexpensive items or for quite expensive ones. The cost per sale of $16.67 shown here assumes that the viral messages sent by customers to their friends will have a higher

Table 5-19 Name Value from Viral Marketing

	Direct mail	Email
Sent	NA	200,000
Cost for each	NA	$0.04
Promotion cost	NA	$8,000
Response rate	NA	2.0%
Responses	NA	4,000
Emails captured	NA	1.5
Emails sent	NA	6,000
Success rate	NA	8%
Sales @ $100	NA	480
Sales	NA	$48,000
Cost per sale	NA	$16.67
Value of a name	NA	$0.24

Table 5-20 Name Value from Newsletters

	Direct mail	Email
Sent	200,000	200,000
Cost for each	$0.50	$0.04
Promotion cost	$100,000	$8000
Response rate	2.00%	1.50%
Responses	4,000	3,000
Average sale	$100.00	$100.00
Profit per sale	$40.00	$40.00
Profit from newsletter	$160,000	$120,000
Net profit	$60,000	$112,000
Twelve per year	$240,000	$448,000
Annual profit per name	$1.20	$2.24

response rate than messages sent to prospects or to customers in general. Viral marketing can be very powerful if it is artfully used.

Newsletters

Email newsletters have become very popular. They save a lot of money. They often get a good response rate. It should be easy for recipients to discontinue them with one click. That is not so easy for the recipients of direct-mail newsletters. Newsletters result in increased retention, sales, and loyalty. They are usually worth the effort if you can put something into them that your customers want to read. The name value is shown in Table 5-20.

Name Rentals

Of course, when you have a file of opt-in names of customers who have agreed that they will accept promotions from your business partners, there is another valuable use of the email names you have collected. Since you are using your names more effectively, you can assume that others will be doing the same. Emails have caught on. Billions of commercial email messages are being sent every week. There is a massive market for opt-in names. If you can rent your direct-mail names 8 times a year, you can certainly rent your email names 10 times as often, or 80 times per year. The price per thousand email names varies widely and will certainly be very different from the time of writing to the time that you are reading this book. Let's take a conservative estimate of $70 per thousand for both direct-mail and email names with permission to use them for partner messages. Table 5-21 shows what you can expect to receive during a year for each name.

Let's summarize again the value of a name in Table 5-22.

Of course, few, if any, companies can use every one of these marketing methods, but your company can certainly use at least half of

Table 5-21 Value of Name Rental

Rental value	Direct mail	Email
Rentals per year	8	80
CPM	$70.00	$70.00
Revenue	$0.56	$5.60
Commissions	$0.14	$1.40
Net revenue	$0.42	$4.20

Table 5-22 Total Name Value

	Direct mail value	Email value
Regular promotion	$0.80	$1.28
Low-cost item promotion	NA	$0.32
Last-minute special	NA	$2.48
Retention messages	$2.40	$3.68
Follow-up messages	$1.20	$9.12
Viral marketing	NA	$0.24
Newsletter	$1.20	$2.24
Rental value	$0.42	$4.20
Total annual value	$6.02	$23.56

them. We can say with some confidence that email names, with permission, are worth at least $15 to $20 each to any company. To my knowledge, no company has done this analysis and therefore knows, with any kind of precision, what emails are worth to it. What does that number tell you in terms of marketing strategy? *You must collect email names and get permission to use them.*

How do you do that? By every means at your disposal:

- Telemarketers must be compensated for capturing these names.
- Every form should be revised to include a space for email names. Don't wait for the forms to run out. Junk them and print new ones.
- Run contests in which, in order to enter, customers must go on the Web to a microsite and enter an email name and provide permission to use it.
- Be creative. You gain $10 per year for every email name captured.
- Lenscrafters gives $10 for each email name provided by customers.

We are in a new millennium, folks, and the rules of the game have changed. Like the invention of catalogs, direct mail, radio, or TV, this new phenomenon, email, has fundamentally changed the nature of marketing, and we must change with it.

Your Action Plan

1. Now that you have read this chapter, go to the Web site www.dbmarketing.com and download all the tables in this chapter. (Incidentally, when you do this, you will be asked to give your email name to the Database Marketing Institute. How's that for email name capture?) Using these tables, figure out how much your company can make by using email more effectively. Determine the value to your company of an email name.
2. Develop an action plan to capture more email names. Get a budget for it and sell it within your company. Establish your schedule and determine when you will get the names.

3. With the names in hand, develop programs that will use these names effectively to build sales and your retention rate.

What Works

- Using test and control groups for all database marketing initiatives
- Determining the value of your email names
- Determining customers' lifetime value and using it to evaluate your marketing strategy
- Capturing customers' email names with permission to use them
- Viral marketing
- Retention marketing
- Emailing last-minute specials
- Emailing follow-up messages
- Emailing newsletters

What Doesn't Work

- Failing to capture customers' email names and use them in your marketing program
- Using database marketing for packaged goods, with some exceptions
- Paying more than half the LTV to acquire a rented name
- Starting any dot com without first computing the value of the email names to be acquired
- Thinking that email response rates will be as high as direct-mail response rates
- Failing to use control groups with any database marketing program

Quiz

1. Compute the lifetime value, after 3 years, of newly acquired customers given these facts: 400,000 customers; retention rates 62 percent, 70 percent, 74 percent; average purchase $320,

$340, $350; cost percent 65 percent, 63 percent, 62 percent; acquisition cost $140; no marketing costs; market rate of interest 7 percent; risk factor 1.5.

2. Develop a second table to show the effect of a 4 percent increase in the retention rate, an increase in annual sales of $12, and marketing costs of $6 per customer per year, with everything else the same.

3. Show the profit or loss to the firm after 3 years if it makes the 4 percent increase. Assume 400,000 customers.

4. Determine the value of these names for resale, assuming brokers' fees of 25 percent and assuming that the buyers use email, with a 1.2 percent success rate. Assume four rentals of names per year. Email costs $0.05 each, and the LTV of the names is the same as that developed in Question 1. Buyers offer 50 percent of the value of the names to them.

5. List five profitable uses for email names in your own situation. Estimate the annual value of the email names resulting from each use.

6. Provide five reasons why regular packaged goods names are worthless.

7. List five specific action steps to be taken in your company (or your client's company) to obtain email names. Estimate how many you will capture during the next 12 months.

8. Come up with a viral marketing plan for your company, listing what you will promote and providing the text of the viral message to be sent by your customers to their friends.

9. Of your current junk emails, find out how to unsubscribe from ten of them. List the percentage that was easy to do and the ones that were hard.

10. Think of a last-minute special email that would work for your company. Write the sender's address, the email subject, and the first five sentences of the email.

CHAPTER 6

THE POWER OF COMMUNICATIONS

Any communication, irrespective of whether or not there is a promotional offer, will increase visits.

Judd Goldfeder, The Customer Connection

Customer communications work. They get people to come back, improve cross sales, and result in upgrades and higher retention rates. And now, because of the Internet, their cost is at an all-time low. To see how communications work, let's look at a few examples.

Business-to-Business Relationship Building

A lighting manufacturer based in Milwaukee used a catalog to market its products to 45,000 contractors and builders. Business was both good and profitable. A consultant at Hunter Business Direct thought that sales could be made even higher through the use of customer communications. His suggestions were greeted with skepticism, but higher management was persuaded to give him a 6-month test. He took the top 1200 customers and divided them into two similar groups: a test group and a control group. The control group was given the same wonderful service that was given to all other customers: Wait for the phone to ring and fulfill the order rapidly.

For the test group, the consultant set up a two-person communications team. A lighting engineer was paired with a customer service rep.

Their job was to call each one of the 600 companies in the test group, find out who the decision makers were, and talk to them. The purpose of the calls was not to make sales. In fact, the team was not empowered to offer discounts. The purpose of the calls was to discuss the customers' lighting needs. Were there new products on the market that they did not find in the catalog? What problems had they had in installations? Where did they see the industry going? Did they need training? Did they have suggestions?

This went on for 6 months, after which the consultant did a complete report on the results. His findings were truly amazing. In the first place, during the 6 months, the test group placed 12 percent more orders than they had in the previous 6 months. The control group placed 18 percent fewer orders!

The test group's average order size grew by 14 percent, whereas the control group's order size shrank by 14 percent. In total, the test group purchased $2.6 million more product than the control group did, spending 27 percent more than they had previously, whereas the control group's total purchases fell by 30 percent. The total cost of the experiment was about $60,000, including the salaries and expenses of the two communicators and the cost of their telephone calls. The increase in sales per dollar spent was a staggering $43.

The heart of this test was the brilliant plan of setting aside the 600-company control group. Without this group, no one would have known how successful the communications program was. This is an experiment that can be repeated in virtually any business-to-business marketing situation.

Consumer Relationship Building

The lighting company's experiment would not have worked with business-to-consumer selling because consumer spending is

- Not continuous
- Far less predictable
- Much lower in volume and margins

However, consumer communications can also produce marvelous results. A chain of restaurants based in San Diego, advised by Judd Goldfeder at The Customer Connection, gave patrons a paper membership card, which was scanned when they arrived at one of the restaurants and used to award them points toward free meals. The program seemed to be working well. After the chain had issued 25,000 cards, it decided to replace the paper cards with plastic ones. When the new cards were ready, they were mailed out with a letter thanking the patron for his or her business. There was no offer or discount connected with the plastic card—just a simple replacement. The results were dramatic. In the week before the cards were sent out, these customers visited the chain 1050 times. During the subsequent 13 weeks, this same group of patrons visited the chain an average of 1400 times per week. Sales to these customers increased by $12,000 per week, or $156,000 in total over the 13 weeks. The increased sales per dollar spent were $8.32.

Keeping the Advertisers

Verizon Information Services was experiencing high attrition in its sales of Yellow Pages advertising. The annual attrition ranged from 10 percent among long-term advertisers to 27 percent among new advertisers. The attrition amounted to over $250 million per year, which translated to over $1.4 billion over the life of the lost advertisers. This loss plus a lower than average acquisition rate was reducing Verizon's penetration in the marketplace.

A study by the Verizon Database Marketing staff showed that there appeared to be two reasons for the high attrition rate:

1. Many small- to medium-sized businesses felt that Verizon had not established a satisfactory relationship with them. The Verizon sales representatives would make contact with their clients only once or twice a year. As a result, some business owners felt that they lacked a close working relationship with Verizon.
2. Small businesses often had difficulty understanding and calculating the value of Yellow Pages advertising. Figuring out how to assess their return on investment was difficult for them.

To address these issues, Verizon wanted to create a retention communications program with these objectives:

- Position Verizon as a business partner for the small-business owner, not just another Yellow Pages provider looking to sell some ad space.
- Educate advertisers about the value of Yellow Pages.
- Target offers and messages to customers providing useful business information.

Verizon's challenge, like that of many other companies, was to get its hands on good customer information in a timely manner. There was an abundance of data on the customers in Verizon's data warehouse, but it was difficult to make that information available quickly enough to enable the company to carry out time-sensitive campaigns. Some of the issues facing Verizon included the following:

- Verizon was unable to coordinate the data with the sales cycle and customer profile. The sales cycle is difficult because Verizon produces more than 1500 different books during the year, with varying closing dates. Some advertisers are in only one book, but many are in two or more books that have different closing dates.
- It was difficult to determine the correct address for advertisers with multiple locations.
- There was no place in the existing database to store model scores or to segment categories.
- There was no process for communicating profile and research information to the supporting groups and departments.

The Verizon Database Marketing staff decided to launch a new program to solve these problems. When the staff began, several solutions were under development or already in place. Behavioral models had been built to predict advertising purchase behavior, including models showing

- Propensity to acquire
- Propensity to cancel, decrease, or increase current spending

- Propensity to buy additional products
- Lifetime value

Some preliminary work had been done on building a data mart, using periodic feeds from the data warehouse. This data mart would be used to organize, summarize, and analyze customer information. Finally, some direct-mail testing had been done, with varying levels of success. Since there was no formalized program in place, these elements were considered nothing more than research and development projects that might or might not yield some long-term value.

From Zero to Hero

The breakthrough solution came as a result of cooperation between information technology (IT) and marketing. A cross-functional team consisting of marketing and IT professionals came together in order to create a "Best in Class" database marketing program.

In order to launch the program, IT revised the data mart so that it could

- Aggregate customer transaction data to an annual level to match the sales cycle.
- Tag customer performance versus the previous year (increase, decrease, cancel, etc.).
- Overlay business demographics (SIC code, number of employees, annual sales, etc.).
- Attach model scores to each customer record.
- Record campaign results attached at the customer level.

When this data mart was combined with campaign management software, it became a powerful tool for direct marketing and marketing research.

While the data mart was being built, customer models were updated and made ready for use in segmentation and targeting. This gave the marketing team the ability to analyze and segment the customer base, design a database marketing program that would target the segments offering the highest opportunity, and create messaging to address those segments.

The final piece of the puzzle was to add a direct marketing agency to the team. The selection of an agency was important in order to ensure

- Strategic input
- Creative insight
- Tactical performance
- Flawless execution

The addition of a direct-mail fulfillment specialist helped to address these issues. Its ability to work with and provide insight to the creative agency, as well as efficiently executing the program's primary direct-marketing campaigns, provided the foundation for success.

The End Result

The strategy was to use the database to send a series of direct-mail pieces that would stand out in the small-business owner's mailbox. The idea was to make them colorful and vibrant, with bold, oversized type on all outer envelopes. Many of the pieces were designed to help the customers calculate their return on investment from a Yellow Pages ad.

Contact frequency and messaging were based on segments defined by the advertisers' tenure and their propensity scores on the various models. A minimum spending level was set as a qualification, so that the marketers could focus their efforts on the top 50 percent of the customer base. All contacts were timed to match various stages of the sales cycle:

- *Tenure.* Advertisers were divided into multiple segments on the basis of seniority. Newer segments received more value-reinforcement and relationship-building messages. Segments that had been customers longer received both relationship and up-selling communications.
- *Propensity scores.* Model scores were then added to the segments in order to further target messaging. Advertisers who were at high risk for attrition received stronger reinforcement communication focusing on educating them on the value of a Yellow Pages ad and

how to measure the success of such an ad. Advertisers who had a high possibility of increasing spending in certain areas were given strong sales messages in those specific areas. Those customers with high scores in both lifetime value and risk of defection received messages showing them how to optimize their product mix and encouraging trial. Those who scored low in all areas received more relationship-building messages.

All mailings were sent first class so that any pieces with bad addresses would be returned. The returned mail was keyed into the database. The impact of the direct-mail communications program was tremendous. The goal was to get a 1 percent increase in sales revenue, or $6 million in additional Yellow Pages ad sales. Control groups that did not get the mailings were set up to measure the results. These showed that the program generated a 3.8 percent increase in overall annual sales revenue, with an additional $13,361,000 in incremental Yellow Pages advertising. Comparing these results with the cost of the mailings and the database, Verizon realized a 1681 percent return on investment.

The success of this program dramatically changed the way Verizon communicated with its advertisers. In subsequent sales cycles, a newsletter was added to increase communication with and education of the customer. Email retention messages were incorporated to make the program more robust. Budgets for these programs were increased in the following year.

The marketing data mart became the cornerstone not just for database marketing, but for all loyalty and database marketing programs companywide. It became the preferred source for information on Verizon customers.

What Has Happened to RFM?

Recency, frequency, monetary (RFM) analysis has been around for more than 50 years. It works wonderfully in managing offers to customers. It is worthless for prospects, however, because it is based on transactions. Companies that use RFM have saved millions of dollars by not sending communications to those who are unlikely to respond. The principles are described in detail in my book *Strategic Database Marketing.*[1]

As an example of the way RFM works, look at Figure 6-1, which diagrams an actual mailing to 500,000 customers coded by RFM.

The company did not break even on those customers in cells below the 0 line; in other words, the profit from sales to them was less than the cost of mailing to them. This type of analysis is done to a small test sample coded by RFM. From the results of that small test sample, you can accurately predict the behavior of 2 million customers coded in the same way. The result was that this firm mailed only to those cells that were profitable. It doubled its response rate. This is the power of RFM. It still is a vital tool in direct marketing using regular mail.

The Web has changed the situation, however. Since emails are so inexpensive, there is little point in restricting offers to existing customers in order to save money. You email to everyone. RFM, however, is still a useful way to categorize customers, even email customers.

Do Communications Change Behavior?

The Air Miles reward program is Canada's largest coalition loyalty program. Over 60 percent of Canadian households have enrolled in the program for free. Under this program, members earn Air Miles reward miles by buying goods and services from a variety of merchants. The Air Miles for Business program allows members to earn reward miles on their business purchases as well as their personal purchases as consumers. In the spring, the Loyalty Group, the creators and managers of the program, offered bonus reward miles to Canadian farmers in a direct-mail campaign urging them to buy products from such merchants as United Grain Growers, John Deere Credit, AgLine, Shell, and Goodyear.

---

[1] RFM software is available free for downloading at www.dbmarketing.com. During the last 5 years, an average of three companies per week have downloaded this software. It works wonderfully for direct mail. In the standard RFM coding, there are 125 cells, from 555 (the most responsive) to 111 (the least responsive).

Figure 6-1   RFM Break-Even Chart

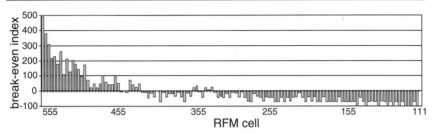

Maria Wallin, marketing manager at the Loyalty Group, arranged for a direct-mail piece to be sent to 50,000 western Canadian farmers who had been active in the program in the 14 months prior to the campaign. In addition, mass media ads for the campaign were placed in six farm publications in western Canada. The goal of the campaign was to achieve a direct-mail response rate of 5 percent and to encourage 2 percent of those contacted to make purchases at one more farm merchant than they had used the previous spring.

Air Miles for Business turned to OgilvyOne Worldwide in Toronto for strategic and creative development of the mailing piece, and to Symcor Direct Response for the laser and letter shop production. Using the Air Miles member database, they developed 72 different combinations of letter copy and 2952 certificate sheet combinations, completely driven by past purchase behavior. The offer of bonus reward miles was designed to encourage increased spending during the promotional period. There was an additional incentive for each farmer to visit one merchant whom he or she had not visited the previous spring.

A control group of 10,000 western Canadian farmers who were members of the program but did not receive any mailings was set aside. The success of the campaign was measured by the overall response rate, the number of farm merchants used, and the number of reward miles earned by those who received the mailing versus those in the control group who did not. The result was that 12 percent of the mail universe responded to at least one of the offers, more than double the first objective. In addition, the number of reward miles earned by those who received the mailing was 59 percent higher than the number earned by the control group during the period of the promotion. The same test had been conducted in the previous year. At that time, the mailing had produced a 46 percent increase over the control.

The second objective was also achieved, as 6 percent of the mail universe made purchases at one farm merchant that they had not used during the previous spring. However, while the objective was achieved, the average number of farm merchants used was the same for the mail and control groups. So, what can we conclude from this? You can successfully use direct mail to get people to do more of what they are already doing. It is much harder to get them to do something different.

Email Communications

The advent of email has changed the equation. Email communications work well. Their costs are much lower than for direct mail, but so are the response rates.

Email customer communications have become more and more acceptable. American Airlines sends weekly notifications of low-cost fares. Amazon sends emails promoting new books. Lands' End promotes new clothing. The economics are powerful.

Direct mail is expensive. If it costs you $30.50 to get a response, as shown in Table 6-1, you had better have something profitable to sell to the responders. On the other hand, with emails, the response rates are much lower, but the costs are dramatically lower.

Because email is so inexpensive, it can be abused. The cost of direct mail, on the other hand, is high, and that is good because the expense weeds out frivolous mailers. You know that the junk mail you receive must be profitable, or the company would not be sending it. Even if you are not interested in what is being offered, there must be thousands of

Table 6-1 Cost per Response: Email vs. Direct Mail

	Direct mail	Email
Sent	400,000	400,000
Cost each	$0.61	$0.04
Promotion cost	$244,000	$16,000
Response rate	2.00%	1.00%
Responses	8,000	4,000
Cost per response	$30.50	$4.00

other recipients who are interested. The cost of direct mail makes it imperative that marketers design something that will be appealing to at least 2 percent of those to whom it is addressed. On the other hand, since email is so inexpensive, thousands of marketers who could not afford direct mail are cluttering the Internet with billions of unsolicited commercial communications. This poses a difficulty for legitimate marketers. Their message gets lost in the clutter of worthless marketing messages.

Direct mail has a lot of problems that are easily solved with email. It takes a long time, sometimes weeks, to know if your message is working with regular direct mail. Another difficulty with direct mail is that there is no practical method for people who do not want to receive the information to remove their names. The mailer who sent a particular piece rented the names from someone else. He probably does not have a database. Telling the mailer to remove your name is like spitting into the wind. The mailer might keep a database of removals and run it against the next list that he rents, but why should he? He will make no money by doing it, and in direct marketing, profits are everything. People don't do things that are unprofitable. You can contact the Direct Marketing Association and get your name entered on its do not mail list, but many mailers do not use this list.

A good emailer, on the other hand, makes it very easy for people to remove their names from the list. Most of the good ones have "one-click" removal. If you click one spot at the bottom of the email, your name is automatically removed from the list. Anyone who does this, however, finds it an endless job. Despite constant grooming, my email is clogged each day with at least 20 emails that I have to delete before I get down to the good stuff. This takes me only a couple of minutes a day, however—certainly less time than it takes me to throw out my junk direct mail. Despite its problems, many companies are now using email very effectively to communicate with their customers and fans.

Promoting Music Using Emails

The Universal Music Group (UMG) is the largest music corporation in the world, with 10,000 artists making CDs for it. For many of its artists, UMG maintains Web sites where fans can come to see pictures of the star in action, listen to snatches of the star's music, and register their names. UMG has been testing the use of these registered names to promote new CD releases. One example is a new CD release called *Essence* by Lucinda Williams on a new label, Lost Highway. The pilot program was designed to determine whether online promotions would have an impact on music sales, and whether database marketing strategies and tactics would work in this industry. This was UMG's first attempt to marry database marketing techniques with e-marketing activities. Universal introduces hundreds of new CDs during any given year. Lucinda Williams was not a well-known artist, and the genre of music called "roots rock" was just emerging as a new music style. This was not a Harry Potter type of marketing effort. UMG's vice president of consumer information marketing, Joe Rapolla, sponsored the promotion and worked with Beth Clough, director of partner relations at msdbm in Los Angeles, to run the project.

The target audience included both existing fans (customers) of Lucinda Williams and prospects who matched the fan profile. The second most important audience was Universal Music managers in UMG's New Media and Common Label Operations departments. These managers had been attempting to prove to management that online marketing could reduce costs and find new customers.

CDs Are Sold in Retail Stores

The Internet was widely used as a channel for music sales through many sites, such as Amazon.com, buy.com, and CDNow.com. However, more than 95 percent of all CDs were sold at retail stores. Most of these CDs were promoted by radio station disc jockeys. The goal of the project, therefore, was not to sell the new CDs over the Web. Instead, UMG wanted to use database marketing strategies to build its email customer base, to gather key information, and to encourage album sales. The market was filled with competing CDs. There were very few radio stations that aired the "roots rock" artists because of the small audience for this genre. Getting rack space for this type of CD was also difficult because it was a new genre of music and a new label. At the time the project began, there were no systems established to measure the success of such a program if success were to occur. UMG management had not given the idea much attention.

The primary objective of the campaign was to develop a successful integrated marketing strategy that would lead to incremental CD sales during the first week of the album's release. The campaign included the following elements:

- Supporting the existing UMG–Lost Highway marketing strategy
- Using online and offline marketing tactics that were trackable, accountable, and measurable
- Proving the value of database marketing in developing fan support and sales
- Developing a model that could be replicated for other UMG labels and artists (see Figure 6-2)
- Using research to create the ideal customer model that would allow Lost Highway to purchase look-alike prospects

All of this had to be done in a situation in which there was no prior research and a very limited existing database of fans. All Joe Rapolla had was a file of a couple of hundred Lucinda fans who had registered 2 years before.

Online Focus Groups

Beth's first task was to develop a customer profile of Lucinda Williams fans based on the names in the existing database. She conducted online focus groups to get qualitative research on the audience for roots rock (see Figure 6-3). The focus groups each contained twelve participants and lasted for 1 hour. Each participant received a $75 cash reward through the mail after the focus group was over. Discussion in the groups centered on the roots rock genre, along with broader topics such as the participant's level of involvement with favorite artists.

Figure 6-2   Lucinda Williams Landing Page

✉ GET A FREE CD with the music everyone's talking about... - Message (HTML)

File   Edit   View   Insert   Format   Tools   Actions   Help

❶ You forwarded this message on 6/6/2001 10:04 AM. Click here to find all related messages.

From: LostHighwayRecords [LostHighwayRecords@list.losthighwayrecords.com]

Jeff Klaasen,

As a music lover, you're always looking for something unique and extraordinary in what you listen to. And the new music coming from Lost Highway Records is what discerning fans are talking about.

Simply click on www.losthighwayonlineclub.com/lucindawilliams/index.cfm? List=A0002&ID=20000, complete the short survey, and you'll have a chance to get a free Lost Highway Sampler* CD AND two free tickets to hear LUCINDA WILLIAMS in a concert near you.

At least 10 sets of prime concert tickets will be given away, so the odds are terrific that you could hear Lucinda, in person, during her current tour. This offer is ONLINE only!
So hurry now to
www.losthighwayonlineclub.com/lucindawilliams/index.cfm? List=A0002&ID=20000
lucindawilliams and complete the short survey. In just a few short weeks you'll be playing your FREE Lost Highway CD.

The free Lost Highway Sampler CD is limited to the first 5000 folks who respond, so please don't hesitate. All responses must be in by August 1, 2001.

(*Tracks slated for the sampler include cuts from Whiskeytown's *Pneumonia*, Lucinda's *Essence*, the soundtrack *O Brother, Where Art Thou?*, Robert Earl

You'll also get a chance to purchase **ESSENCE**, Lucinda Williams' brand-new CD, at the lowest price available, another way of

Figure 6-3   Focus Group Page

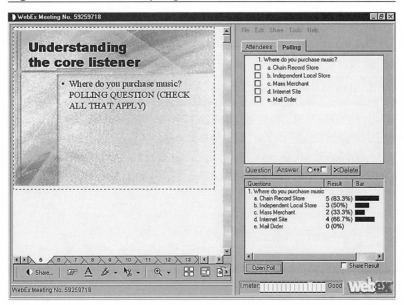

The advantage of an online focus group is that participants can "attend" from their home or office. UMG and msdbm managers were able to communicate directly with the moderator during the sessions. Unlike normal focus groups, online groups require no travel expenses or logistic setups such as meals or the renting of a hotel room. Turnaround time was faster than with traditional focus groups.

Online Microsite

Based on this analysis, msdbm created an online microsite and database to deliver the promotion, capture the data, and report the results. The microsite included an online survey to capture information from the registrants (see Figure 6-4).

The second phase focused on program execution. Beth created a model that used the profile to point to the ideal prospect. Next, she did the research necessary to find email lists of prospects who matched the Lucinda Williams fan profile.

Figure 6-4   Reward for Survey

Email Campaign

The subsequent email campaign consisted of a series of targeted communications, beginning with an outbound email campaign to fans and prospects promoting the release of Lucinda Williams's album and a special offer for those who completed an online survey. Joint online promotions were conducted with the UMG sister company MP3 to expand the reach of the effort. In addition, UMG conducted guerrilla marketing efforts collaboratively with the company M80, which used the promotion to create excitement in the marketplace, increase sales and airplay of the CD, and ultimately drive traffic to the online promotion site.

Data on every responder were stored in the database, and the responder was profiled to see if he or she matched the anticipated type of listener. Responders to the special offer got a follow-up thank-you email with another survey (see Figure 6-5) and further promotion of the *Essence* album, encouraging them to purchase the CD.

Special direct links to Amazon.com's purchase page were developed so that visitors to the microsite who wanted to do so could make a

Figure 6-5 Survey

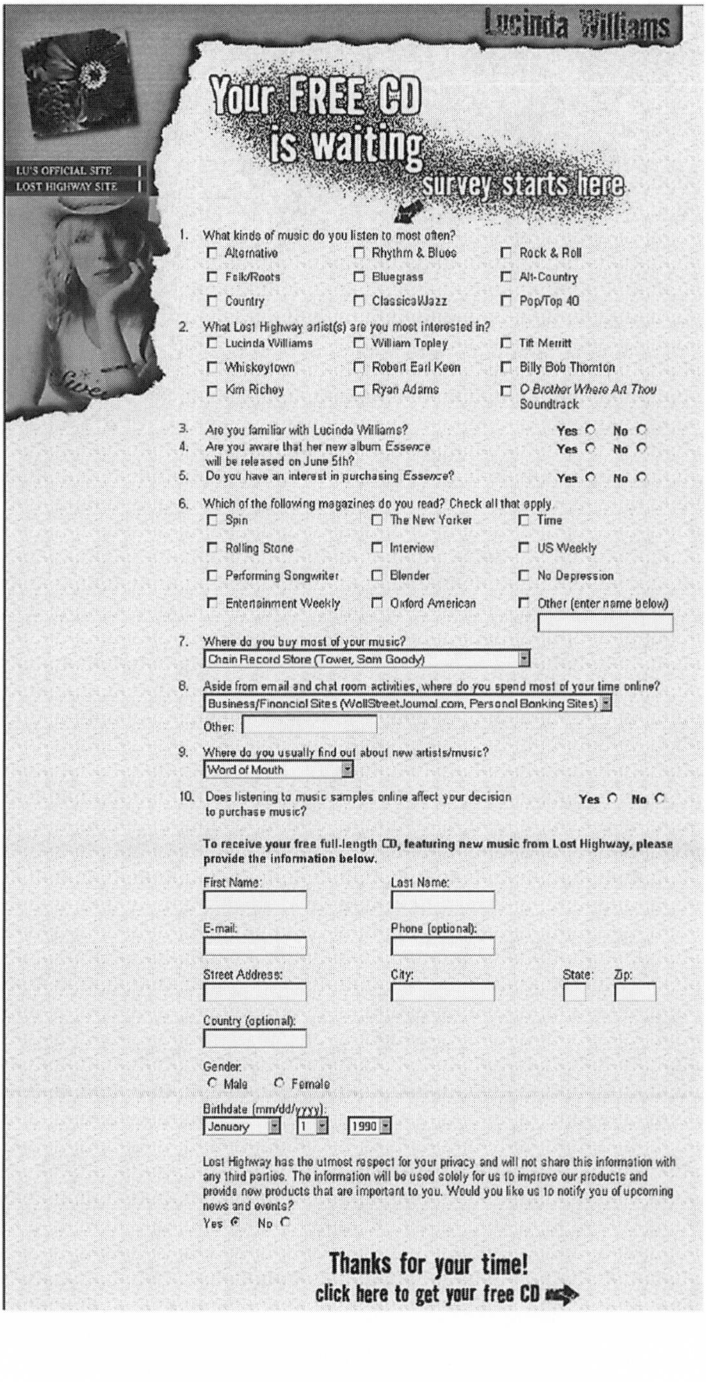

Lucinda Williams

LU'S OFFICIAL SITE
LOST HIGHWAY SITE

Your FREE CD is waiting
survey starts here

1. What kinds of music do you listen to most often?
   - Alternative
   - Rhythm & Blues
   - Rock & Roll
   - Folk/Roots
   - Bluegrass
   - Alt-Country
   - Country
   - Classical/Jazz
   - Pop/Top 40
2. What Lost Highway artist(s) are you most interested in?
   - Lucinda Williams
   - William Topley
   - Tift Merritt
   - Whiskeytown
   - Robert Earl Keen
   - Billy Bob Thornton
   - Kim Richey
   - Ryan Adams
   - *O Brother Where Art Thou* Soundtrack
3. Are you familiar with Lucinda Williams? Yes No
4. Are you aware that her new album *Essence* will be released on June 5th? Yes No
5. Do you have an interest in purchasing *Essence*? Yes No
6. Which of the following magazines do you read? Check all that apply.
   - Spin
   - The New Yorker
   - Time
   - Rolling Stone
   - Interview
   - US Weekly
   - Performing Songwriter
   - Blender
   - No Depression
   - Entertainment Weekly
   - Oxford American
   - Other (enter name below)
7. Where do you buy most of your music?
   Chain Record Store (Tower, Sam Goody)
8. Aside from email and chat room activities, where do you spend most of your time online?
   Business/Financial Sites (WallStreetJournal.com, Personal Banking Sites)
   Other:
9. Where do you usually find out about new artists/music?
   Word of Mouth
10. Does listening to music samples online affect your decision to purchase music? Yes No

To receive your free full-length CD, featuring new music from Lost Highway, please provide the information below.

First Name: Last Name:

E-mail: Phone (optional):

Street Address: City: State: Zip:

Country (optional):

Gender:
Male Female

Birthdate (mm/dd/yyyy):
January 1 1990

Lost Highway has the utmost respect for your privacy and will not share this information with any third parties. The information will be used solely for us to improve our products and provide new products that are important to you. Would you like us to notify you of upcoming news and events?
Yes No

Thanks for your time!
click here to get your free CD

quick purchase. In addition, the site provided the names and addresses of local retailers who sold music. A music sampler was embedded into the site to give prospects an idea of the quality of the new artist and the new genre.

When the campaign was over, responders were sent a postcampaign follow-up email to determine which of them had purchased the CD and why or why not. Based on these responses, Beth conducted a post-campaign analysis measuring customer satisfaction and intention to purchase the Lucinda Williams CD.

Lucinda Williams was constantly on tour during this period. The gradually increasing fan database was used to send targeted city-specific emails to people who lived near places where she was holding her concerts (see Figure 6-6).

As part of the database-driven microsite development, msdbm developed a real-time report that was tied directly to the database (see Figure 6-7). Through this real-time report, msdbm tracked response information, including response by list source, publication, links, and statistical response to the online survey. UMG and Lost Highway were issued user names and passwords so that they could access the report at any time. The report also featured drill-down functionality so that the client could view response by segment, such as specific lists, publications, and so forth.

As a result of the campaign, the fan database grew 960 percent during the 3-month promotion. This campaign proved the value of email database marketing strategies in the music industry. UMG management was stunned by the results of this coordinated effort. It loved the real-time reporting and the ability to have a data-driven Web site. The overall campaign response rate (combined direct and indirect) for the 172,744 people who received emails was 15.5 percent, of which 50 percent reported that they had bought the new CD. Instead of a few hundred registered fans, the Lucinda Williams database developed nearly 26,718 registrants who could be used in further database marketing initiatives. UMG management, impressed with the results, decided to use this method for promoting new artists and staying one step ahead of its competition.

Using direct emails plus MP3, the campaign exposed Lucinda Williams to over 3 million people. The *Essence* CD ranked number one

Figure 6-6   Concert Tickets Email

Lucinda Williams

She's rocking the USA . . .
Got your tickets yet?

[Dear Robert McKim,]

THE REVIEWS ARE IN . . . and they're exceptional. Lucinda Williams' US tour is in progress, and the critics are raving that this double Grammy winner is better than ever. *Rolling Stone* magazine's Richard Skanse raves, "her spell wouldn't be half as wicked if not for the depth and beauty of her songwriting," and Robert Christgau commented, "Lucinda Williams is one of the rare contemporary artists who can make it real."

IT'S NOT TOO LATE . . . for you to see the phenomenon they're talking about . . . Lucinda Williams on tour! In fact, she'll be at a location near you within TWO WEEKS! See and hear Lucinda at . . .

Lancaster, PA   The ABC Concert Hall   Thursday, June 7, 2001

Tickets are going fast, so go now to Lucinda's tour site . . . concerts are being added throughout the summer, so visit her site regularly.

HEAR LUCINDA'S NEW CD . . . to hear a cut from her groundbreaking new CD, *ESSENCE*, visit the Lost Highway online club. While you're there, be sure to take advantage of the LOW PRICING for *ESSENCE*. Amazon.com tells us this CD was already a best seller in prerelease alone — so order your CD now!

AND, don't forget to check out the Lost Highway Online Team

If you received this message in error or would like to unsubscribe, go to Unsubscribe

on Amazon.com and MP3.com for several weeks in a row during the promotion. The campaign generated interest and excitement among other UMG labels, which wanted to execute similar campaigns for other artists. It became the standard by which subsequent UMG campaigns were measured.

Figure 6-7   Online Campaign Reports

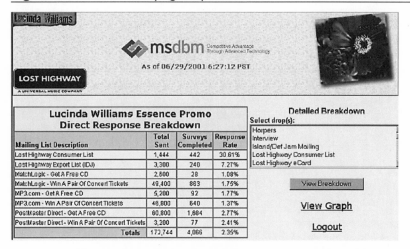

Six months later, the same technique was used for the UMG launch of an album by roots rock artist Shelby Lynne. This campaign:

- Reached 1.4 million fans and/or prospects with direct (email) communications plus another 1.6 million via partner and offline efforts.
- Achieved 75,749 survey respondents, including 40,097 opt-ins, increasing the Shelby Lynne fan database by over 600 percent in approximately 2 months.
- Achieved an 11.2 percent response rate from Shelby Lynne fans and a 6.8 percent response rate from the Lucinda Williams list.
- Encouraged 20 percent of the respondents to use the viral marketing idea by referring the promotion to others. Of those referred, 10 percent went on to complete the survey.

Emails from Racing Fans

Emails are the most inexpensive method of communication with customers ever to come along. The cheapest form of direct mail—a postcard—will cost you at least $0.35. Email to your own customers is almost free. But how do you collect email names? That is difficult. Here is how one company went about the process.

Horse racing was once the most popular sport in America, but attendance has dropped significantly over the years. Other gambling and sport viewing options have proliferated, hurting attendance. The National Thoroughbred Racing Association's challenge has been to increase track attendance and fan involvement in horse racing. It turned to e-Dialog of Lexington, Massachusetts, to help it use the Internet to develop a deeper relationship with core fans and to attract new fans to the sport.

At first, the NTRA had no opt-in email addresses. e-Dialog recommended a campaign that would create an email database: the $1,000,000 Breeders' Cup Challenge. The challenge was launched 8 weeks before the actual race. The contest was straightforward, but not easy: Correctly pick the winner of each of the Breeders' Cup races and win $1 million. A unique hurdle for this program was that the final roster for each of the eight races was announced just 72 hours before the big day. All contestants had to submit their eight picks during that 72-hour window. For this reason, it was critical to develop a communications program that would keep fans engaged throughout the 8 weeks between registering for the contest and submitting their picks.

The solution was a weekly email campaign called "Countdown to the Breeders' Cup." Contestants registered for the contest through an online form that included seven segmenting questions. The final email in the program, sent just hours after the rosters were finalized, contained a link to the actual "pick your horse" page.

To drum up interest in the contest, a combination of online, offline, broadcast, and direct media was used. There were TV ads, emails with "forward to a friend," and signage displayed at racetracks.

The seven weekly emails to registrants created an overall click-through rate of 41 percent and an unsubscribe rate of 2 percent. Over the 7 weeks, the campaign registered 23,407 people, of whom 87 percent, or 20,863 people, opted in to receive additional communications and offers from the NTRA.

Stride Rite Shoes

Stride Rite Children's Division had approximately 135 corporate retail stores nationwide. Stride Rite's marketing director, Julie Lehman, turned to her account team at PreVision Marketing, LLC, in Lincoln, Massachusetts, to create a strategy for filling the stores with customers during the pre-Easter (traditionally a peak sales period) and April (historically an off-peak selling season) time frames. The goal of the strategy was not only to drive sales during these two periods, but also to understand the impact of a second communication on the targeted households reached.

The campaign consisted of two direct-mail pieces: a March peak catalog and an April sandals postcard. The catalog was designed to display the depth and breadth of Stride Rite's product offerings and to drive the key pre-Easter store sales. The follow-up April sandals postcard was designed to increase store sales during the off-peak selling season by focusing on a particular shoe product, sandals, to drive incremental sales at the company's retail stores.

For the campaign, PreVision used the Stride Rite customer database for 70 percent of the households mailed and compiled prospect lists for the remaining 30 percent to support newly opened Stride Rite stores. The March peak catalog's performance was measured over a 5-week period during which a special offer featured in the catalog was valid ("Buy two pairs, save 15 percent; buy three or more, save 30 percent"). The April sandals postcard had no special offer, but its performance was also measured for a 5-week period to ensure comparable results.

To test the effectiveness of each communication alone as well as the incremental impact of the second communication, PreVision set up a test design to enable the following comparisons:

- Compare those who received only the catalog to a no-contact control group.
- Compare those who received only the sandals postcard to a no-contact control group.
- Compare those who received both mailings to those who received only the catalog.

The no-contact control groups matched the audience selection criteria of the mailed households, but did not get any of the communications.

To know who responded, each customer was tracked through name and address capture at point of sale. These point-of-sale data were loaded into the Stride Rite customer database and subsequently matched to the outgoing mailing files. In this way, PreVision was able to identify which of the purchasers had received one communication, which had received two communications, and which had received nothing.

The results, shown in Table 6-2, were very interesting. What do these results tell us? First, both the catalog and the postcard as stand-alone pieces successfully increased both shopping rate and sales, resulting in a positive return on investment (ROI). It is important to note that the ROI for the March peak catalog was not as great as that for the April sandals postcard, as the cost to produce the catalog was significantly higher than the cost of the postcard.

The March peak catalog capitalized on a historically strong season for selling shoes, as evidenced by a high natural shopping rate during that time period. The catalog, which featured a large selection of shoes and show-cased new styles, effectively increased the average basket size of those who received the mailing compared to those who did not. In addition, the catalog successfully drove additional customers to shop at Stride Rite. The April sandals postcard drove additional traffic during a typically slower shoe-selling period but did not significantly increase average basket size.

The dual-contact strategy was also successful. The second contact drove additional households to shop, especially if they had not shopped

Table 6-2 Stride Rite Results

	March peak catalog vs. no contact	April sandals postcard vs. no contact	Dual contact vs. catalog only
Number of households in mail group	354,000	86,000	220,000
Number of households in control group	25,000	20,000	17,000
Lift in shopping rates	9.12%	20.93%	4.53%
Lift in sales	15.16%	20.82%	3.27%
Lift in average basket size	6.12%	NA	NA
Return on investment	1.28:1	1.91:1	1.22:1

after receiving the first communication. The lift in sales and traffic came primarily from households that had not previously shopped. Because the cost per piece for the postcard was low, there was a positive return on the investment. The second communication paid off because it was a cost-efficient piece.

Because of the success of this program, PreVision has recommended dual-contact communication strategies during other selling seasons as well, so that Stride Rite could maximize the effectiveness of its marketing dollars and communicate effectively with its customers.

Constructing an Email Test

If you are like most marketers, you have yet to do an organized email promotion to your customer base. Here is how to go about it.

To begin with, you probably have a database of names and addresses, but you probably have email names for only a few (or none) of your customers. Your first job is to get the email names into your customer records. As you know from this book, this process takes a long time and involves revising all your forms and telemarketing scripts to be sure you start capturing these email names, with permission to use them.

To jump-start the process, you can get opt-in email names appended. You can get help with this. CSC Advanced Database Solutions, for example, has access to a database of more than 50 million households that have provided their email names to various vendors and given written permission for their use for commercial promotions. You can ask CSC or some similar vendor to run your house file against this list and append your customers' email names to your database records. This will cost you about $250 per thousand, or about $0.25 each. (This may sound expensive to you if you have not yet read Chapter 5, "The Value of a Name." After reading that chapter and doing your homework, you will know whether spending $0.25 per name is worth it for you.)

There are dozens of other methods of gaining customer email addresses. You should be sure that customer service and telesales always ask for the emails and for permission to use them. There should be a space for an email address on every form that customers fill out. Some companies have contests for their customers, with email addresses required for entry.

Opt In or Opt Out

When you get customer email addresses, you should be sure that the customers have given you permission to use them for communications. There are two methods for ensuring permission:

- Opt In requires customers to check a box saying that they want to hear from you. The result of using Opt In is often a 5 or 6 percent customer email acquisition rate.
- Opt Out requires customers to check a box saying that they do not want to hear from you. The result of using Opt Out is usually an 80 to 90 percent customer email name acquisition rate.

In both cases, customer privacy is protected. Customers can easily show their unwillingness to hear from you. Don't use Opt In. You will never get enough customer email addresses to create a viable email marketing program.

Of course, you must make it easy for customers to discontinue further emails at any time by providing a "one click" option on every single email you send to them:

- "To discontinue receiving any further promotional emails from our company, Click Here."

Should you get permission to sell the customer's email name to others? Of course you could. But do you want to? Many established businesses find that the revenue gained from renting customer names is small compared to the negative perception of the company being in the name rental business rather being a customer-friendly supplier. You will have to decide what image you want to project to your customers.

Let's assume that one way or another you have gotten email names and permission to use them for 100,000 of your existing customers. How do you go about developing a promotion test?

For direct mail, you would probably test two different packages, sending them out simultaneously to 50,000 people each to see what the response will be. You might even segment your file into 10 different segments of 10,000 each, with slightly different copy, offers, and packages. After 6 weeks you would know which segment did the best job and had the highest return on investment.

That is not at all the way email campaigns are run. In the first place, you seldom, if ever, should send to your whole 100,000 at once. The best plan is to divide your file into 20 different segments of 5000 each. Then spend some time crafting the right appearance for your emails on the customers' screens. Figure 6-8 shows some samples of senders and subjects.

Which of these grab you? How many of them would you delete without reading them? I would say most of them. Only two caught my eye: VAR Business and AOL. I subscribe to *VAR Business* and I am a paying member of AOL, so I might open these two. In fact, I have no interest in sending emails in five languages or in news about Computer Associates, so I would delete those two also. Figure 6-9 shows another group.

There's not much that looks interesting in this group either, except possibly the message from Cyber9014 about processing online transactions. That might be a legitimate offer.

Figure 6-8   Email Sample I

Email Address	Subject
VARBusiness_Insi	CA Denies Federal Inquiry
Byealways7	i was thinking about something
freehgh732111@ho	Tired Of Dieting? Learn About HGH And Permanent We
UnknownSender@Un	Your future needs protection! V8m00j
Whistle779	Need A Credit Card? Everyone Approved !!!
AOLSpecialOffers	datamktins, Send email in 5 different languages!
modgepop@gethold	Improve Clarity and Reception On Your Wireless
needtoknow0128n5	finally 5808WKvs4-134kTOyl16
11k1_@123india.c	FREE CELL PHONE - Your Approved in 60 Seconds!
kmitch3865@8ways	I found this site for men and women, good products
winners25153@yah	Re: Your Confirmation Number... JfauMba9

Figure 6-9   Email Sample 2

Email Address	Subject
Lauren.Arden@ec-	ec-OurCity is Opening its Largest Shopping Mall
viapro2002@msn.c	re: FREE FOR YOU NOW
AOLSpecialOffers	datamktins, you deserve the best of both worlds!
sayheh656@donald	give this a try..it's free
jlio@henerycommo	free vacations & free tour
SexySaraHWantsU2	Hiiii
cyber9014@yahoo.	Processing Online Transactions will SKYROCKET You
CreditFix372375@	Repair Your Credit Online
XLeary057X	XXX
WelcomeRelatiosh	Online Relationship Master
idaho@thecoolguy	Do you have credit card debts? PXy2eSIA19

Lauren Arden sounds like someone's name. It could be a legitimate email that would be of interest. I decided to open that one. It *was* interesting. It began:

> *As a full Web-service provider, we are helping vendors sell their products directly to consumers. Therefore, prices for some of the products are the lowest available. All 500,000+ discounted items can be found by visiting www.ec-OurCity.com.*

Let's try another group (see Figure 6-10).

What stands out here is the Account Specialists with a subject Email Centre. Why the English (rather than American) spelling of Centre? It caught my eye. The email said:

> *The "@aol.com" part of your email address is owned by someone else and is known as a Domain name. You will have datamktins@aol.com as long as you subscribe and pay each month. You never really own your email address, someone else does. You just rent it.*

It went on to offer the firm's services to help me own my own email name.

Figure 6-10 Email Sample 3

Email Address	Subject
TaraDRosenthal45	Your attention: Subscription request, please read
cashnotice@natio	Read This And You Won't Regret It!
HoTt CoLoMblaNa	whats up!
dmckin324@yahoo.	Accept Credit Cards with Zero Money Down!...
joedavis50@yahoo	Homebased Business Owner?
GiftRemndr	Valentine's Day is right around the corner!
dmckin324@yahoo.	Find Out The Background of a SUSPICIOUS NEIGHBOR
AccountSpecialis	Email Centre
Roofre	National Defense & Aviation Stock Opportunity
alabama@kappamai	Home Workers Urgently Needed 805D450lfr
Matty51077	Bondage

The Valentine's Day reminder also looked interesting. Notice that dmckin324 is sending me two emails: one on credit cards and one on background checks. He has destroyed his credibility by sending two emails so close together.

What do these things tell us about emails?

- There is a lot of competition, particularly from really junk email.
- Junk email is much more widespread than junk direct mail. Email is so cheap to send that any worthless smut purveyor can afford to send millions per day.
- People look first at who sent the email and second at the subject. They seldom look at the text of your emails at all, unless the email address and subject pass a validity test.
- You need to give a lot of thought to what your email address should look like.
- Then spend some time figuring out how to present your subject. Settle on three different email addresses and three different subjects.
- Once you are happy with these six, you can begin to worry about what to say in the email. (I am reminded of experts at Ralston Purina, who reportedly spent more than 6 months designing the appearance of the perfect cereal box before they got around to figuring what to put into the box!)

Designing the Text

Once people have opened your email and read your copy, what do you want them to do? You have to make it easy, obvious, and compelling. Here is how one merchant did it:

Click here to search our database with no obligation.

This takes you directly from the email to the merchant's Web site, where it offers its services (see Figure 6-11). This is very seamless and compelling copy.

Figure 6-12 shows the text of the Valentine's Day email. Each underlined section of text is an automatic link to a professional Web site. This is the way to go.

Few email texts are this organized. Most of them make you work at filling out forms and emailing them to someone, with a response generated in a few days.

Beginning Your Test

Your first step is to send 5000 emails in a head-to-head test of two different email addresses and one subject (2500 to each). You will know within 48 hours which of the two produced the better result in terms of click-throughs, responses, and sales.

Figure 6-11   Web Site for Designing Your Web Address

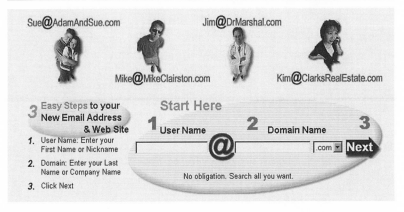

Figure 6-12 Text of Valentine's Day Email

AOL Reminder... Valentine's Day is only 4 days away!

Hi Arthur Hughes,

Don't forget that Valentine's Day is Thursday, February 14th and there's still time to send that special person something! Select the perfect gift from our Valentine's Day Shop.

If you can't find what you're looking for there, RedEnvelope can still deliver in time for the big day! Check out their unique gift collection now!

When in doubt, you can always find something at Target! Shop today.

Now take the better of the two email addresses and try two different subjects with the next 5000 names. Save the best email address and the best subject. Experiment not only with the email addresses and the subjects, but with different texts and different days of the week for your mailing.

Gradually, over the next couple of weeks, you can work your way through your 100,000 customers, getting better and better response rates as you go. You may start with a 0.5 percent response rate (12 responses out of 2500). At the end of 10 tests, you might have worked your way up to 2 percent (50 responses out of 2500)—that is four times better than the rate you started with. You might even do much better. Many companies that use emails to market to their existing customers have achieved response rates of 20 percent or more.

The key to success here is constant testing. You simply cannot do this with direct mail. With email, if you do it right, you can achieve tremendous success in a very short space of time.

Summary

Communications to customers work. Used correctly, communications will

- Increase your retention rate and reduce attrition
- Increase cross sales and up sales

- Increase referrals
- Increase profits

The advent of email has given marketers a tremendously valuable new communication channel that will revolutionize database marketing. The one-to-one communications that we talked about in the 1990s are being carried out in the new century. From now on, anyone who is not using emails will lose out in the competitive race to build customer loyalty.

What Works

- Communication with customers through direct mail and email
- Capturing email names with permission to use them
- Creating Web sites where customers and fans can register their support of artists and products
- Online focus groups
- Real-time reports on the results of email communications
- Getting customers to fill out personal profiles online
- Personalizing emails and Web sites
- Testing emails on small groups to get the right email address and subject

What Doesn't Work

- Email blasts to unknown (and angry) people to get them to buy legitimate products.
- Direct mail promoting low-margin products.
- Database marketing for packaged goods.
- Customer communications programs without the use of a control group. You cannot prove that they have done any good.
- Trying to get your name eliminated from unsolicited email commercials.

Quiz

1. What was the breakthrough solution in the Verizon case study?
   a. Building a warehouse
   b. Segmenting the data
   c. Cooperation between IT and Marketing
   d. Building a data mart
   e. Sending mail first class
2. Figure the cost per response for an email campaign that costs $0.05 per email and gets a response rate of 1.16 percent.
3. A bank tried two communications programs. One was to mutual funds customers and was aimed at getting them to buy more mutual funds. The second was to those who did not have a home equity loan, asking them to apply for one. Which was likely to get the larger response rate and why?
   a. Home equity loan offer.   It is easy to qualify for one.
   b. Mutual fund offer. It is easier to get people to do more of what they are doing than it is to get them to do something else.
4. If RFM can double the response rate in direct-mail campaigns, why would it not be equally valuable for email campaigns?
   a. RFM does not work with email.
   b. There is no control group.
   c. Domain names are unavailable.
   d. Emails are so inexpensive you can concentrate on maximizing profits.
   e. None of the above.
5. Propose a budget for your company for an online focus group. List the two things that you would most like to get out of the focus group.
6. Make a chart for a warranty expiration program, comparing the costs of email warranty notification with telemarketing at a cost of $5 per call. Assume that the emails cost $0.06 each. What was the cost per order of each, assuming that the telemarketers got 8 orders out of 100 and the email program got 3 orders out of 100? What was the return on investment? Which method would you choose?

7. List the four most important things to capture on a customer profile completed through the Web.

8. What one factor, if it had been left out of the lighting manufacturer's test, would have ruined the program?
   a. The customer rep
   b. The lighting expert
   c. The test group
   d. The control group
   e. None of the above

9. In the case of the restaurant chain with the frequent diner card, what did the program cost the chain over the 13 weeks?

10. Which is the most important item in an email promotion program?
    a. The offer
    b. The timing
    c. The copy
    d. The subject line
    e. The domain

CHAPTER 7

CUSTOMER RESPONSE

The best response to a promotion is a sale. Typically, you want customers to visit a store and buy your product or service. In the absence of this fruitful response, until recently there were four other ways in which customers could respond to a promotion. They could

- Call on the phone
- Send a letter through the mail
- Send a fax
- Send an email

These four methods are still used for both consumer promotions and business-to-business marketing. They work well, and they will continue to be an important part of direct marketing. But all four have a drawback: They are moderately expensive two-step procedures that require additional effort to complete the sale.

In the last few years, Web response has been developed. It has many advantages over these four methods. With Web response, the customer goes to a Web site, gets more information about the product, and places the order personally. This method swamps all the others in terms of

- Reduction in fulfillment cost
- Capture of data along with the sale
- Immediacy of response information
- Personalization and speed of response
- Accuracy of the data captured

Here is how the process works. In the promotional message, the customer is given the name of a Web site to contact. If the promotion is an email, the Web site address can be contained in the message itself. All the user has to do is to click where it says click here, and she jumps to the site automatically. Once she arrives at the Web site, if the process has been set up correctly, she sees a greeting: "Welcome, Susan" or "Welcome back, Susan." She also finds information about the product that was featured in the promotion. At that point, she can

- Buy the product directly on the site or make a reservation (rather than a sale)
- Get the names and addresses of local dealers who sell the product
- Talk directly to a local dealer
- Talk to a live operator
- Get detailed answers to her questions about the product or service
- Answer some survey questions designed to help her make a decision about which product is best for her needs
- Complete a personal profile that provides her preferences and some demographics
- Provide her address, email name, and credit card number
- Send messages to friends about the product or service
- Learn about other products sold by the supplier and order them
- Provide permission for further correspondence

In fact, in many ways, her visit to the site is *better* than a visit to a local store. If the site is set up properly, it provides the supplier with a wealth of information about the prospect or customer that would be difficult or impossible to get during a store visit or with any of the other four response methods except the phone call.

"Welcome, Susan"

How do you manage to say, "Welcome, Susan"? This is one of the secrets of modern database marketing using the Web. You begin with a list of prospects who are to receive your direct-mail or email promotion. You assign a unique four-character code to each person on your list. A typical code could look like this: R34Y. With a four-character coding system, you can assign unique codes to 1.5 million people. A five-character code gives you 52 million unique codes. You make your Web site address as simple as possible: www.Nikkon.com/R34Y. When Susan enters this address in her Internet browser or clicks on it, your site functionality immediately checks the last four characters against a lookup table that is stored in memory and is able to respond, "Welcome, Susan." Your software, with Susan's permission, will leave a cookie on her computer so that when she comes back the next time, you can say, "Welcome back, Susan."

If your promotion is via TV, radio, or print, the address will be different. You might tell the customer to contact www.Nikkon.com/BAR2. The "B" might tell you that this is a mass communication promotion, and the AR2 tells the Web site which of 42,000 particular ads on a TV or radio station or in a periodical prompted Susan's response. In this case, of course, you cannot say "Welcome, Susan," but you can know exactly what prompted Susan to pay the Web site a visit.

Setting up a Microsite

Web response involves a Web microsite that is set up specifically to receive customer responses to promotions. A microsite differs from a regular company Web site in that it is constructed with a particular group of promotions in mind. The setup cost is much lower. A major company Web site, like www.marriott.com, costs millions of dollars to create and maintain. (This site, by the way, is one of the best on the Web.) Every company needs a main Web site, although most do not need a site that is as complex and powerful as the Marriott site. What we are describing in this chapter is a microsite that can be set up for a one-time fee of $3000 and maintained for $400 per month or even less. This microsite has a database associated with it on the same server. In fact, the two are really part of the same system.

As an example of such an email connecting to a microsite, Figure 7-1 shows an email that I developed after one of my speeches. It was sent to all the attendees who gave me their business card during the speech.

Figure 7-1   Sample Microsite

Where to find the speeches/slides	**UCEA Conference Follow Up - Arthur Hughes**
How to get email appended to your customer database	At the UCEA Conference in San Francisco that we attended together last week, a number of people asked me about the various email and Internet techniques that I recommended in my two talks. Since there
Emailing to your customers	was such interest, I thought that I would pass on some ideas that you might use in implementing some of these techniques.
Next Best Course	
Maintaining your database	**Where to find the speeches/slide**. If you are interested in the presentation slide shows, click on the links below:
Building your registration web site	⬛ UCEA Mini-Workshop on Database Marketing (2.1 MB)
Consulting on database marketing	⬛ Building Bridges: Reach Your Customers and Keep Them Coming Back (1.9 MB)
Contact Arthur	If you are interested in buying any of my books or downloading the free RFM software that I mentioned in the talk, please click here. You can also download Lifetime Value Tables.

Any data entered into the microsite are stored immediately in the database. Also, the database provides the lookup table for the PIN codes that may be contained in the outgoing email or direct-mail promotions. There are editing procedures stored in the microsite software that keep erroneous data from being entered. As a result:

- U.S. zip codes are always numbers, and Canadian postal codes are letters and numbers.
- Phone number area codes always match the address.
- Email names given by customers are always correct because the responder gets a reward that is distributed by email.
- The site does not accept erroneous product codes.
- Dates, ages, and incomes are always within reasonable limits. For example, customers' ages are not listed as being over 120 years, and birth dates are not later than today.
- Data are converted to the proper case, usually upper- and lowercase.

Finally, the microsite always has a seamless link to the company's main Web site.

Table 7-1 Comparative Media Results

	Mail	Email	Fax	Phone	Web
Incoming costs	$0.35	$0.00	$0.15	$0.70	$0.00
Data entry	$0.60	$0.60	$0.60	$3.50	$0.00
Cost per 100,000	$95,000	$60,000	$75,000	$420,000	$0
Time in weeks	3	1	1	0	0
Information gained	Medium	Medium	Low	High	Highest
Possible errors	Moderate	Moderate	High	Low	Very low
Interactivity	None	None	None	Very high	High
Personalization	None	None	None	High	High

The beauty of Web response is that the customers do all the work. The cost savings are tremendous. Table 7-1 gives the relative costs per response.

With mail, email, or fax, it is necessary for a data entry clerk to read and retype the information in order to get it into the company's order fulfillment and database system. There is always an error rate. Some companies report an error rate as high as 30 percent, and lots of data are not captured—email name, phone number, or correct address, for example. The time delay is significant. To keep costs down, data entry is done in batches. As each batch is completed, it is sent electronically to the fulfillment and database system. In these systems, there is a limit on the amount of information that you can ask for and reasonably expect to get.

The telephone is by far the best of the five systems. Until recently, most call center operators typed their data into an internal software system and sent the responses to the client's fulfillment system in batches. In modern database marketing, the operators have access to the Web and can type the data directly into the client's fulfillment and database system through the Web, so there is no delay. Products can be sent out the same day. Operators can make suggestions and cross sales. They can answer questions and coax a customer into buying more. You pay a lot for phone service, but, when it is done well, you get a lot for it. For most companies, it is still the best possible customer response system.

How the Web Can Trump the Phone

Where Web response comes into its own is in the sophistication it makes possible and the very low cost. Once your Web microsite is set up and running, the variable costs of each customer response are exactly zero. We should note that we are not factoring in the setup costs here. Web setup can be expensive, but it is much less expensive than call center software. It is comparable to the elaborate arrangements that are necessary to receive, open, and enter data from phone, fax, or email.

The tremendous cost savings from use of the Web are possible only if customers are willing to go to the Web to respond. Whether they do so depends on how good the Web site is. If using the Web site is a superb experience, word will get around, and customers will flock to it. If the experience is annoying, unhelpful, uninformative, slow, or confusing, people will stay away in droves. For the present, do not expect the majority of your customers to respond via the Web. The phone will be the response mechanism of choice. But this is changing every day as Web use grows. For the Web to be successful in database marketing, your company is going to have to put a lot of effort into making the experience satisfying for the responder. Here are some of the things that you are going to have to provide:

- *Personal greetings.* Find a way to greet customers personally, particularly business-to-business customers. As already discussed, you absolutely must use cookies, unique site addresses, or PINs. The goal is to make the Web site better than a live operator.
- *Quick loading.* Do away with flash pages that take a long time to download. Most consumers today are still on modems, not broadband DSL, and this will be true for some time to come. You system has to be designed for your current customers, not for the customers of the future. If you cannot make your current customers happy, you may have no future.
- *A site designed for the customer.* Design your site with your customers in mind. Put yourself in their shoes. Don't say, "What do I want to sell them on this site?" Instead say, "What would I want to see if I came to this site as a customer who knows very little about our company and its products and who is trying to find information or get prices on a specific item?"
- *Search boxes.* Provide a search box prominently on every page. Make that search box very informative. Nothing is more annoying than going to a Web site looking for something and not being able

to find it. I went to the Hewlett-Packard Web site trying to find toner for my HP Laserjet 4—the most common printer in the United States. I couldn't find it. Even if you don't have what you assume many people will be looking for, give them an answer. HP could have said, "We don't sell toner for our printers. Go to www.Staples.com/HPToner."

- *Three-click rule.* Use the three-click rule. Make it possible for anyone to find anything on your site with just three clicks.
- *Constant modification.* Study the things that people are asking for every day, and update the site so that it answers the questions that are asked. That is what call centers do. If a number of people ask the call center operator, "Is your product made in the USA?" he will quickly ask around to be sure his answer is correct. You have to design your Web site to do the same thing. In designing and managing your Web response site, spend a few hours a week sitting next to a call center operator and listening to the questions and the operator's answers. Your site has to be that good.
- *Pictures, lists, and diagrams.* Capitalize on what you can do on the Web site that a live operator cannot possibly do. You can have pictures of things, maps, references, articles, lookup tables, and diagrams. Incidentally, while I am at it, let me take a swipe at Acrobat. Many Web sites use Acrobat software to display pictures and text. It produces attractive results, but you cannot copy it or download it easily. I prefer screen content that you can print directly on your PC printer or copy directly into Word. Acrobat is annoying and turns me off. Figure 7-2 shows the entire process in a nutshell.

Of course, there are still millions of Americans who do not yet make a habit of going to the Web in response to promotions. That number is going down by thousands every day. Before you finish reading this chapter, several thousand additional U.S. households will have come online. Today nearly everyone above the poverty level has a computer. Just about everyone is using email at work or at home. While people are looking at their email, it is an easy step to click on a Web site contained in the email to respond to your promotion.

Figure 7-2   Customer Service Link through the Web

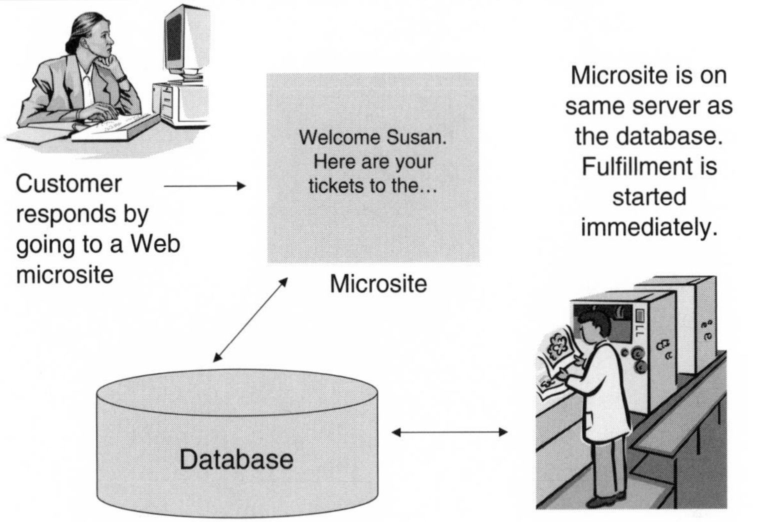

Customer responds by going to a Web microsite

Welcome Susan. Here are your tickets to the...

Microsite

Database

Microsite is on same server as the database. Fulfillment is started immediately.

Generating Web Response

I am often asked what the typical response rates to a promotion are. There is, of course, no answer to this question. It depends on the audience, the offer, the package, the copy, the timing, and a host of other factors. Some promotions to customers have generated response rates of 40 percent or more. Most promotions to prospects are lucky to achieve a 1 percent response rate. An important aspect of promotion response is the method selected for receiving the response. Is it mail, phone, email or Web? As this book demonstrates, Web response is the most cost-effective and powerful method. Let's take a look at a couple of cases to demonstrate this point.

Direct-Mail Response

An automobile manufacturer designed a credit card for its automobile customers. It created two different cards: a Titanium card with a $100 annual fee and a Gold card with no annual fee. The Gold card included a $50 reward package and an initial APR of 3.9 percent.

The direct-mail promotions were sent only to the owners of the company's cars, not to the general public. The automobiles were designed for and sold to an upper-income segment that appreciated their performance and style. The owners were loyal to the brand. The promotions took place at a time when the credit card market had been saturated with offerings for the previous four years. Few cards were generating significant response rates.

Overall, there was a surprising difference in the response to the two cards, as shown in Table 7-2. From these numbers, it is clear that the Titanium card was a loser. The acquisition cost of $297 per account was really uneconomical. You can't subtract the $100 annual fee from this number because the fee will be paid only at renewal time, 1 year hence. At that time, if this card is like most cards, less than 50 percent will pay the $100 to renew.

The Gold card, on the other hand, produced an unusually good response rate. Since the overall industry average acquisition cost for credit cards is well over $100, this automobile company made excellent use of its customer database to promote these cards, as its cost per account was only $57.

The response to the cards was by phone or mail. No opportunity for Web response was offered. This could have been a serious mistake.

Direct Mail versus Email

A major manufacturer of business-to-business computer products created an innovative Web site that was designed to

- Teach IT managers about the value of the company's services
- Get them to register
- Profile them for the sales force

Table 7-2 Card Response

	Titanium	Gold
Low response	0.15%	1.01%
High response	0.40%	4.71%
Total response	0.25%	1.60%
Cost/response	$317.50	$49.96
Approval rate	107.00%	87.22%
Cost/account	$297.25	$57.28

A creative direct-mail piece was sent to 186,000 IT professionals drawn from lists of customers and rented lists of computer magazine subscribers. It directed people to go to the Web site. Parallel to this, an email campaign was launched to 56,000 IT professionals. The email lists were primarily lists of trade show attendees. The results comparing the various lists used, shown in Table 7-3, were quite interesting.

What Table 7-3 shows is that the email promotion did very well against the direct-mail promotion. The response rates were lower and the percent registering was much lower, but the cost per registrant was almost half that of direct mail. What can we conclude from this?

- Direct mail is not dead. It will continue to be a useful and effective direct marketing technique.
- Email gets lower response rates, but it produces results at far lower cost.

There is one really powerful lesson from this case that does not show up in the numbers presented so far. That lesson concerns the responses that came from an unknown source, as shown in Table 7-4. This is where the company was a real winner.

Table 7-3 Cost per Registrant

	Direct mail	Email
Cost per piece	$0.76	$ 0.14
Number sent	186,361	53,250
Low response	0.26%	0.00%
High response	4.03%	7.79%
Total response	1.42%	1.04%
Percent registering	1.01%	0.29%
Cost per registrant	$75.25	$48.28

Table 7-4 Responses from an Unknown Source

	Direct mail	Email	Unknown source
Number of log-ons	2,639	553	1,288
Number registered	1,885	153	882
Cost per registrant	$75.25	$48.28	$00.00
Gross revenue	$942,500	$76,500	$441,000
Marketing costs	$141,846	$ 7,387	$0
Net revenue	$800,654	$69,113	$441,000

Where did all of these "unknown source" registrants come from? Analysis of this situation tells us a lot about modern direct response techniques.

The Value of Web White Mail

In a traditional direct-mail campaign like the credit card example, the responses arrive via a toll-free number. When you call this number, an operator asks you for your source code. Good operators can usually worm this number out of the respondents, even though they may not have it with them when they call. When the operators cannot determine the source, they dub the source "white mail"—responses from an unknown source.

On the Web site, it is different. In this example, responders were supposed to enter their PIN when they came to the site as a result of an email or a direct-mail piece. If they did not remember their PIN, they were invited to visit the site and register anyway. As you can see, 1288 of them visited the site, and 882 registered.

We will never know whether these 1288 people came as a result of the email campaign, whether they came as a result of the direct-mail campaign, whether they stumbled on the site through the recommendations of a friend or associate at work, or whether they came because of a combination of these reasons. But that points up a difference between live phone operator response and Web response: the fact that an entertaining Web site with a relevant quiz can lead people to visit the site to see what it is. There is no commitment. You can be anonymous, and disappear if you are not interested.

On the other hand, practically nobody calls a toll-free number just to see what it is like. There it is tough to be anonymous. You know you will be talking to an operator. You don't want to waste her time. Therefore,

- Web response will generate a lot more white mail than phone response.
- This response can be the most valuable output of the entire process.

Selling Trucks to Existing Customers

Isuzu makes midsized commercial trucks that sell for about $33,000 each. Recently, the truck marketplace was moving very slowly. Furthermore, at that time, Isuzu had no new truck models to offer with which it could beat the competition. As a result, Isuzu had to rely on better marketing and improved ability to target prospects and customers.

At the time, Isuzu's marketing budget had been cut back. On the bright side, however, American Isuzu Commercial Vehicles had just completed two major database projects using an updated customer database created by msdbm in Los Angeles. The first project was to profile customers, and the second was to model customer purchase behavior. Based on these models, a numerical scoring methodology was developed to indicate purchase behavior. Scores were then grouped into three ranges indicating a high, medium, or low likelihood of purchase. If the methodology was accurate, then customers who received a high score would be more likely to purchase in the near term than customers who received a low score. It was also felt that the company was more likely to be successful at selling a new vehicle to a current customer than at trying to convert a prospect.

Msdbm developed a scoring methodology to predict the behavior of Isuzu Commercial Truck owners. The model predicted the propensity to purchase based on four variables:

1. Number of people employed by the business
2. Vocation—e.g., landscaping, electrical contractor, towing, etc.
3. Time since last purchase
4. Total number of trucks owned

Using the model scores, the customers were divided into three groups based on the likelihood of their purchasing a new truck:

1. High probability
2. Medium probability
3. Low probability

Isuzu decided to use the models to create a mailing designed to drive selected customers to Isuzu dealers. The goal of the mailing was to

- Test the model to determine whether the scoring methodology could correctly separate the customers into the three segments.
- Use the same creative material for all segments—low, medium, and high scores—in order to get a valid test.
- Provide a mechanism for collecting and updating data and offer a purchase incentive.
- Sell 150 trucks.

The data in the legacy system had many flaws. They were over a year old. Much of the contact management history had not been recorded. The majority of the customers were small vocational companies, such as Joe & Jim's Landscape Company in Keokuk, Iowa. The vocation of many other companies was difficult to identify. The data used for the model were put together from multiple sources of data: R. L. Polk, InfoUSA, and in-house transaction files.

There was an additional problem of determining who the real driver of the truck was. In a typical situation, the sale of a truck might have been financed by GE Capital, then the truck was delivered to Ryder Truck, leased with a new truck body to Joe & Jim's Landscape, then driven by Mac McKenzie. Who is the decision maker for the purchase of a new truck?

What Was Sent to the Customers

Msdbm created a direct-mail package that included a cover letter, a fax-back form asking specific purchasing questions, a four-color product information sheet highlighting the features and benefits of the most popular truck model (N Series), and a purchase certificate for an additional gift if a truck were purchased. The completion of the fax-back purchase information form guaranteed all respondents a gift of a briefcase, while the purchase of a new or used vehicle guaranteed the buyer a set of seat covers and floor mats for use in the vehicle. Respondents were given only 60 days to take advantage of the offer. The total quantity

Table 7-5 Trucks Sold

	Group totals	Companies buying	Buying rate	Trucks sold
High score	1899	97	5.10%	107
Medium score	1855	32	1.70%	34
Low score	1890	15	0.80%	16
Control group	520	3	0.60%	3
Total	6164	144	2.30%	160

mailed was 6000. In addition, 520 companies were set aside as a control group to monitor the success of the promotion. These 520 companies did not get the promotions.

This test mailing proved that the scoring methodology that had been developed was highly accurate; the results are shown in Table 7-5. As a result, Isuzu used the same methodology to score the entire customer file for a follow-up mailing. This gave Isuzu the ability to target key customers and ensure the sale of a vehicle at very little cost, compared to normal prospect acquisition costs.

The marketing and sales departments were initially dubious about the mailing. Based on their previous experience, they had expected to sell only 85 trucks to 6000 prospects. After they saw the results, they could see that their future success was going to be tied to database marketing. Being able to accurately predict which companies were likely to buy, so that they could direct their marketing and sales efforts at those companies, proved to be a powerful advantage.

As a result of the test campaign, the company sold 160 trucks, for a total of more than $5,600,000, with an investment, including the model, printing, mailing, and generation of creative material, of $80,000 (see Table 7-6). The industry estimates that, in general, it costs a manufacturer about $1000 in marketing and sales effort to sell one midsized truck. Using the database, Isuzu was able to sell the trucks for half that amount.

Web-Based Employee Recognition Program

ScotiaApplause was designed by the Carlson Marketing Group to be a platform that would support a customer-centric employee recognition

Table 7-6 Overall Truck Promotion Results

Description	Results/response
Total number of trucks sold in 60 days	160
Overall customer sales conversion	2.1%
Overall sales conversion on total trucks purchased	2.8%
Overall forecasted sales conversion	1.5%
High-score sales conversion on trucks purchased	5.1%
Medium-score sales conversion on trucks purchased	1.7%
Low-score sales conversion on trucks purchased	0.8%
Cost of program	$80,000
Program cost per vehicle sold	$500
Control group (520)—3 sales	0.5%
Total delivered mail quantity	5,644

program for 20,000 branch employees of Scotiabank, Canada's third largest bank. The purpose of the Applause program was to promote, recognize, and reward certain customer-centric behaviors defined by the bank. To focus and articulate the brand vision, a statement of the bank's core valves was developed. The core purpose was considered critical in sustaining the bank's position as a leading international Canadian bank.

The core purpose statement was

To be the best at helping customers become financially better off by finding relevant solutions to their unique needs.

Carlson and Scotia management designed ScotiaApplause to encourage employee behaviors that demonstrated the desired core values. The Applause Principles for employees were identified as

- Respectful
- Straightforward
- Insightful
- Spirited

Background of the Program

Historically, employee incentive programs at Scotiabank had been used sporadically and had had a strong emphasis on driving volumes. Many of these programs encountered difficulties ranging from lack of implementation to inequitable competitive groupings. Most of them lacked a strong reinforcement for building customer relationships. The worst characteristics of these programs were the following:

• They were strictly sales incentives.
• The areas where the bank's budget was biggest, rather than customers' needs, got most of the attention.
• They offered few benefits for the sales and support staff.
• They did not benefit most employees, and as a result they did not lead to discernible changes in employee behavior.
• They lacked consistency in the communications delivering recognition or rewards.
• They did not address the primary employee behavioral problems.

From a review of past programs, Carlson concluded that a program designed around recognizing and rewarding *leading* indicators of performance activities and behaviors, as opposed to *lagging* indicators or results, was required.

Strategy and Design

Many Scotiabank branch employees had been with the bank for 15 to 25 years. Securing their buy-in for a new incentive initiative was not easy. The core idea of the program was that establishing a recognition system that rewarded employees for adhering to the identified core values would lead to an increase in customer service, resulting in customer retention and growth while minimizing attrition.

ScotiaApplause was designed to be completely Web-based, with employees accessing the Web site from work or from home. By means of emails and intranet connectivity, employees could electronically submit both online recognition and personalized certificates. Certificate nominees and recipients were eligible for monthly reward draws for Applause points, which were redeemable for reward merchandise.

ScotiaApplause gave the bank

• An ability to offer district vice presidents and branch managers a motivational program

- A recognition program that was integrated among the various channels—call centers, the branch network, and management
- Flexibility by recognizing both team goals and individual achievement
- Success with online training
- Real-time reporting for management and staff

Results after 6 Months

The initial goal was to get employees to register for the program. The target was to get 75 percent to register by the end of the fiscal year. Six months ahead of schedule, the program had achieved 91 percent registration, with about 70 percent of those who had registered being active in the program. The goal for certificate issuance was 660 per week. In fact, the program actually achieved 2844 per week.

- More than 100,000 recognition certificates were issued.
- More than 7000 rewards were ordered.
- Desired activities and behaviors were rewarded, and the result was an increase in these activities and behaviors.
- There was consistency in communication channels and messages.

The program received significant recognition throughout the bank. It rapidly became the bank standard for employee recognition and rewards. The success of the program contributed to the bank's being rated the number one bank in Canada in overall quality of customer service by the Customer Service Index (CSI) survey, published by Market Facts, a leading U.S.-based market research firm.

Moving a Loyalty Program to the Web

A major long-distance provider asked KnowledgeBase Marketing, an integrated marketing solutions company, to develop a new loyalty database and redesign a rewards program for the company's highest-value customers. The goal of the program was to prevent churn and provide cross-selling opportunities. For 9 years, the long-distance provider had maintained a customer retention program on a mainframe, operating in batch mode. In Phase I, KnowledgeBase Marketing upgraded the system to a true real-time transactional database. Customers now could redeem loyalty points in real time through a call center, through an automated telephone system, or through the travel division. In addition, the new system provided the ability to offer more exciting rewards efforts, cross-selling opportunities, promotional tracking, and enhanced customer interaction with the company.

How the Loyalty Program Worked

Reward program members accumulated points through monthly long-distance phone usage. In addition, they were awarded quarterly and anniversary bonus points, as well as points for responses to special promotional campaigns. The accumulated points could be redeemed for invoice credits, travel options, and gift certificates for additional products and services.

Objectives of the Shift to the Web

KnowledgeBase's real-time database was a very effective system for this long-distance provider. However, there were opportunities to improve costs and deepen the customer relationship by bringing the loyalty initiative directly to the rewards membership. Therefore, in Phase II, KnowledgeBase Marketing created an online redemption functionality for the loyalty platform, with the following objectives:

- Provide a Web-enabled interactive interface for the rewards program through the company's own Web site, crossing through firewalls, to the KnowledgeBase loyalty database.
- Deliver the new system in 30 days.
- Increase retention and cross-selling opportunities with the new system.
- Reduce the operating costs of the loyalty program.

With the new system, customers could go online to obtain information, review their transaction history, and redeem loyalty points. Customers received email confirmation of their redemption seconds after the transaction, further creating a "live link" with the customer. Analysis of the rewards program, such as determining the type, frequency, and medium (Web, IVR, call center, etc.) of redemptions, is performed using a reporting database into which customer redemptions and other data are fed. IVR, of course, is Interactive Voice Response, the process of pushing buttons on a telephone keypad to get the information or the person you are seeking from an automatic phone answering system.

In the first week after the program was launched, the company had a 40 percent increase in point redemption. In subsequent weeks, Web redemptions grew by 5 to 10 percent. Web redemptions, of course, replaced phone redemptions. The average cost of a phone redemption was about $6. The marginal cost of a Web redemption was only a few cents. In the first year of the Web redemption program, the long-distance provider's costs for maintaining the loyalty program were cut in half. Churn was reduced, and cross-selling initiatives were enabled through customer-friendly Web marketing efforts assisted by KnowledgeBase Marketing.

Summary

Web response beats phone, mail, email, and fax in

- Reduction in cost of fulfillment
- Data captured along with the sale
- Immediacy of response information
- Personalization and speed of response
- Accuracy of the data captured

Web response involves the creation of a special microsite where customers can be recognized and greeted by name, using a PIN or a cookie.

Direct-mail promotions usually get better response rates than email promotions, but the cost per response may be higher.

The Isuzu case showed that models can correctly predict which business customers are most likely to respond and which probably won't.

The Scotiabank Applause program shows that internal Web programs can be highly effective in reaching employees and obtaining employee participation, even with a mature group.

The KnowledgeBase program showed that long-distance customers will respond productively to an online program, saving the cost of phone response.

What Works

- Getting your Web site to do things that a live operator cannot do
- Using the three-click rule and having a search box on every page
- Reaching employees through an internal Web program
- Online response

What Doesn't Work

- Flash pages that take more than 5 seconds to download
- Searches that don't provide what customers are looking for
- Sites that are designed to sell, rather than being designed to provide what customers want
- Mainframe legacy databases in support of online operations

Quiz

1. Why do Web response campaigns produce more white mail than phone response campaigns?
    a. People are curious about the offering.
    b. Operators cannot worm source codes out of callers.

    c. On the Web you can't easily capture source codes.

    d. All of the above.

2. Which of the following is not suggested as a way of improving a Web site?

    a. A high-tech flash page

    b. Personal greetings

    c. Search boxes

    d. The three-click rule

3. What is the cost per registrant of an email campaign that costs $0.11 per email and produces a 0.67 percent click-through rate and a 48 percent registration rate?

4. What was the essential lesson in the Isuzu truck case?

    a. You can sell a lot of trucks through direct mail.

    b. You can accurately predict response rates.

    c. You need a customer database.

    d. Truck buyers are business-to-business customers.

    e. The control group beat the tests.

5. The Scotiabank Applause program proved all but which of the following?

    a. The power of the Web.

    b. That long-term employees will buy into a new program.

    c. That employees will work to receive rewards.

    d. That employee rewards program work.

    e. None of the above; it proved all of them.

6. In the KnowledgeBase case study, the key goal was

    a. To create a profitable Web site

    b. To increase customer transactions

    c. To deliver a new system in 60 days

    d. To reduce call center costs

    e. To reduce churn

7. Which of the following was not suggested as something to have on your Web site?

    a. Pictures

    b. Maps

    c. Articles

    d. Diagrams

    e. Video clips

8. Which has the highest rate of errors as a response mechanism?

    a. Email

    b. Fax

    c. Phone

    d. Web

    e. Mail

9. Which has the lowest cost per 100,000 as a response mechanism?

    a. Mail

    b. Phone

    c. Email

    d. Fax

    e. All have the same cost

10. Which has the highest level of interactivity as a response mechanism?

    a. Phone

    b. Web

    c. Email

    d. Fax

    e. Mail

CHAPTER **8**

MARKETING TO CUSTOMER SEGMENTS

To develop a relationship program, you still have to put individuals into groups, and develop products and strategies that will keep them loyal. That, in my opinion, is where companies have the most difficulty. Even when you say to them, "I can help you to identify your key customer segments." They respond, "Well, great. But tell me, what to do with them once they are identified. How do I manage each segment?" Marketers are not yet sophisticated enough to know what to do with the information.
—Stephen Shaw, *Canadian Direct Marketing News*

Since one-to-one marketing is seldom possible, most successful direct marketers aim their marketing efforts at segments. A segment is a group of customers or prospects that you have identified for marketing purposes. In your mind, you think, "What are these people like? What would appeal to them and get them to buy? How can we track their response to our promotions?" Then you set about getting the information that you need in order to define the segment and design marketing programs just for it.

Creating marketing segments is an art, not a science. Expert marketers spend a lot of time dreaming up segments and consulting their database to see if these segments really exist. Then they spend time coming up with marketing programs and testing them on the segments. To determine whether they are successful, they always carve out control

164

Segment Marketing versus One-to-One Marketing

The idea in one-to-one marketing is to store in a data warehouse enough information about each customer to enable you to develop an individual marketing program designed just for that customer. True one-to-one marketing is real time: If a customer buys something this morning, your communications to that customer this afternoon will reflect that fact, along with everything the customer has purchased since the beginning of the relationship with you, plus what you know about the customer's demographics. You don't have five marketing programs; you have 2 million marketing programs for your 2 million customers. It is a very nice idea. So why isn't everyone doing it? Because, in most cases, the lift in sales that you get from one-to-one marketing does not pay for the cost of the warehouse and the communications. There are very, very few situations in which real one-to-one marketing is economically profitable.

Segment marketing, on the other hand, is relatively easy to achieve. You still need a database of customers that includes their demographics, preferences, and transactions. Your next step, however, is to divide customers into segments on the basis of profitability: Best Customers, New Customers, Lapsed Customers, and Occasional Customers. You develop a marketing program for each segment. The actual communication with each customer can be personalized using the data on that customer that you have in your database, but the segment determines the overall approach. The cost of segment marketing is a fraction of the cost of one-to-one marketing.

groups, members of the segment who do not receive the promotions that are sent to all the other members of the segment. Then they measure their success by comparing the purchases made by the members of the segment to whom the promotion was sent against the purchases made by the control group. To determine the return on investment, they have to take the incremental revenue gained from the segment to which the promotion was sent and subtract it from it the cost of the promotion and the rewards given to the members of that segment. Many times the return on investment is negative. In this chapter, we will begin with the process of creating a segment: coming up with the idea and finding the data to measure whether the segment is performing as you intend. Then we will look at some case studies involving marketing to segments. So, let's begin with getting data about segment members.

Two Kinds of Data

There are two kinds of data: demographic and behavioral. Demographic data include age, income, presence of children, lifestyle, geography, type of housing, and other such things. In the case of business-to-business files, the demographic data are SIC code, number of employees, annual sales, and so on. Behavioral data usually consist of transactions—responses, purchases, redemption of certificates—plus preferences and survey responses. In business-to-business marketing, transaction data are usually very easy to acquire, since most businesses have accounts with their suppliers. With consumers, the data are often difficult to get your hands on, particularly if the product is purchased at retail stores or through dealers.

There are two ways to obtain demographic data: You can have them appended to your database records by an outside source such as Experian, or you can get the information directly from the customers by asking them to fill out a survey or a profile. The profile method has become so important that a whole chapter, Chapter 14, has been devoted to the subject.

To market to segments, you need a database that includes transaction history. The difficulty is in capturing the data. Many retail stores try to do this with a proprietary credit card. All large department stores issue cards, which they hope their customers will use. In fact, only the most determined customers use these cards. It is a nuisance to carry around 10 or 12 store cards in addition to your MasterCard, Visa, or

Figure 8-1 iDine

Amex. The solution to this problem is to get customers to register their bank credit cards with you, so that when the customers use these cards, you will know that they have made a purchase.

iDine (see Figure 8-1) has made a successful business out of this idea.

Members register their credit cards with iDine. Then, whenever they go to any of the 7500 restaurants in the country that are associated with iDine and pay for their purchases using one of these cards, iDine finds out about it and either gives them a credit on their credit card or gives them airline miles. The customers don't have to say to the restaurant, "Be sure to let iDine know that I am eating here!" The process is so simple that it is amazing that more retailers have not caught onto the idea.

Reverse Phone Matching

In the absence of a registered credit card to identify their customers—and because it is often more effective—many retailers use reverse telephone matching to capture customer data. The Sports Authority, the largest full-line sporting goods equipment retailer in the United States, is a good example.

Retail sales are often driven by the calendar. People are in a buying mood before Christmas. The mood is entirely different a month later. The Sports Authority, which operates 198 full-line sporting goods super-stores in 32 states across the United States, wanted to respond to existing and new customers in key markets during the busy holiday shopping season. Like most retailers, The Sports Authority gathered information about customers at the point of sale. However, by the time information on a customer made its way to the company's marketing department for use in follow-up or promotions, at least a month had elapsed. To capture repeat business before the 4-week holiday season ended, Jeff Handler, senior vice president, advertising and marketing, challenged the company's customer relationship management (CRM) software vendor, Harte-Hanks, to shorten this time to 1 week.

The goal was to identify the customers, and then, using print-on-demand functionality, react to those customers with an appropriate direct-mail offer, all within 1 week after any store visit. Few retailers in America have ever accomplished such a feat. The Harte-Hanks customer contact strategy, dubbed "Retail Daily Sales Builder," involved analysis of point-of-sale data, interaction with the full customer database, and creation of customized marketing communications.

The Sports Authority centers its holiday promotions around the first week in December. For this program, The Sports Authority focused on its in-store customers, as opposed to Web or catalog customers.

The Objective: Repeat Business

To make the most of the holiday season, The Sports Authority uses both mass marketing and targeted, focused direct mail to bring shop-pers into the stores in December. Retail Daily Sales Builder was designed to cost-effectively bring customers back one or more times before Christmas, a time period when repeat business may be difficult to achieve because customers have many choices. Without special incentives or relevant messages, they may not return to stores where they have already spent money for some of their holiday purchases. The key is to provide compelling offers in a timely manner. Without a truly sophisticated system, compelling and timely offers are not possible. The

Sports Authority's goals were to get a printed, customized direct-mail piece into customers' and prospects' hands within 1 week following a store visit, and to reward early purchasers during the holiday season

The most difficult elements of the project were getting the program in place by November 30, given that the starting point was early November, and then being able to quickly turn around a second offer to customers and prospects. Part of the process involved matching the in-store customers to their mailing addresses. The team used a reverse telephone number appending process. Each clerk at each point-of-sale station captured the buyer's telephone number as part of the transaction. Every night, these data were transmitted from each of The Sports Authority's stores to the central database, where the phone numbers were matched to mailing addresses using reverse appending. With its Retail Daily Sales Builder process, The Sports Authority and the Harte-Hanks team were able to do that within 1 day of the purchase. Many of the names and addresses were already in The Sports Authority's customer database. Other names and addresses came from rented telephone appending lists.

The Offer

The day after any purchase, Harte-Hanks was able to identify the name and address of almost every person who had provided a phone number the day before. It was then able to print a targeted direct-mail certificate and mail it so that it would arrive in the shopper's mailbox within 1 week of the shopper's visit to the store. The project started in November with the mailing of a holiday gift guide to all existing retail customers near each store. In certain key markets, there was some targeted prospecting as well. People who made a purchase based on the gift guide would receive a second standard postcard offer within 1 week.

The Sports Authority says that approximately 5 percent of the shoppers who received the initial gift guide came to the stores and used the certificates included in the guide. The follow-on mailing to anyone who responded to the first holiday mailer had double-digit response rates, essentially tripling the industry norm for response rates and, most important, bringing those customers back to shop again before Christmas.

Why did this program work? Because of its recency and a solid offer. The customer who is most likely to respond to any promotion is the customer who has made a purchase most recently. The increased sales were so significant in comparison to the cost of the program that The Sports Authority made it a permanent part of its marketing program.

Creating the Segments

Once you have captured the customer transaction data, you need to divide your customers into some sort of usable segments so that you can create a marketing program for each. How do you set up the segments? This is a problem that separates the good marketers from the indifferent ones. There are dozens of ways to do this. For example:

- Senior citizens, college students, families with children, empty nesters
- High spenders, occasional shoppers, lapsed customers
- Profitability segments
- RFM (recency, frequency, monetary analysis) segments
- SIC groups (for business-to-business marketing)

Bringing Them Back

The School of Continuing Studies at the University of Toronto is a self-sustaining academic division of the university that welcomes about 15,000 adult learners each year and offers courses in three program areas: business and professional studies, arts and humanities, and English as a second language.

Recently, the school had to replace its existing registration system. This system had been in place for more than 12 years, and, although it could generate business reports and track registrations, the actual customer data were locked within its tables. The new system was Oracle-based. The school's director saw this as an opportunity for the school to take advantage of its customer data and employed Terri O'Connor as the school's first database marketer.

Making Sense of the Data

Terri put the customer records from both the old and the new registration systems into a separate database. In order to make sense of the data, the records from the two systems were merged to create a unique customer record that provided a profile of the customer. During this process, Terri used RFM to help summarize the customer data.

The frequency indicator provided the school with its first database surprise. The administrators had always known that they had a significant number of long-term customers, but they were very surprised to learn that some customers had purchased more than 50 courses in the previous 12 years. Terri termed these the *high-value* (HV) customers and started to track their retention rates and the types of courses they were purchasing. The breakdown is shown in Figure 8-2.

Recency and LTV

The school used several methods to distribute its course calendars. One of the most effective methods was to mail them directly to customers

Figure 8-2 Currently Registered HV Customers by Start Date and Program Area

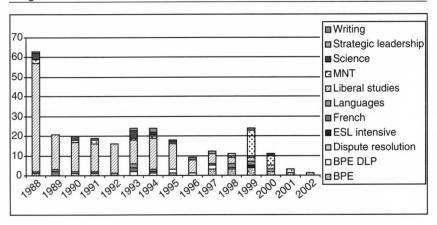

who had registered within the previous 2 years. When Terri started to assemble the first house list using the new database, she assigned a source code to each customer for tracking purposes. The addition of the source code meant that the list and the individual customer cells could be tracked separately. She reviewed the customer records and was able to locate and include a group of customers who had a high lifetime value (LTV) but had not purchased courses for 3 or 4 years. Normally this group of customers would be excluded, since it is too costly to mail calendars to customers who haven't purchased in 3 or 4 years. But by targeting only the customers in this group who had a high LTV, Terri was able to keep the mailing costs manageable while she attempted to reactivate their business. The result was that 8 percent of those who were targeted purchased courses, and their purchasing habits were as high the second time around as they had been originally. The reactivated HV group bought an average of three courses each per year compared to the school's overall average of 1.45.

The impact of recency on course purchases is obvious in Figure 8-3. By assigning RFM indicators to the customer base, Terri was able to find new revenue from "lost" customers and to gain some valuable insights into the school's best customers.

Marketing to customer segments by direct-mail promotions is relatively easy. Going beyond that by appointing segment managers and

Figure 8-3 Sales Rates for the House List Calendar Mailing

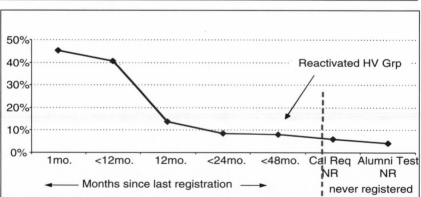

managing segments on a daily basis is much more complicated and seldom profitable. Let's take a look at one enterprise that succeeded.

Targeting Customer Segments

While many companies have failed at managing customer segments on a day-to-day basis, National Australia Bank (NAB) succeeded at this task. The lead franchise in NAB was National, a Melbourne-based bank serving more than 4.5 million customers. With the help of Beth Ann Konves of the Teradata Division of NCR, Fernando Ricardo, head of customer knowledge management at the bank, identified six major customer segments composed of individuals and businesses. Each segment was managed as a global business. The system, called National Leads, identified leads within the bank's database based on significant changes (events) in a customer's transaction pattern, such as balance changes, large transactions, or loan renewals. The system also calculated each customer's propensity to buy a product or to respond to an offer. The bank's database was maintained on an NCR Teradata computer using Teradata's CRM analytical software, which was used for the National Leads system.

The National Leads system prioritized events and alerted the appropriate bankers each morning so that they could take appropriate action. The system also served as a communications gatekeeper, managing the frequency, content, and channel used for customer interactions during marketing campaigns. The goal was to ensure that customers were contacted with meaningful opportunities at the right times through the right channels.

The six major customer segments used by the bank were common to many other banks and financial institutions:

- Custom business
- Packaged business
- Agribusiness
- Private
- Premium
- Retail

Each segment was managed by a vice president. Every National customer was assigned to one of the segments on the basis of a financial needs analysis and profitability assessment. Within each of these major segments, further refinements were made based on current profitability, the bank's share of the customer's wallet potential, and the customer's demonstrated financial needs. As a result of this analysis, there were more than 200 subsegments that were used for target marketing. The system worked this way:

- The Teradata warehouse was updated with an average of 2.2 million transactions per day.
- Every night, queries "trawled" the warehouse to search for any unusual changes. The queries involved complex logic, scanning hundreds of millions of rows in the database and joining from six to ten tables at a time.
- Once a month, each customer was scored, using a model that predicted the customer's propensity to purchase various products and propensity to respond to product offers. The best leads were selected and sent to the bankers.
- Every night 250 communication vectors combining the events detected and the propensity predictions were run. The software recommended the action to be taken via ATM, email, mail, or leads to call centers, branches, or package business bankers, who followed up with a phone call or personal mail.
- The system captured all feedback and responses, measuring them against the opportunities developed. Each offer was placed in a location in a three-dimensional "cube," with the three axes being the segment, the channel, and the offer. The system moved customers from one location in the cube to another based on their response to offers.

In a typical scenario, the system might direct a banker to contact a customer with an offer, such as a financial planning appointment or the renewal of a loan. Armed with this lead, the banker would contact the customer to gather financial profile information, using the standard financial needs assessment process developed by the bank. Bankers were given incentives to gather pieces of profile information every time they spoke to their customers. The bankers typed the collected data into a customer needs record in the database, using a terminal on their desk.

The way it worked was this: A customer might tell a banker that he was currently renting, but that he planned to purchase a home in about 9 to 12 months. The banker would enter this information into the system. Eight months later, the banker would receive a message generated by the database to recontact this customer to discuss home loan options.

The Results

- During the first year, more than 1 million leads and $4 billion in growth opportunities were sent to National bankers.
- During the next 6 months, 570,000 new leads were sent, which resulted in the closing of $4.4 billion worth of new loans.
- During the second year of the system, premium sales of banking products increased by 25 percent over the previous year, while sales of wealth management products increased by 40 percent.
- The close rate for leads increased by five times over the close rate before the new system began.
- The bank achieved a $391 million return on investment on one campaign.

Quadrant Marketing

One valuable method of segmentation is by quadrants. The idea in quadrant marketing is to take two variables, such as spending and income, and divide all customers into four groups based on these variables. For example, let's take a bank. Most banks and financial institutions have learned to use a variety of inducements to capture the names and transactions of all their customers. What they may not have is their customers' incomes and ages. These can be obtained as appended information from Experian or other sources. Armed with these data, they can develop four quadrants based on income and amount borrowed. The resulting quadrants might look like Table 8-1.

Table 8-1 Quadrant Marketing

Q2 high income, low asset		Q1 high income, high asset	
Population	356,331	Population	69,778
% of total	41%	% of total	8%
Income	$138,665	Income	$136,778
Marital	79%	Marital	78%
Average age	38	Average age	52
Average asset	$855	Average asset	$44,556
Total assets	$304,663,005	Total assets	$3,109,028,568
% of assets	5%	% of assets	51%
Q3 low income, low asset		Q4 low income, high asset	
Population	377,221	Population	58,996
% of total	44%	% of total	7%
Income	$55,669	Income	$56,993
Marital	53%	Marital	54%
Average age	29	Average age	61
Average asset	$766	Average asset	$40,221
Total assets	$288,951,286	Total assets	$2,372,878,116
% of assets	5%	% of assets	39%

This bank has about 860,000 customers. Its total bank assets are about $6 billion. They are divided into four quadrants: high income, high bank assets; high income, low bank assets; low income, low bank assets; low income, high bank assets

It is interesting that the high-income customers tend to be married, whereas fewer of the lower-income customers are married. Also, the people with high assets tend to be much older than the people with low assets. We will set these facts aside for a moment and concentrate on the incomes and assets.

Here's how to do the math for a quadrant analysis. For income, look at all household incomes. See if there are some at the top that are outrageous: $1 million, for example. Exclude the few outliers like this. Then add all the incomes together and divide by the number of people. For the data used to construct Table 8-1, the average income was $68,230. Then divide customers into two groups: those with incomes above and those with incomes below $68,230. Get the average income for those above, which was about $136,000, and for those below, which was about $56,000. Do the same thing with the average assets.

When you have done this, sit back and think about your table for a day or two. What is it telling you? What are these segments, and what can you do with them?

- *Quadrant 1 marketing plan.* Begin with the high highs. These people have a lot of money, and a lot of it is in your bank. What is your goal for these people? Retention. There is no point in marketing to them. They are maxed out. All the money they have is in your bank, and they can't give you any more. But you don't want to lose these people. They are your Gold customers. So you design a retention program for them and put them in it. Give them special benefits that come with being Gold customers. They shouldn't have to do anything. They should be able to just sit there and let the benefits roll in. Thank-you letters from the branch manager. Birthday cards. Greetings whenever they come into the branch—each employee is taught to recognize them and use their name. The branch manager jumps up from his desk and shakes their hand whenever they come in. If he sees them waiting in a long line, he goes up to them and asks them to come to his desk, where he handles their transaction personally. I have enjoyed that treatment at my bank, and I love it. It works. I would never go anywhere else.
- *Quadrant 2 marketing plan.* These are the high lows. They have a lot of money, but your bank has very little of it. They probably have their money somewhere else. Here is an opportunity. Marketing is going to work here, because these people have assets that they can manage, with your help. You might tell them the benefits that come with Gold status at the bank, and show them how easy it would be to reach Gold status by shifting deposits, buying mutual funds, or engaging in other activities that would benefit them.
- *Quadrant 3 marketing plan.* These are the low lows. Here is a group of really worthless people, as far as you are concerned. They have very little money, and they don't put much of it in your bank. Marketing to them would be a waste of your money, since they don't have much to work with. Here is a wonderful opportunity to reduce your marketing expenses. These are 44 percent of the bank's customers. Spend your money somewhere else. You will have money left over to concentrate on the other quadrants.
- *Quadrant 4 marketing plan.* Here is a really interesting group: older people with a lot of money in your bank, but relatively low incomes. Who might these people be? They are mostly retired, of course. They have worked all their lives and they have saved

(or they inherited money), and they have something to show for it. So what should you do? Well, in the first place, you don't want to lose these valuable people, so you try to get inside their heads and think as they do. Focus groups would help here. Many of them will need help with their wills. This is a free service that you can provide for them. The bank might be the executor if they have no one else. Most of them are not interested in getting rich fast; they just want to keep what they have. Long-term care insurance would be an obvious offering if you handle insurance. If they are in anything risky, talk to them about moving into something more stable, so that you don't lose them in a downturn. Become their financial adviser.

These may not be the best quadrant plans in the world, but they illustrate the power of this technique. They show what you can do with your customer base to make it come alive and to let you direct your efforts to areas where you can make more money for your company and make your customers happy at the same time.

Reaching Mothers-to-Be

Kmart ran into some financial troubles in 2002, but that does not mean that we cannot learn a great deal from some of Kmart's excellent marketing programs. One of these programs focused on prospective mothers. There is a lot of money to be made from selling to this group. Mothers-to-be spend $18 billion annually, and 80 percent of that amount is spent before the baby is born. For a 2-year period families spend thousands of dollars in a category in which they have not recently been spending and in which they are unlikely to spend again until the next child arrives. Kmart and other retailers have understood the power of this segment for some time and have made major efforts to capitalize on it.

Kmart developed a comprehensive strategy for targeting this segment. Using its database, it was able to reach one-third of all U.S. moms-to-be before the baby was born. The basic strategy was this:

- Use the database to identify moms-to-be through their purchase of maternity apparel and other prebirth items.
- Be the first to market before the baby is born, through database-targeted direct-mail communications.
- Integrate with other departments as a cross-functional team to change merchandise assortments and the arrangement of merchandise in the stores so that the items purchased by mothers-to-be are within easy reach.

Actual shopping behavior plus multiple regressions were used to determine which customers really were mothers-to-be (as opposed to grandmothers or friends shopping for a baby shower). The data explored the cross shopping of each individual, her market basket, her known age, and her previous shopping history.

Armed with this information about the moms-to-be, Kmart developed test groups that got the special promotions and control groups that did not. Comparison of the purchasing behavior of the two groups clearly showed the advantage of the special targeting.

The Results

The program increased store sales by over 15 percent while reducing mailing costs by 35 percent. In Hispanic markets, store sales of baby products increased by over 25 percent, while sales in adjacent highly cross-shopped departments increased by 35 percent over the prior year.

On a customer level, over 21 percent of the top-decile moms-to-be shopped at Kmart during the mail event, increasing their spending more than 40 percent over the prior year. Targeted customers outperformed the control groups by 4 to 1 and spent over 20 percent more per visit during the promotional event.

As a result of this experiment, the use of the database to drive promotions was expanded into many other departments at Kmart. According to Tom Lemke, vice president of database marketing at Kmart, "Our mission is to 'Mail Less and Sell More.' To accomplish this, we use the intelligence of customer data to create improved response rates and lowered mail volumes."

How Many Segments Should You Create?

Everyone who tries to create customer segments runs into the problem of numbers. By using recency, frequency, monetary (RFM) analysis, it is possible to come up with hundreds of different RFM cells. By using SIC codes, you can create hundreds of types of customers that you can market to. By using profitability, you can subdivide your customers into deciles, for example, from the most profitable to the least profitable. How many segments make up the right number?

To get the answer, you need to consider the imagination and creative genius available in your marketing organization. Every new marketing idea requires time and resources for its execution. Few organizations can develop and support as many as five or six simultaneous marketing efforts. Therefore, the sector marketing strategy must end up creating and marketing to just a few sectors.

Are Your Segments Viable?

OK. You have divided your customer base into five segments, and you have developed a marketing program for each of the five. Let's say you divided your customers by level of total spending (rather than by age, income, product categories, etc.). Were your segments the most profitable that you could have devised? How can you know?

One good way to find out is to create a universal control promotion that you use with your segment control groups. This is a good promotion that has worked in the past and resulted in a lot of sales. It is used to test the marketing promotions designed for each segment. Table 8-2 shows a possible result of a mailing to your segments based on total spending.

Here's how we did the math for the lift in sales. We subtracted the sales rate for the control group from the sales rate from the test. In the Gold segment, for example, we subtracted 7.94 from 8.10 and got 0.16 percent. Then we multiplied that 0.16 percent by the number of people in the test segment—in this case 100,000—to get the lift in sales. What this tells us is that the creative material we used with the Gold

Table 8-2 Testing Segment Promotions

Customer segments	Number promoted	Sales rate	Lift	Lift in sales
Gold	100,000	8.10%	0.16%	160
Control	20,000	7.94%		
Silver	100,000	6.60%	0.19%	190
Control	20,000	6.41%		
Bronze	100,000	5.01%	0.41%	410
Control	20,000	4.60%		
Lead	100,000	2.34%	−0.06%	(60)
Control	20,000	2.40%		
Total	480,000			700

people resulted in 160 more sales than we would have gotten if we had sent them the control package.

Unfortunately, this segmentation scheme is a self-fulfilling prophecy. The high spenders spent a lot. The low spenders spent a little. You knew that when you set up your segments. You could not think up enough creative things to say to the Gold customers, for example, to differentiate their behavior from that of the Gold customers who got the same message that was sent to everyone else. This is bad segmentation strategy.

Suppose we were to create our segments in a different way. We might do it by the age of the customer. We create special promotions for people in their teens, people in their twenties and thirties, people in their forties and fifties, and senior citizens. We want to see if we can design messages that reach these segments and do better at selling to them than a generic message. Table 8-3 shows a possible result.

As you can see, we have the same number of people, but they are divided into age groups. The lift from our promotions is very much more pronounced. The teen message really scored well and produced a 4025-customer lift over the control groups. We can't say the same for the work that our creative staff did for people in their forties and fifties. From this you can see that the way you create your segments often determines your results.

You should experiment with several segmentation schemes before you settle on the one that you will use for a long time.

Table 8-3 Age Segment Promotion

	Number promoted	Sales rate	Lift	Lift in sales
Teens	115,000	9.50%	3.50%	4,025
Control	20,000	6.00%		
20s and 30s	145,000	7.70%	1.90%	2,755
Control	20,000	5.80%		
40s and 50s	75,000	5.00%	−0.70%	(525)
Control	20,000	5.70%		
Seniors	65,000	4.00%	0.90%	585
Control	20,000	3.10%		
Total	480,000			6,840

Rules for Segment Marketing

Based on this discussion, how do you go about profitable segment marketing? There are several rules:

- Build a customer database with demographics and transaction history. Find a reliable way to get regular updates on transactions and responses.
- Come up with a profitable method for creating customer segments that you can market to.
- Select just a few segments and design a marketing program for each segment.
- Set up control groups that have exactly the same characteristics as the groups selected for marketing, but that do not get the promotional material. Measure the performance of the segment that received the promotion against that of the control group.
- In the marketing campaign for each segment, use the database to create personalized content: emails, direct-mail pieces, telephone calls, Web response pages, and so on. Monitor the response from each segment and each response method and record them in the database.
- Constantly test new methods of marketing to each segment, recording the results and increasing the resources devoted to those methods that work.

Summary of Case Study Results

- From iDine, we learned that you can track consumer behavior by using registered credit cards. It is easy to do. You can get many people to participate if you make it worth their while.
- From the National Australian Bank, we learned that Teradata computers and software permit you to "trawl" customer accounts every night to find people who have had significant changes in their bank accounts. We use segment marketing to develop rules to market to each situation.
- From Kmart, we learned that you can identify mothers-to-be based on their shopping behavior. Marketing to this segment was very profitable for Kmart, and was worth the effort.
- From the University of Toronto, we learned that you can reactivate lost customers using a creative database marketing strategy.

What Works

- Dividing your customer database into a few segments based on some logical scheme and developing a marketing strategy for each segment.
- Always setting aside a control group in each segment that gets a generic marketing promotion (or none at all) so that you can measure the effectiveness of the promotions.
- Differentiating the promotions to each segment by personal data in the database. "Since you bought the ski outfit last October, you may want to consider a flannel nightgown to wear on those cold evenings."
- Finding a way to collect the data on what happened after you sent the promotions. If you can't get the data, you may be wasting your money on the promotions.

What Doesn't Work

- Creating more than eight or nine segments. Even the largest companies don't have the marketing staff to think up and implement unique marketing programs for lots of different segments. If you have divided your database into 10 or more segments, you have made a serious mistake.
- Forgetting to create and use control groups. An advertising agency created a "frequent user" segment with special benefits for a client. The client spent more than a million dollars promoting to the segment, and it seemed to work. After 2 years, the client asked the agency to provide the value the client had received for the million dollars. Unfortunately, there was no control group, so the agency could not provide this information. The agency lost the account.
- Not revising your segments after each promotion. We are supposed to learn something from the segments. If you just promote and promote, and never revise, you may be wasting your money and not learning anything.
- Collecting a lot of data about customers that you never use for anything. Everything has a cost. Getting and updating data is expensive. Every time you add a piece of information to your database, ask, "How are we going to use this to make money? How can we use this right away to modify customer behavior?" If you haven't got a good answer to these questions, don't collect and store the data.
- Spending too much on building a data warehouse that will never pay its way in terms of increased sales through promotions based on the data in the warehouse.
- Creating segments that are self-fulfilling or that do not allow your creative team to create a significant differentiation.

Quiz

1. Why do most marketers choose segment marketing over one-to-one marketing?
   a. One-to-one marketing does not work.

    b. Segments are easy to create.

    c. They don't know how to do one-to-one marketing.

    d. Segments cost less but produce similar results.

    e. One-to-one marketing produces a much higher lift in sales.

2. Which of the following are not considered demographic data?

    a. Age

    b. Preferences

    c. Ethnicity

    d. Income

    e. Value of home

3. What technique does iDine use that most marketers are not using today?

    a. Creating customer segments

    b. Credit card matching

    c. Air miles as a reward

    d. Cash as a reward

    e. Transactions viewed on the Web

4. Which is not listed as a feature of the Australian National Leads program?

    a. Web customer response

    b. Customer segmentation

    c. Nightly trawling of the data warehouse

    d. Prediction of customer propensity to purchase

    e. Offers based on transactions

5. What is the best strategy for Quadrant 3 – the low lows?

    a. Retention

    b. Expansion

    c. Ignoring them

    d. Repricing their services

    e. Rewards for good behavior

6. Which was not a result of the Kmart mothers-to-be program?

    a. Hispanic baby product sales were up 25 percent.

    b. Cross shopping was reduced by 35 percent.

    c. Twenty-one percent of top-decile shoppers increased their spending by 40 percent.

    d. Targeted customers outperformed the control by 4 to 1.

    e. None of the above; all were results of the promotion.

7. Compute the lift in sales in the following table.

	Number promoted	Sales rate	Lift	Lift in sales
Teens	100,000	8.80%		
Control	20,000	7.00%		
20s and 30s	100,000	6.60%		
Control	20,000	5.80%		
40s and 50s	90,000	7.20%		
Control	20,000	6.00%		
Seniors	60,000	5.10%		
Control	20,000	4.30%		
Total	430,000			

8. Which of the following is the best number of segments to create for segment marketing?

    a. 100

    b. 80

    c. 50

    d. 12

    e. 6

9. What is the best way to design segments?

    a. Something that you can relate to and design programs for

    b. RFM groupings

    c. LTV segments

    d. SIC segments

    e. None of the above

10. When should segments be revised?

    a. Monthly

    b. Quarterly

    c. Never; keep them consistent

    d. After each promotion

    e. Once a year

CHAPTER 9

HELPING BUSINESS CUSTOMERS TO BECOME PROFITABLE

Most manufacturers sell their products through wholesalers, dealers, brokers, or agents. They don't have to deal directly with the ultimate consumer of the product. This situation has both a good and a bad side. The good side is that the manufacturer is selling in wholesale quantities. It has hundreds instead of millions of customers to worry about. The bad side is that if the intermediaries are not good at their business, sales will falter, and there is not much that the manufacturer can do about it. It is hard to introduce new products when you cannot communicate with your ultimate consumers.

Database marketing has provided a new method of handling the marketing of business products. If the manufacturer can just get its hands on the names and addresses of the ultimate consumers, it can correspond with them, introduce them to new products, and drive them to the dealers. Many dealers resist this approach. Their fear is that the manufacturer will use this information to go around them and sell products directly to the ultimate consumers.

This situation almost drove Compaq out of business. Compaq had a network of wholesalers and retailers that were the exclusive marketers of its computers. Beginning in the middle 1980s, Compaq developed an excellent database of registered users of Compaq products. The company knew their names, their addresses, their positions in business, their occupations, the software they used, and scores of other pieces of information about them. But it never once contacted any of them directly, for fear that its retailers would stop promoting the Compaq name.

Meanwhile Dell, Gateway, and then IBM began to sell PCs directly to the public, stealing market share away from Compaq. When Compaq finally woke up to its losing strategy and began to sell direct, it was too late. Compaq had dropped to the back of the pack.

With database marketing, the ideal strategy for a supplier is to work to make its dealers, agents, and brokers successful. The supplier wants to help them to succeed in their business. As a result, the dealers will push the sale of the supplier's products. Presented in this chapter are several case studies in which suppliers have done just that.

Top 10 Prospects

A manufacturer of industrial components made 40,000 different products and had $400 million in sales through 1800 independent agents. While $400 million may sound like a lot, it was less than 1 percent of the $87 billion in annual sales in this business category. The independent agents handled the products of many other manufacturers in addition to this firm's. Some agents were very good at pushing this firm's brand. Others were not so good. The company wanted to stand out from the crowd. It turned to Scott Brostoff of CSC Advanced Database Solutions to come up with a method of helping its agents succeed.

Each agent had a unique territory. The firm had compiled a list of hundreds of thousands of ultimate customers based on their deliveries over 3 years. CSC decided to take this database and add Dun & Bradstreet data to it, showing for each customer the SIC code, annual sales, number of employees, and actual products that the customer had purchased.

What types of data are available from Dun & Bradstreet for appending to a business-to-business file? Some different types are listed in Figure 9-1.

Scott decided to feed the D&B information into a model that showed which products in which quantities customers in each SIC code bought. Armed with that information, CSC decided to use the D&B data to identify prospects in each agent's territory that were not currently buying the firm's products. The model was designed to score each prospect in order to determine the 100 prospects in each agent's territory that would be

Figure 9-1   Dun & Bradstreet
Data

**Dun & Bradstreet Appended
Business Data**

Company name and address
Business family linkage
SIC codes
Line of business
Territory covered
Number of employees
Trends
Year business started
Bank relationships
Contact names
Net worth
Annual sales
Financial stress scores
Energy demand: electricity, gas
Telecom demand
Number of PCs
IT spending
Propensity to lease
Market penetration

most likely to consume the largest amount of the firm's products. The resulting prospect database of 180,000 companies was designed to list the top 10 prospects in each agent's territory and the particular products that these prospects were most likely to buy. The model was also designed to predict the next best product for each of the existing customers in each agent's territory. The next best product was the product that the customer was not now purchasing that the model predicted was most likely to be purchased and to have the highest sales.

This was information that the agents did not have and could not easily develop without CSC's help. CSC's next job was to get the agents to buy into the idea and subscribe to the top 10 prospects and next best product information. Experience in other situations had convinced CSC that agents will use valuable information like this only if they pay for it. If it is offered free, they will consider it worthless. How do you get 1800 independent agents to sign up for such a service and pay for it?

Scott decided to develop a major campaign to sell the agents. He started with the few agents who he knew would buy into the idea from the start. Their success in using the top 10 prospects could be used to convince the others that they could profit by signing on.

The delivery system for the names was interesting. CSC decided to install Epiphany software on the database which could be accessed by the 1800 agents through the Web. Each participating agent received an ID and a PIN so that its employees could sign onto the database and see a Web page that was designed just for them and that featured information about their sales and commissions, their top 10 prospects, the next best product for each of their existing customers, and a chart that compared their sales with those of other agents in their region and in the nation. A contest was designed for the agents who made the most effective use of the top 10 prospects, with prizes for the winners. By making its independent agents profitable, the manufacturer would increase its sales and profits.

How to Determine the Next Best Product

One of the most practical and useful applications of database marketing for a business-to-business company is determining its customers' next best product (NBP). The NBP is a guide for the sales force. Typically, the sales force tries to get companies to buy more of what they are already buying. That makes sense, and it is logical and easy to do. What many salespeople have found, however, is that their best customers are "maxed out" in certain categories. They are already placing all their orders for a category with this one supplier, and so pressures to buy more may not be effective. So what else do you sell to this company? Suppose you have 40,000 different products in your catalog. Which ones do you push? Until the advent of database marketing, the answer depended on intuition, observation, and luck. To these three, we can now add one more: next best product analysis. Next best product analysis will tell you what to sell to whom. It divides customers into similar buying groups, examines what each group is buying now, and then scores each customer on the basis of the relationship between sales to the customer and sales to other members of its group. It can be a very powerful guide for the sales force.

For a business-to-business application, how do you go about determining the next best product for each of your customers? Let us assume that you already have a database with information on your customers and their purchases for the past 2 years and that you have overlaid your file with SIC codes, number of employees, and annual sales. These data can be obtained from D&B.

Your first job is coming up with meaningful SIC categories. For each SIC group, determine your total sales. You may have to do some grouping to get something to work with. For example, Table 9-1 gives just a few out of perhaps a hundred SICs.

I would not waste time on SICs B and F. They should be combined with others. You might want to collapse SIC E as well. You will end up with perhaps 40 meaningful SICs or even fewer.

Then I would divide the final SICs into categories on the basis of either number of employees or annual sales, depending on your preference. We can divide them into three categories as shown in Table 9-2.

We now have divided our customer base into 21 different groups on the basis of SIC group and size.

Table 9-1 Sales by SIC Groups

SIC	Your sales	Number of companies	Average sales
A	$1,889,000	14	$134,929
B	$23,000	1	$23,000
C	$4,599,000	18	$255,500
D	$102,000	3	$34,000
E	$56,000	15	$3,733
F	$124	1	$124
G	$3,445,220	178	$19,355

Table 9-2 Customer Companies by Number of Employees

SIC	Your sales	Number of companies	Number of employees Under 400	401–1000	1001+
A & B	$ 1,912,000	15	$ 552,001	$ 200,000	$1,159,999
C	$ 4,599,000	18	$ 45,000	$ 456,000	$4,098,000
D, E, F & G	$ 3,603,344	197	$2,001,000	$ 500,000	$1,102,344
H	$ 1,002,000	41	$ 200,000	$ 62,000	$ 740,000
I	$ 4,567,000	101	$1,002,000	$ 890,000	$2,675,000
J	$ 2,089,000	43	$ 45,001	$ 1,998,000	$ 45,999
Total	$17,772,344	415	$3,845,002	$ 4,106,000	$9,821,342

What Do They Buy?

Next, we turn our attention to the products sold to these companies. We have to do some consolidation here as well. Some companies are buying 100,000 different products, and others are buying only 4 or 5. To make sense out of these numbers, we have to break these products down into meaningful categories. By meaningful, I mean that not only do they have to have sufficient sales to be worth bothering with, but they also have to have some relevance to one another. For example, we might have categories like those shown in Table 9-3.

Looking at these categories, I might concentrate on the four product categories in which the average sale per buyer is $27,000 or more. Depending on the situation, you might also combine some of the categories.

Now it is time to use a sophisticated model. We take each of our 415 current customers and determine that customer's sales in each of our major product groups. We look at the SIC group and the employee size category. The model will create a next best product for each of the 415 different customer companies based on that company's product purchases relative to those of the other companies in its SIC and company size group. Each of the 415 different company scorecards will look like Table 9-4.

Table 9-3 Average Sales by Product Type

	Total sales	Total buyers	Average per buyer
Hoses	$ 6,001,000	220	$27,277
Fasteners	$ 778,001	198	$ 3,929
Valves	$ 1,002,000	18	$55,667
Pipe	$ 9,001,000	144	$62,507
Wire	$ 339,000	201	$ 1,687
Switches	$ 603,000	22	$27,409
Connectors	$ 46,001	32	$ 1,438
Total	$17,770,002	415	$42,819

Table 9-4 Next Best Product for XYZ Company

	Total average annual sales				
	Hoses	Valves	Pipe	Switches	Total
SIC group average	$38,002	$60,003	$42,001	$2,002	$142,008
This company	$22,001	$78,003	$ 1,001	$8,990	$109,995
Next best product			$42,001		

What Table 9-4 says to the sales force is that the next best product to sell to XYZ company is pipe and that the annual sales could amount to $42,000 per year, based on the purchases made by other similar companies.

These numbers can be produced for every company and given to the sales force. Each salesperson can be measured not only on total sales but on the ability to increase sales in these conquest categories.

Computing the 10 Best Prospects

Suppose that you are a business-to-business manufacturer with a sales force, each member of which has an assigned territory. Some of the salespeople are doing well, and some are not doing so well. The sales force may be company-owned, or it may consist of independent agents. In either case, you want to equip your salespeople with the most productive data to help them in their efforts. One vital sales assist is the NBP described previously.

Even more powerful can be a top 10 prospects list developed for each unique sales territory. Here is how such a list is developed. A part of the next best product determination was the creation of SIC categories, broken down by small, medium, and large companies. Using that analysis, you can rank each of your existing customers by annual sales. This might produce a ranking for a single territory that looks like Table 9-5.

For the top 10 analysis, we may arbitrarily confine our attention to companies that have annual sales of over $100,000. There are three such

Table 9-5 Ranking of Sales within a Territory

Company	Sales
G	$1,992,001
B	$ 889,445
C	$ 102,004
D	$ 56,002
E	$ 1,245
A	$ 317
F	$ 77
Total	$3,041,091

companies in Table 9-5. Because of the NBP analysis, we know the product that we sell the most of to each of these three companies and the companies' total annual purchases from us, and we have categorized them as being large, medium, or small companies. We also know what categories of products the top three companies in this territory buy (see Table 9-6).

Now let's go to D&B to find all the companies (that are not current customers) in this particular sales territory that match the profiles of companies G, B, and C (the companies with over $100,000 in annual purchases from us). We may find that there are 34 such companies. Table 9-7 indicates what the analysis will show us.

Prospects that resemble company G are clearly the best prospects for future sales. And we know what to offer them: hoses. That is a no-brainer. Where do we come up with the next four to round out our top ten? We have to pick, arbitrarily, four of the eight companies that are similar to company B. We can offer them switches.

The way top 10 prospects works, however, we are not yet through with our analysis. In a typical process, each agent is linked to the central database by a Web interface. When an agent logs on to the database, he sees a list of all his customers, together with the next best product for

Table 9-6 What the Top Three Customers Buy

	Total sales	Total buyers	Average per buyer	Company G	Company B	Company C
Hoses	$ 6,001,000	220	$27,277	$ 889,554	$227,665	$ 19,882
Fasteners	$ 778,001	198	$ 3,929	$ 19,646	$ 3,929	$ 1,965
Valves	$ 1,002,000	18	$55,667	$ 478,003	$ 55,667	$ 27,833
Pipe	$ 9,001,000	144	$62,507	$ 312,535	$ 62,507	$ 37,253
Wire	$ 339,000	201	$ 1,687	$ 8,433	$ 1,687	$ 843
Switches	$ 603,000	22	$27,409	$ 276,881	$545,667	$ 13,705
Connectors	$ 46,001	32	$ 1,438	$ 7,188	$ 2,434	$ 719
Total	$17,770,002	415	$42,819	$1,992,240	$899,555	$102,200

Table 9-7 Top Products of Prospect Companies

Company	Sales	Similar companies	Best-selling product	Average annual buys
G	$1,992,001	6	Hoses	$889,554
B	$ 889,445	8	Switches	$545,667
C	$ 102,004	20	Pipe	$ 37,253
Total		34		

each company. He also sees a list of the 10 best prospects, along with the product that he should sell to them. By clicking on each prospect, he gets the name and address of the company, the contact information, company data, and so on.

Let us suppose that this particular agent has already canvassed some of these prospects and knows that he cannot win them over. They are already locked into the competition for some solid reason. The agent needs more prospects. No problem; he clicks on a "Do Not List" column opposite each of these prospects, and then clicks on a "Refresh" button. The top 10 prospect software goes back to the prospect pool and redoes the analysis, dropping the "Do Not List" companies and adding new companies from the pool. Within a few minutes, the agent has a refreshed list of top 10 prospects. He can do this as often as he wishes, working his way down all the prospects reported by D&B within his territory.

This is an example of the way modern database analysis supports business-to-business marketing and sales. The information shown in these tables could not have been developed without a customer marketing database. Once you have that database, the software to produce next best product and top 10 prospects is complex, but achievable.

Using the Web Correctly

BenefitMall.com is an online exchange for buyers, sellers, and providers of employee benefits for companies with 100 employees or less. Through BenefitMall, insurance brokers can access active accounts and receive accurate real-time quotes, reducing the total sales cycle from more than a month to less than an hour in most cases. As well as the Internet, BenefitMall also supports brokers with traditional in-market call center and sales support. The Mall's quote engine lets brokers quote multiple carriers and multiple products in a single proposal.

There is a large community of brokers in the United States that focuses on providing insurance and benefits contracts to small businesses. Also, there are many companies that offer small-company benefit packages, with many different product offerings. The challenge for a broker is to be able to access information on a variety of options in a timely fashion. Since brokers usually have small budgets and cannot afford sophisticated systems, they find companies like BenefitMall to be quite helpful. Going directly to a carrier can require a lot of paperwork and take weeks to process. By the time it's all completed, the client may have chosen to purchase from some other broker.

BenefitMall's director of marketing, Patty Harris, asked SmartDM Chief Analytics Officer Bill Franks to help the company make a major expansion of both its online and its offline capabilities and staff. With more than 50,000 brokers in the company's database, they decided to launch a program to increase the share of business obtained from brokers.

The goals of the initiative were to

- Set up a new Web-based database marketing system across several channels, including direct mail, email, fax, and Web surveys.
- Provide regular updates to broker segment classifications and respond rapidly to changes in the broker profile.
- Begin marketing to brokers through programs based on the type and frequency of business that they have done with BenefitMall.
- Allow easy collection of broker information, including communication preferences, demographics, and customer satisfaction feedback.
- Have responses tracked and results quantified so that the effectiveness of marketing efforts can be rapidly determined and the efforts adjusted as needed.
- Personalize broker communications with the data collected and the name of the broker assigned to each broker.

To set up the new system, there were several obstacles to be overcome:

- The BenefitMall database was not "marketing-friendly." Getting data out of it was difficult.
- BenefitMall had not done sophisticated database marketing in the past. It was difficult to sell the concept to management.
- There was no historical information that could be used to benchmark the response to new programs.

- Management, once it was sold on the program, demanded an aggressive implementation process, with not enough time for testing.

Program Communications

To set up the new system, Franks and the SmartDM team set up a number of new communications aimed at building relationships with brokers:

- Welcome kit mailings to new brokers when they first register on the system.
- Activation emails encouraging brokers to make their first quotes and sales.
- New customer thank-you mailings to thank brokers for their first BenefitMall sale.
- Thank-you satisfaction surveys emailed to each broker after each sale. The email links the broker to a Web microsite that asked questions about the experience. The emails came from the regional vice president of sales for the broker's region.
- Reactivation emails, letters, and phone calls of two types: one for those who stopped selling, and one for those who stopped quoting.
- Broker newsletter emails: nine regional monthly versions.
- Special regional postcard/email/fax promotions. These were special communications aimed at getting information such as new carrier announcements, rate changes, and so on to brokers in a short period of time.

Database Changes

For its marketing database, BenefitMall used SmartDM's DirectTR@K system, which got updates every 2 weeks from the BenefitMall system. This database stored all the information about each broker: past transactions, past marketing communications received, when the broker became a customer, and so on. The DirectTR@K system sent the emails automatically. It tracked who opened the emails, who clicked on the various links, and what emails bounced. While the DirectTR@K system sent the email communications directly, lists for the direct-mail and fax communications were extracted and sent to SmartDM's production division for execution.

The communications were personalized and customized to include transaction data, sign-up date, and the sales rep and sales manager and their contact information. In this way, the communications appeared to have been sent to the broker by the rep whom the broker knew.

New Systems

This program was entirely new for BenefitMall. It required setting up

- A Web-based, multichannel, marketing system that tracked customer activity and response.
- Data of much higher integrity than had previously been maintained. It was necessary to pull lists on the same day as the request, which was very new to BenefitMall.
- User interfaces for generating queries, examining data on individual brokers, managing campaigns, and viewing marketing reports.
- Broker profiles, including type of practice, product sales, and transaction types. This information had not been available before.
- Customer satisfaction data from the Web surveys, which enabled BenefitMall to identify strong and weak personnel within the company.
- One-on-one direct marketing communications across several channels (email, direct mail, fax, phone, and Web microsite).

With the new program, the company added a BenefitMall custom proposal, a Microsoft Excel–based software tool designed to make it easier for brokers to customize insurance coverage proposals for clients. The goal of this free software was to help brokers customize proposals so that they could sell more insurance. The Web system (see Figure 9-2) permitted brokers to

- View side-by-side rate and benefits comparisons for multiple policies.
- Add coverage options to help clients compare rates and benefits.

Figure 9-2   BenefitMall Web Site

- View preloaded, preset spreadsheets and reports.
- Create final presentations right on their laptops, then view the proposal on the screen or print it out and discuss it.

After a 120-day development process, BenefitMall was able to start its first month of the new system by sending

- Welcome kits to 2500 new brokers, personalized for the individual broker and the broker sales representative for each of the 11 regions.
- Activation emails to all new quoting brokers and all new selling brokers. BenefitMall was able to convert 5 to 10 percent of these brokers to full customers within the first 2 months. This was true even though typical sales cycles are 3 to 6 months. It is anticipated that this percentage will at least double over time.
- New customer thank-you letters and gifts to all first-time selling customers in all regions.
- Thank-you satisfaction surveys to all brokers completing sales each month; 25 percent of the brokers reached in the emails participated in the surveys.
- Reactivation emails, letters, and sales phone calls to all lapsed brokers, those who had stopped quoting and selling. BenefitMall

was able to reactivate more than 5 percent of these brokers within the first 60 days. This percentage is expected to at least double, since typical sales cycles are 3 to 6 months.

- Email newsletters to all brokers with 45 to 55 percent open rates for HTML. (Open rates refers to the percentage of people who open and read an email instead of just deleting it.) There was a 5 percent click-through rate on links to the Web site and an opt-out rate of 0.3 percent over an 8-month period.

- Eighty special regional postcards, faxes, and emails, all within 48 hours of the event, improving the turnaround time by 62 percent. These communications gave brokers updates on price changes, seminars, new carriers, or other time-sensitive news items.

In the first 8 weeks of the new program, BenefitMall generated over 2000 new quotes and 80 new sales.

Postcard Direct

Isuzu dealers sell midsized trucks that are used in a variety of occupations, including landscaping, plumbing, manufacturing, and materials distribution. Because of the differing vocations for which the trucks are used, the engines are the same but the appearance of the trucks varies considerably. To sell a truck to a nursery or an electrical contractor, it is useful to show the prospect a picture of what the truck will look like. To solve this problem, Isuzu worked with msdbm of Los Angeles to create a program called Postcard Direct.

Isuzu asked its dealers to provide it with scores of testimonials from satisfied Isuzu truck owners, complete with photographs of the trucks being used in various vocations. Msdbm helped Isuzu to assemble the best of these testimonials and photographs into a group of oversized postcards designed to be sent to customers in various vocations. Msdbm worked with Dun & Bradstreet and Isuzu to compile a database of small and midsized businesses and prospects, coded by business type. These names were put into a database with the latitude and longitude recorded in each record. In addition, the database contained the names, addresses, phone numbers, and logos of all the Isuzu dealers in the United States.

To launch the program, msdbm created a mailing to all Isuzu dealers, inviting them to come to an Isuzu microsite (see Figure 9-3) to order custom postcards to be sent to customers and prospects in their trade area. Dealers could come to the site and select the vocations that they wanted to promote, select the number of names they wanted to mail to, and view the test front and back of each postcard.

After dealers selected the postcards they wanted to send, they would see the number of prospects and customers whose offices were within a close radius of the dealership (see Figure 9-4). They could order the cards right on the Web. Dealers would click on the number of prospects they wanted to mail to and then would see a form for placing the order (see Figure 9-5).

The program proved to be an outstanding success. Fifty percent of the Isuzu dealers in the United States logged on to the Web site and ordered postcards. After 1 year, a total of 128,000 postcards had been ordered using the system, at an average cost to the dealer of $0.25 each.

Figure 9-3   Postcard Direct

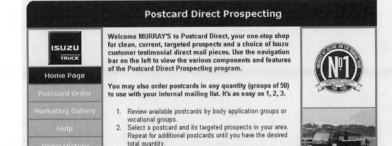

Figure 9-4   Order Form for Postcard Direct

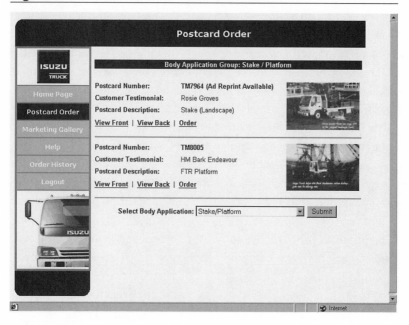

Figure 9-5   Postcard Order Details

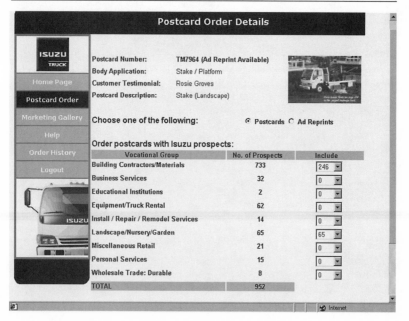

Along with the postcards, the dealer got printed labels to affix to the postcards. The dealer could mail the cards on whatever schedule was suitable to keep the sales force busy.

This program was an extremely effective use of the Web. There was no other way that such a program could have been run in such a cost-effective manner. Direct mail would have been much more costly. Phone would not have worked, because the dealers would not have been able to view the postcards. Once the dealer ordered the cards, they were mailed within a week, together with the labels. The dealer got an immediate email thanking him or her for the order. The dealer was also able to get an email list of the names and phone numbers of the prospects to which the cards were to be sent so that the salespeople could follow up.

Secret Double Agents

Winning the hearts and minds of travel agents is one of the keys to running a successful hotel chain. Agents are barraged by faxes, brochures, and advertisements from hotels, airlines, rental car companies, cruise lines, and destinations. The information changes daily as rates are revised and promotions generated. If a hotel wants to get the attention of travel agents, it must break through this information overload and promise something more.

To increase booking activity for Radisson Hotels during slow travel periods, Gail Recker of the Carlson Marketing Group created a "hurdle" promotion to motivate travel agents. Using the Radisson travel agent database, Gail created a specific "confidential" and achievable goal for each agent's booking of Radisson hotels between March and May. The goal varied based on an analysis of the agents' past activity with Radisson. Upon reaching the goal, the travel agents would be rewarded with "double points" for bookings made through August. The points earned by the travel agents would put them into a sweepstakes drawing. Eight agents would be selected in the drawing for an all-expenses-paid, 2-week trip to one of several exotic spots as a training exercise.

Because the reward for agents offered double points, the program was called Secret Double Agent, with spylike teasers and a mission for each travel consultant.

Phase 2 of the promotion focused on the slow travel period just before the holiday season, with successful agents being rewarded with double points for future bookings made in October and November. Radisson and Country Inns & Suites general managers received a mailing to alert them to the programs.

How the Hurdles Were Determined

The program was launched by sending a self-mailer with customized hurdles to 80,000 U.S. and Canadian travel agents. The hurdle levels were determined by segmenting agents into 10 tiers based on past booking patterns, probability, and liability. A control group of 20,000 agents was identified that was not included in the promotion. This gave Carlson the ability to measure the incremental value of the program.

The Radisson database, which had been built up over 9 years, included 250,000 travel agents worldwide. The database was used to communicate monthly with the agents.

The goal of the program was to increase incremental revenue from the 80,000 targeted agents by between $1.5 and $3 million over a 6-month period. The results were far greater than anticipated. The incremental revenue increased by $4.5 million, with 15 percent of the targeted agents reaching their hurdle and receiving the double points as an incentive.

Supply Chain Management

Probably the most important new use of database marketing and the Web is in supply chain management. There are many different inputs that manufacturers need in order to make their finished products. Keeping the warehouse full of parts entails high interest payments and requires lots of space and employee management.

Now that everything in the world is bar-coded, it has been possible to introduce vendor-managed inventory. The system works as follows: A manufacturer keeps its inventory records on a computer that can be accessed by its suppliers through the Web. It works out arrangements with its suppliers so that they can use the Web to learn electronically every hour what parts have been used and which remain on the manufacturer's shelves. The manufacturer discloses its sales plan so that the suppliers can estimate how many of which items will be needed each day. Then they can arrange just-in-time shipments to keep the inventory to an absolute minimum, but always sufficient so that the production line is never halted for lack of a part. Before the Web, some manufacturers used a system called EDI (Electronic Data Interchange), which served some of the same functions as vendor-managed inventory. EDI, however, was much more difficult to install and operate than the Web.

Using the vendor-managed system allowed Dell to hold less than 8 days' worth of inventory at any given time. Without the system, Compaq had to maintain 3 weeks' worth during the same period. This gave Dell a tremendous cost advantage. Intel shipped products to Dell three times a week without Dell's having to process a single request—Intel could forecast Dell's needs based on Dell's sales forecasts and current stock usage.

Let's see how a supplier might profit from using vendor-managed inventory and "forward-deployed" products for 400 of its 1000 best customers. These customers spend much more than other customers— that is why they are the best. Figure 9-6 shows what the new system might look like if you were the supplier.

Your products will be stored in the customer's warehouses and in your nearby warehouses, with title still remaining with you. Every time your customer takes your products from its shelves or from your warehouse, your vendor-managed inventory system will know this. Shipping

Figure 9-6   Vendor-Managed Inventory

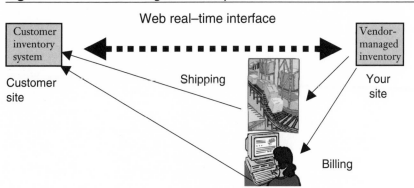

will be notified if it is necessary to replenish products in inventory. Billing will be notified to bill the customer. Using this system, the following things will happen:

- The customer will save money: It no longer has to manage its warehouses, nor does it have to pay for any inventory until that inventory is actually used. This is a very large dollar saving to the customer.
- The retention rate for customers using this system will approach 100 percent. Customers' spending on your products will also substantially increase, since, if they like the system, they may begin to shift to your company's products instead of competitors'.
- Your costs will not increase. Of course, you have to maintain inventory at remote sites, but you were doing that anyway.
- We assume that your customers already have an inventory system that keeps track (using bar codes) of the disposition of each product in the warehouse. You can use the Web to poll this system and get hourly reports on the movement of inventory. You have to add the vendor-managed inventory software, which
  - Does the hourly polling of inventory status at each customer site
  - Automatically replenishes products when they run low and recalls products when they are not moving
  - Forecasts usage and automatically increases or decreases minimum stock quantities
  - Automatically bills the customer for products taken off the shelves
  - Provides complete reports for you and for all your customers

Table 9-8 shows what your 400 best customers will look like before you introduce vendor-managed inventory. What does VMI cost? That depends on the complexity of your operation. Let's assume that it costs $1 million to set it up, which annualizes to $350,000 per year, as shown in Table 9-9. What could happen to the 400 best customers who adopt this system? See Table 9-10. The effect of the new system on total profit

Table 9-8 Base LTV

	Year 1	Year 2	Year 3
Retention rate	75%	80%	85%
Customers	400	300	240
Annual spending	$50,000	$52,000	$64,000
Revenue	$20,000,000	$15,600,000	$15,360,000
Costs	70%	68%	67%
Operating costs	$14,000,000	$10,608,000	$10,291,200
Acquisition cost ($400)	$ 160,000		
Marketing cost ($50)	$ 20,000	$ 15,000	$ 12,000
Web site costs	$ 270,000	$ 270,000	$ 270,000
Total costs	$14,450,000	$10,893,000	$10,573,200
Profit	$5,550,000	$4,707,000	$4,786,800
Discount rate	1.10	1.19	1.28
NPV of profit	$5,045,455	$3,955,462	$3,739,688
Cumulative NPV of profit	$5,045,455	$9,000,917	$12,740,604
Lifetime value	$12,613.64	$22,502.29	$31,851.51

Table 9-9 Annual Costs of VMI Software

Software development	$1,000,000
Annualized	$350,000

Table 9-10 Improved LTV

	Year 1	Year 2	Year 3
Retention rate	90%	93%	96%
Customers	400	360	335
Annual spending	$54,000	$56,000	$68,000
Revenue	$21,600,000	$20,160,000	$22,766,400
Costs	70%	68%	67%
Operating costs	$15,120,000	$13,708,800	$15,253,488
Acquisition cost ($400)	$ 160,000		
Marketing cost ($50)	$ 20,000	$ 18,000	$ 16,740
Web site costs	$ 270,000	$ 270,000	$ 270,000
VMI costs	$ 350,000	$ 350,000	$ 350,000
Total costs	$15,920,000	$14,346,800	$15,890,228
Profit	$5,680,000	$5,813,200	$6,876,172
Discount rate	1.10	1.19	1.28
NPV of profit	$5,163,636	$4,885,042	$5,372,009
Cumulative NPV of profit	$5,163,636	$10,048,678	$15,420,688
Lifetime value	$12,909.09	$25,121.70	$38,551.72

Table 9-11 Profit Gain with New System

	Year 1	Year 2	Year 3
LTV after	$12,909.09	$25,121.70	$38,551.72
LTV before	$12,613.64	$22,502.29	$31,851.51
Increase	$ 295.45	$ 2,619.40	$ 6,700.21
With 400 customers	$ 118,182	$1,047,762	$2,680,084

for these top 400 customers is shown in Table 9-11. The result is a profit of $2.6 million over 3 years.

Do these numbers prove that Web pages for your best customers and vendor-managed inventory for your very best customers will work in your case? Of course not. You will have to work out the numbers for yourself. What this chapter shows you is how to go about it. Develop tables like these for yourself to see if these systems will work. Then, if the numbers look good, go ahead and see if you can

- Find the software you need at a price that will make the numbers profitable.
- Sell your best customers on adopting such a system. This will be the most difficult part of the job.

Panduit's Vendor-Managed Inventory

One of the pioneers in vendor-managed inventory is Panduit, which makes 60,000 different electrical products such as switches, fuse boxes, connections, and so on. The company markets solely through 1800 distributors. For its largest customers, Panduit set up a fully automatic computer-to-computer management system. The distributor and Panduit establish mutual goals for service level and inventory turns. The distributors then transmit a daily report on changes in inventory. Without human intervention, the system automatically

- Forecasts demand for each part number monthly.
- Determines the optimum replenishment quantity.
- Creates purchase orders in Panduit's and the distributor's business systems.

- Ships and transmits replacements and the associated electronic paperwork.

The advantage of this system is that Panduit has solved its customer's business problems by having

- Freight costs reduced.
- Human errors eliminated.
- Operating costs minimized.
- Out-of-stock conditions eliminated.
- Profits increased.
- Distributor loyalty maximized—the distributors become relationship buyers.

FedEx Shipping Partnerships

National Semiconductor, a major maker of computer chips, handed over its logistics management to FedEx. Before the transfer, National shipped products from its six factories to seven warehouses around the world. FedEx set up a single warehouse in Singapore to house all of National's output. National's customers place orders with National's order center in Santa Clara, California. Many of these orders are placed directly on National's Web site, www.national.com. When the orders come in, they are processed electronically and sent to the FedEx shipment center in Memphis. There the orders are routed electronically to the FedEx warehouse in Singapore, where the products are picked, packed, and shipped by FedEx to National customers throughout the world. The result of this system has been:

- A reduction in the customer delivery cycle from 4 weeks to 1 week
- A reduction in National's distribution costs from 2.9 percent of sales to 1.2 percent of sales
- Elimination of the seven National regional warehouses in the United States, Asia, and Europe

The FedEx–National partnership enabled National to get a jump on its competitors by building profitable relationships with its customers. By combining vendor-managed inventory with FedEx shipment, National could concentrate on its main jobs—designing, manufacturing, and selling chips—rather than storing and shipping the chips.

Summary

What do these case studies tell us about how database marketing and the Web are helping suppliers to make their customers profitable?

- In the first case, CSC decided to analyze the firm's customer database, append D&B information, and determine the next best product and top 10 prospects for 1800 independent agents.
- BenefitMall.com used the Web to help thousands of independent brokers determine the best benefit systems for their customers, signing up 2500 new brokers in the process.
- Isuzu used the Web to provide its dealers with customized postcards to be mailed to prospects in their area.
- Radisson Hotels used the Web to encourage 80,000 independent travel agents to increase bookings by $4.5 million, benefiting both the agents and Radisson.
- Intel used the Web to conduct vendor-managed inventory for Dell, thus reducing Dell's inventory to 8 days, while Dell's competitor Compaq had an inventory level of 3 weeks.
- FedEx used the Web to help National Semiconductor cut the time required for delivery of parts to customers by 3 weeks per order and cut delivery costs in half.

None of these activities would have been possible without a customer database or without the Web. The combination of the two has created a powerful shift in the relationships between suppliers and their customers.

What Works

- Vendor-managed inventory over the Web that permits suppliers to manage their customer's inventories.
- Providing agents with specific next best products for each customer and top 10 prospects.
- Finding out more about the customer's business and solving the customer's business problems.
- Creating a database of prospects and serving them up to agents via the Web.
- Taking over logistics management for customers, so that they can concentrate on their core business: designing and manufacturing products.

What Doesn't Work

- Old-fashioned business-to-business ordering systems using fax and phone to order products that are used daily and in quantities.
- Manufacturers not concerning themselves with the business problems of their agents.
- Assuming that intermediaries can do their job without your help. Maybe they can, but why take a chance?

Quiz

1. In the CSC business-to-business case, how were the top 10 prospects for each agent selected?
   a. Agents were asked to select them.
   b. Existing customers were modeled.
   c. Prospects were surveyed.
   d. Prospect sales were modeled.
   e. D&B provided prospect purchase intentions.

2. Which of the following is not typically part of D&B business-to-business data?
   a. Market penetration
   b. Number of employees
   c. Prizm cluster codes
   d. Annual sales
   e. SIC codes

3. Which of the following was not a feature of the BenefitMall case study?
   a. Broker newsletters
   b. Satisfaction surveys
   c. SIC analysis
   d. Welcome kits
   e. Reactivation emails

4. In the Isuzu case study, what percentage of dealers logged on to the site and ordered postcards?
   a. 2 percent
   b. 4 percent
   c. 6 percent
   d. 12 percent
   e. 50 percent

5. Which of the following is not a benefit of vendor-managed inventory?
   a. Vendors do the selling for their customers.
   b. Vendors own the products in their customers' warehouses.
   c. Vendors can call back slow-moving items.
   d. Vendors can predict customer product usage.
   e. Inventory costs for customers are down.

6. In the Radisson Hotels case, what did the "hurdle" mean?
   a. A goal for total sales
   b. A minimum that was the same for all agents
   c. A level that only top agents could achieve
   d. A rate calculated using the agent's previous sales
   e. None of the above

7. In the Isuzu Postcard Direct program, what was the best way for agents to order the postcards?
   a. The Web
   b. Emails
   c. Direct mail
   d. Phone
   e. Fax

8. What was the advantage to National Semiconductor of the FedEx arrangement?
   a. National cut shipping costs by 8 percent.
   b. National eliminated eight warehouses.
   c. FedEx took over some of National's shipping responsibilities.
   d. National cut delivery time to customers to 1 week.
   e. All of the above.

9. Who owns "forward-deployed" products?
   a. The supplier
   b. The customer
   c. The taxpayers
   d. The marketing department
   e. The IT department

10. Why is the discount rate in year 1 of a business-to-business LTV table seldom equal to 1?
    a. Business marketing costs are higher.
    b. The SIC codes are often unknown.
    c. Business customers usually pay long after shipment.
    d. The annual sales to businesses are greater than those to consumers.
    e. Business databases are usually smaller than consumer databases.

CHAPTER 10

CUSTOMER MANAGEMENT

Once you have a customer database, you can use it to manage your customers. What does "managing customers" mean? Marketers have found that they can

- Identify their Gold customers and work hard to keep them.
- Identify their Silver customers and persuade them to buy their way up to Gold status.
- Identify the customers who are most likely to defect and get them to change their minds.
- Reactivate lapsed customers.
- Get customers to refer others, who also become customers.
- Determine the next best product for each customer, and get customers to buy the product.
- Manage the second sale to one-time buyers.
- Manage leads to get them to become buyers.
- Develop loyalty programs to maintain customers' interest.

Most of these things were only dreamed of in the 1980s. Some companies became proficient at customer management in the 1990s. Today, using the Internet, database marketers are learning to do all these things.

A Little Restraint

A little restraint is required. Just because, theoretically, you can manage all your customers using your database does not mean that you should. Managing the top 20 percent is quite easy. Managing the next 20 percent is a bit harder. Managing the bottom 20 percent may not be worth the effort. In direct response, 80 percent is about the most important number. Using this number, you can increase your response and your sales while lowering your cost per sale. Let's see how valuable 80 percent is to you.

Gold customers (the top 20 percent of your customers) bring in 80 percent of your revenue. These people are really your company. Lose them, and you lose it all. Spend a small amount of money on retaining them, and you keep 80 percent of your total business. How does this work?

When you hear people complaining that database marketing is too expensive, you will find that they are talking about 100 percent. Suppose you develop a retention program consisting of birthday cards, thank-you letters, appreciation emails, and special customer services and benefits for certain customers. If you were to do these things for all your customers, the costs would be quite high. The benefits you would receive might not pay for the cost of the extra services. But why not concentrate on the Gold customers—those who bring in 80 percent of the revenue but represent only 20 percent of the customers? The cost of a program for Gold customers is only one-fifth the cost of a similar program for all customers, but it safeguards 80 percent of your revenue.

The 80 percent rule also applies to your database cleanup. Your database is a mess. Many of the names and addresses are wrong. Many entries lack phone numbers or email names. Cleaning it up will be costly. But wait a minute. Why clean it *all* up? Why not clean up only the easiest 80 percent? Your programmers will tell you that those 80 percent can be cleaned up in an afternoon. Getting the remaining 20 percent correct will take several months. Go ahead and clean up the 80 percent right now. Get it done. Then clean up the remaining 20 percent at your leisure, in the most inexpensive way possible or, better yet, *apply the 80 percent rule to them.* What does that mean? Run through the remaining 20 percent of bad addresses and pick out the Gold customers. Clean those up. As for the rest, forget about them for now.

You want to send out emails to your customers. But some of them are on AOL and can read only text. Others can read HTML. Still others want their copy in Spanish. It is a big job, costing a lot of money and resources. How can you solve this problem? Use the 80 percent rule. Pick the easiest 80 percent of your customers and get your message off to them right away. If you have a consumer database, AOL probably represents 80 percent. If it is a business-to-business (B2B) database, 80 percent can probably read HTML. Design your email for the 80 percent and get something done now. If the email is a success, then figure out how to reach the remaining 20 percent. If it is a failure, don't bother with the remainder. Either way, you have kept your costs down.

Building a Data Warehouse

Building a data warehouse for 100 percent of their customers and those customers' data has proved to be very expensive for many companies. Most large companies that have built such a warehouse have spent at least $20 million on the project. Why is it so expensive? Because a data warehouse is designed by a committee. It has to include all the data that an organization ever conceivably uses: data on customers, prospects, leads, transactions, promotions, responses, products, prices, models, and employees. Since the accountants are involved, the data in the warehouse have to balance to the penny. Since IT is involved, the warehouse is built by in-house programmers who have never built a warehouse before; they are very excited by the idea, but they have no experience at all.

As most people who have studied data warehouses will tell you, these warehouses almost never pay for themselves in terms of increased profits. Why not? Because the benefits of using a warehouse are incremental. The warehouse will enable you to do better targeting of your communications. Instead of getting a 2 percent response rate, you will get a 2.1 percent response rate. The question is, will the profits from the 5 percent increase in the response rate pay for the cost of the warehouse?

In most cases, they won't, and you can prove it to yourself with a simple Excel spreadsheet before you begin to build your warehouse.

Suppose your company is taking in $156 million per year in direct sales to customers. The benefits of a warehouse are shown in Table 10-1. That's very nice. Your warehouse has brought in 30,000 more sales, totaling $7.8 million more per year. But let's look at the incremental profits. Suppose you are making a 30 percent profit on direct sales. Table 10-2 shows what would happen.

Your warehouse will lose you about $1.1 million per year. So what should you do? Use the 80 percent rule. Don't build a data warehouse that will retain all the data you could ever possibly need. Build a simple data mart that meets 80 percent of your marketing needs. Even the largest corporation in America can build such a data mart for less than $1.5 million total, with an annual cost of about $800,000. Table 10-3

Table 10-1 Warehouse Costs

	Current	Warehouse	Increase
Number of offers	100,000,000	100,000,000	
Response rate	2.0%	2.1%	
Number of responses	2,000,000	2,100,000	100,000
Sales conversion	30%	30%	
Number of sales	600,000	630,000	30,000
Average sale	$260	$260	
Sales	$156,000,000	$163,800,000	$163,800,000

Table 10-2 Increased Profits from Complete Data Warehouse

	Increased sales	Profit rate	Increased profits
Annual warehouse benefits	$7,800,000	30%	$2,340,000
Annual warehouse costs			($3,500,000)
Loss from warehouse			($1,160,000)

Table 10-3 Increased Profits from Data Mart

	80% increased sales	Profit rate	Increased profits
Data mart benefits	$6,240,000	30%	$1,872,000
Data mart costs			$ 800,000
Gain from data mart			$1,072,000

Table 10-4 Warehouse Costs

Step	Cost
Build warehouse	$6,000,000
Amortize over 3 years	$2,000,000
Annual maintenance	$ 500,000
Customer communications	$1,000,000
Total	$3,500,000

shows the result of the 80 percent solution. You have converted a $1 million loss into a $1 million profit increase by using an 80 percent solution.

Where did the $3,500,000 annual cost for a warehouse come from? Here is a simple way to measure data warehouse costs. If it costs you $6 million to build the warehouse, you can amortize these costs over 3 years, for $2 million per year. Maintenance of the warehouse will cost you at least $500,000 per year. Once the warehouse is built, you need to use it to communicate with your customers—otherwise, what is the warehouse for? Let's say that you spend only $1 million on customer communications per year. Then the warehouse will cost you at least $3,500,000 per year, as shown in Table 10-4.

Whenever you or any of your colleagues at work come up with a proposal for a large direct response project, Web site, or warehouse, ask this question: How much could we save by concentrating on the easiest 80 percent and postponing the rest for later? You will be amazed at the profitability of the answers.

Risk/Revenue Analysis

There is another way of cutting the costs of customer management besides using the 80 percent rule. That is applying risk/revenue analysis. For this to work, you have to have done two things:

1. Determined the lifetime value of your customers and divided the customers into high, medium, and low lifetime value segments.
2. Determined the likelihood that customers will leave you and divided the customers into high, medium, and low likelihood of defection segments. When you have done this, you can develop a simple table that looks like Table 10-5.

Table 10-5 Risk/Revenue Analysis

	Likelihood of Defection		
Lifetime value	High	Medium	Low
High	priority A	priority B	priority C
Medium	priority B	priority B	priority C
Low	priority C	priority C	priority C

Assuming that all your segments are of equal size, you will have 44 percent of your customers in priority A and priority B and 66 percent of them in priority C. Customer management is not free. It costs money for communications, benefits, recognition, and rewards. Why waste a lot of money on managing your priority C customers? They are in one of two categories:

1. Of very low lifetime value to you
2. Very loyal and unlikely to defect

In either case, spending a lot of resources trying to modify their behavior is likely to be a waste of money. This means that you can concentrate your energy on managing (modifying the behavior of) only 44 percent of your customers, instead of 100 percent. This concentration on the real customer management problem will pay dividends in many ways.

In the first place, if you try to manage everybody, the resources you can devote to any one customer will be limited. Let's say that you have a customer management budget of $1 million and a customer base of 1 million customers. That is $1 per customer per year. You can't do much to change a customer's behavior with $1 per year. That's two letters and an email at best. Suppose you concentrate on only priority A and B customers. You will have $1 million to spend on 44 percent of your customers, which comes to $2.27 per customer. Even better, if you devote $4 per customer to priority A customers, you will still have $1.67 left for each of the priority B customers. You can do a lot more with $1.67 than you could have done with only $1, and much more with $4.

This chapter presents several case studies of different methods of customer management. All of them look appealing, and they are, because they have worked well for some companies. How can you determine whether they would work for you?

Table 10-6 Increased Return

	Present	With customer management	Cost of customer management	Net increased return
Leads	500,000	500,000		
Conversion rate	30%	36%		
One-time buyers	150,000	180,000		
Conversion rate	50%	60%		
Two-time buyers	75,000	108,000		
Annual revenue	$200	$240		
Total revenue	$15,000,000	$25,920,000	$4,000,000	$6,920,000

There is a relatively easy answer. Plug your own numbers into Table 10-6 to determine whether customer management will work for you. Begin by asking yourself what success you are having today with

- Conversion of leads to buyers
- Conversion of one-time buyers to two-time buyers
- Cross-selling products to existing customers

We are assuming here that you develop a customer management program that costs you $4 million a year to run. It consists of a database with communications to the customers and to the sales force that is managing the program. A successful customer management program should increase the lead conversion rate, the conversion rate of one-time buyers to two-time buyers, and, through cross selling, the annual revenue from two-time buyers.

What will these customer management communications be? This is up to you. At this point, you know that you want personal communications based on data in your customer database. You want to capture email names so that most of the communications are essentially free. In the rest of this chapter, there are several valuable case studies showing how some companies have been able to manage their customers to produce results like those shown in the previous tables.

Loyalty Programs

One of the most wonderful ways of managing customers is to set up a loyalty program. The basic idea is that customers earn some sort of points or miles based on their purchases, and these points or miles earn them rewards. The best loyalty programs also include status levels. Customers work hard to achieve various status levels.

Those who have read my previous books know how hard I worked to become Gold on American Airlines and how happy I was when I achieved this level. It meant that I got to upgrade to first or business class whenever I flew. I got to go on the planes first, with the little children and the old people. I earned bonus miles. I had a special 800 number just for us Gold folks, and I had Gold printed on all my boarding passes so that flight attendants and others would treat me with the appropriate respect. Readers will be happy to learn that because of all these books, I continue to fly all over the world. I have now become Platinum for Life on American. For some reason US Airways, which had joint arrangements with American for a couple of years, gave me Silver Preferred.

Now what is the effect on me of these loyalty programs? Well, they have me hooked. I never fly United or Delta or any other airline if I can help it. Why would I want to sit jammed into the back of the plane? So the effect of a successful loyalty program is that you get as close to 100 percent of your customers' patronage as the customer can get. Now that's customer management.

So how do loyalty programs apply to you, since you are not an airline? This is something that's worth thinking about. Hotels and rental cars get into the act by awarding airline miles. The effect is not as powerful as it is for airlines, but the loyalty program really helps. Lately I have always sought out Hilton hotels because they let me double-dip. I get both air miles and Hilton points.

But most of the readers of this book are not in the travel business and want to know whether loyalty programs will work for them. I can report that loyalty programs seem to work in a number of areas, including

- Retail stores, such as shoe stores, dress stores, and department stores.
- Supermarkets.
- Car washes, auto lubes, and dry cleaners.
- Hallmark Gold Crown stores and similar establishments.
- Banks— by rewarding customers with high or increased balances and holders of multiple accounts.
- Business-to-business firms.

- Restaurants.
- Telephone companies, cell phone providers, and long-distance carriers.
- Credit card providers. I have three credit cards from Citibank that award American Airlines miles. I use them instead of cash or checks whenever I can.

What do you need in order to get started?

- A valid idea for some easy way to award points when customers spend money with you. This may take some doing in the retail area. At present, most people's wallets are crammed with various plastic cards. Few people will want to add more. How, then, can you award points? My suggestion is the iDine method discussed in Chapter 9: by getting people to register their credit cards with you. Then you can award them points whenever they use these cards with you.
- Some practical plan for providing benefits. There are really two types of benefits:
    - Immediate rewards, sometimes including preferred treatment
    - Long-term rewards (like air miles), where the customer is saving toward an achievable long-term goal
- A lifetime value analysis that permits you to determine in advance whether the plan will make you more profitable or make you go broke. Some stores, like supermarkets, operate on very thin margins. They can't afford to give away anything substantial. Yet they have made loyalty programs work very well for them, as we will see.
- Some sophisticated software that maintains the points and redemptions, handles monthly reports to the customers, and reports to you. In most cases, companies have outsourced their loyalty programs. You really should work with a firm that has been through this process before and knows what can go wrong.
- A Web benefits microsite where customers can come to see what they have earned and redeem points for rewards. Try, if possible, to use this Web site for your loyalty program instead of live operators. The customer service costs can eat up the profits from the program if you are not careful.

- Reports to the members that are made available on the Web, or sent by email if your customers prefer it. If you send monthly statements, your report can be printed on the statement. Airlines send statements through the mail and have found them to be quite costly. They are all trying to shift to Web-based reporting.
- A clear expiration date that is announced when your program begins, so that if it is not working out, you can gracefully exit. You can always extend the deadline, but you can get in real trouble if you try to cancel a program while many customers are holding onto hard-earned points.
- A promotion plan that aims at a very high utilization rate. The place to start is with your employees. Enroll them in the plan from the start—with special benefits. You want all your employees to look the customer in the eye and say, "You really should be in this program. It is great. I am in it myself." Promote the plan in every possible way. The purpose of the plan is to modify customer behavior. You can do that only if customers are enrolled.
- Status levels, if appropriate, with appropriate status rewards. The reason for status levels is to get customers to work hard to achieve them. The Platinum program for American was 50,000 miles in a calendar year. I used to go crazy trying to meet this goal. I would take two legs on an American flight when a direct flight was available on other airlines just so that I did not end the year with 46,000 miles.

Let's look at some examples of nonairline loyalty programs.

Supermarkets

Most supermarkets today give their customers plastic frequent shopper cards. These are scanned at the checkout counter and permit the supermarket to build a valid database, giving it information on when and where you shop and how much you spend in each department. How do the supermarkets reward loyalty? There are several ways:

- Few of them provide miles or points. The margins in supermarkets are too thin to allow them to give anything away.

- Many of them use straddle pricing. They price many items in the store a small percentage higher than the price charged at other stores, but they let their members have the items at a small percentage below the market price if a loyalty card is used. These items, and there can be hundreds of them in a store, are usually marked with their occasional shopper price and their member price. Some of these member-priced items are things that food manufacturers are trying to promote; others are just items that the store management has decided need a lift. The effect of straddle pricing is to reward loyal customers while making occasional customers who are not members pay for the rewards. It is a wonderful system. A nonmember won't care that much that his milk costs $1.05 while members pay $0.95. If he does care, he can always sign up for a card and get the price break then and there. Members, of course, see their membership benefits at the bottom of the cash register receipts that are printed out for them: "Today you saved $4.24 by using your VIC card." The beauty of this system is that the store did not have to provide this $4.24. It was provided by occasional shoppers.
- Stores use their loyalty programs to modify customers' behavior in other ways. Members get free ice cream on their birthdays. If they spend $50 a week in the 6 weeks before Thanksgiving, they get a free turkey. Members who come in on Tuesday night get an additional saving, since Tuesday is a slow night.
- Members who shop only in the deli and not in the produce department will get a special certificate giving them $1 to spend in the produce department. This will get luncheon shoppers to buy stuff to take home. This $1 is awarded only to the deli-only shoppers. Other certificates will get produce shoppers to use the deli.
- Lapsed members who spent a lot but who have stopped buying for 6 weeks will get a special offer to encourage them to come back to the store.

Specialty Stores

Shoe stores, dress stores, department stores, bookstores, and other types of stores have used loyalty programs with some success. Here, however, the process is more complicated and often less rewarding than it is for supermarkets or travel-related businesses. Let's take the DSW Shoe Warehouse. I bought four pairs of shoes from its store in Fort Lauderdale. The store gave me a DSW paper card that I could use to get further benefits. I have never used it since—after all, I am not the shopper in our house. Helena is. But what has happened is that I now think of DSW when I think about shoes. It is because of the card, I think. I am sure that this card does affect customer behavior in a positive way. The rewards to the retailer are:

- Some people will return and use the cards to buy more products.
- Some will remember the store because of the card, and may buy more products.
- The store gains a mailing list, and hopefully an email list, that has real value.
- As we know from this book, the store can calculate the value of each customer who gets a card and determine whether this covers the cost of issuing the cards.

Surveys by the Carlson Marketing Group have shown consistently that while only 40 percent of consumers participate in loyalty programs, those who do participate have higher-than-average incomes, and, once they are involved, their behavior is affected by the cards.

Let's see what a loyalty program could do for a retail store chain. Table 10-7 gives the picture of customers before the program is introduced. It costs $32 to acquire a new customer who makes an average of 1.4 visits per year and spends $50 per visit. The modest lifetime value of $3.00 in the first year rises to $29.42 in the third year.

Let's now plan a loyalty program. We are giving on-the-spot benefits to members in order to modify their behavior. We are seeking to

- Increase the number of visits per year
- Increase the spending per visit
- Increase the overall retention rate

To get these benefits, we are prepared to spend $5 per customer in the first year, with the amount increasing to $10 per customer for loyalists who have been with us into the third year. Table 10-8 shows what could

Table 10-7 LTV before Loyalty Program

	Year 1	Year 2	Year 3
Retention rate	40%	45%	50%
Customers	200,000	80,000	36,000
Visits per year	1.4	1.6	1.8
Spending per visit	$50	$60	$70
Revenue	$14,000,000	$7,680,000	$4,536,000
Cost percentage	50%	49%	48%
Costs	$ 7,000,000	$3,763,200	$2,177,280
Acquisition cost ($32)	$ 6,400,000		
Total costs	$13,400,000	$3,763,200	$2,177,280
Profit	$600,000	$3,916,800	$2,358,720
Discount rate	1	1.12	1.32
NPV of profit	$600,000	$3,497,143	$1,786,909
Cumulative NPV of profit	$600,000	$4,097,143	$5,884,052
Lifetime value	$3.00	$20.49	$29.42

Table 10-8 LTV with Loyalty Program

	Year 1	Year 2	Year 3
Retention rate	50%	60%	65%
Customers	200,000	100,000	60,000
Visits per year	1.6	2	2.4
Spending per visit	$55	$70	$80
Revenue	$17,600,000	$114,000,000	$11,520,000
Cost percentage	50%	49%	48%
Costs	$ 8,800,000	$6,860,000	$5,529,600
Acquisition cost ($32)	$ 6,400,000		
Database costs	$ 500,000	$ 250,000	$ 150,000
Loyalty program	$5.00	$8.00	$10.00
Loyalty program costs	$ 1,600,000	$1,600,000	$1,440,000
Total costs	$17,300,000	$8,710,000	$7,119,600
Profit	$300,000	$5,290,000	$4,400,400
Discount rate	1	1.12	1.32
NPV of profit	$300,000	$4,723,214	$3,333,636
Cumulative NPV of profit	$300,000	$5,023,214	$8,356,851
Lifetime value	$1.50	$ 25.12	$41.78

happen. The program has cost us in the first year, but the third-year profits are substantial. Third-year lifetime value has risen to $41.78. The total profits from the program are given in Table 10-9.

If you look closely at these numbers, you will see that a loyalty program is not a sure thing. If it works, we will get $2.4 million pure profit out of it. But for it to work, the number of visits per year has to go up, the

Table 10-9 Gain in LTV from Loyalty Program

	Year 1	Year 2	Year 3
Old LTV	$3.00	$20.49	$29.42
New LTV	$1.50	$25.12	$41.78
Change	− $1.50	$4.63	$12.36
With 200,000 members	− $300,000	$926,071	$2,472,799

spending per visit has to go up, and the retention rate has to go up. Will your loyalty program have these results? You had better test the program on a small scale at one store to see what will happen before you make a big mistake.

A loyalty program is not a lead-pipe cinch. For more on this subject, read Brian Woolf's excellent book *Customer Specific Marketing*. A key point that he makes is that without adequate promotion to the customers and adequate benefits, the program will fail. This type of program is really directed at the frequent shopper who is not as interested in long-term benefits, such as a trip to Hawaii, as in immediate rewards.

Automatic Trigger Marketing

IMarket, a D&B company, sells data to companies that want to get business leads and learn more about their existing customers. IMarket initially delivered data on a CD-ROM (CD) with a meter attachment for the user's PC that permitted the user to select records from the CD for a given price per name. To use the system, companies had to install the CD and register with iMarket.

The arrival of the Internet gave iMarket a new channel for delivering product—by the Web rather than by a CD. Zapdata.com, iMarket's Internet product, provided a much wider market for the company's product. However, Zapdata.com required the company to develop new marketing strategies to acquire, retain, and cross-sell products through both the Internet and the desktop.

IMarket's objectives were twofold:

- To create a database that would provide a complete view of iMarket's customers and prospects, both those using the desktop and those using the Web.

- Set up a one-to-one automated marketing program that would enable the company to understand past behavior and the response to past promotions, and to gather new information through the Web.

These objectives had to take into account the fact that iMarket was a small company with limited in-house resources. Therefore, iMarket created an in-house customer and lead information database that was segmented using

- RFM analysis
- Logistic regressions based on business demographics
- Software that permitted the merging of records from different units of the same companies and the elimination of duplications from those records

The resulting segmentation system was used to create 10 meaningful RFM segments: Virtuoso, Prodigy, Student, Toddler, Precocious, Challenged, Infants, Newborn, Lost Opportunities, and Inactives. These segments are shown in Figure 10-1.

Figure 10-1 iMarket Prospect Segmentation System

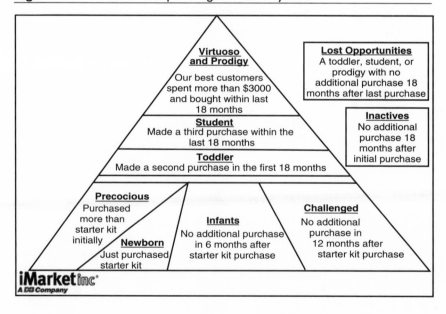

Table 10-10 Prospect Report

	Conversations		Messages		Responses to
	Total	Active	Sent	Opened	questions
Zap registrant surveys	5516	792	15	5	3
Zap registrant nonbuyers	300	207	209	50	10
Buyers invited to training	430	170	123	0	0
CSR survey	2195	142	772	368	149
Corporate billing contract usage	137	14	147	0	0

Automated marketing programs were set up to move customers into higher-value buying segments. The programs consisted of a large number of dialogs, which were directed and monitored by Revenio's Dialog software. A sample report is shown in Table 10-10.

The database provided the sales force automation software with lists of customers and prospects to contact, indicating the segment they were in as well as demographics and model scores and the prior history of all calls and contacts. The communications included a variety of different messages, such as:

- Welcome letter
- Welcome call
- Training fax
- Customer support survey
- Meter credit promotion
- Renewal fax
- Nonrenewal fax
- Upgrade promotions
- Inactive revival
- No-contact call

IMarket set up automated trigger marketing campaigns for the contacts in its database. These contacts had "raised their hands" by attending one of the company's seminars, registering at the company's Web site, responding to an ad, or visiting iMarket's booth at a trade show. Once they are in the database, the company markets to both leads and customers through phone, fax, and email. Customers can choose their preferred delivery medium.

The new database program was used to

- Eliminate duplicate records of customers and leads
  - Mailing costs were lowered.
  - Customers were no longer treated as leads.
  - Different salespeople were no longer assigned the same companies.
  - Fights between salespeople over leads were reduced, and commission payments were lower.
  - The entire company had increased confidence in the quality of the data.
- Have a unified view of customers across online and offline channels
  - There was a better understanding of customers' needs.
  - The sales force was now able to view the customer's entire history and sell more confidently.
  - Cross-selling opportunities increased.
  - Unified company reporting became available.
- Create automated marketing programs
  - Batch marketing was replaced by messages triggered by customer buying behavior.
  - The "traffic cop" feature prevented customers from receiving different messages at the same time.
  - Instead of being based on the marketing department's timetable, programs were based on customers' buying and demographic characteristics.
  - The number of programs run was no longer based on the number of marketers available, since the technology could add new programs easily.

As a result of the new system, iMarket

1. Increased its revenue by 50 percent per quarter and increased the value per customer by 35 percent per quarter for seven quarters in a row.
2. Decreased the cost of customer acquisition by 30 percent per quarter over seven quarters.

3. Reduced the marketing staff while creating 17 new programs that were executed daily.

Building Loyalty for a Lottery Program

Golden Casket Lottery Corporation Limited is a world leader in providing innovative lottery games. It has offered entertaining lotteries in Queensland, Australia, for 85 years and today operates the popular games of Wednesday and Saturday Gold Lotto, Oz Lotto, Powerball, The Pools, Casket, and an extensive range of Instant Scratch-Its tickets. The games are sold through an agency network of approximately 1150 retailers.

Golden Casket's loyalty program is called Winners Circle. The program has more than 1 million unique Winners Circle members, or 38 percent of the adult population of Queensland. Players use the Winners Circle card to register their Lotto purchases for the benefits of security (unclaimed prize checks are mailed to them), convenience (the card can store up to 20 sets of their favorite numbers), and reward (every $1 spent gives them another chance to win the weekly $10,000 bonus draw). The loyalty program captures 80 percent of all Lotto revenue and provides Golden Casket with invaluable marketing information. The gaming market in Queensland is very competitive, with scores of gaming options available—casinos, gaming machines, horse racing, sports betting, keno, and so on.

Analysis of Golden Casket's customer database showed that its approach to branding was eroding player loyalty. The brands were competing with one another for the same customers, which undermined player loyalty to the corporation as a whole. Golden Casket asked Acxiom to build computer models that would assist Golden Casket in building customer loyalty.

Acxiom built three customer models, which are now rescored every quarter. They are

- Future value model
    - Using a neural network, 2 years' worth of data, and 133 variables, Acxiom built a model that predicted the combined

future value of 96.2 percent of all customers on the database with 96.8 percent accuracy.
- Acxiom allocated the customers to low, medium, and high future value bands. Using these segments, Golden Casket:
  - Created a retention strategy for customers whose future value was likely to decrease.
  - Continued the current strategy for those whose future value was not likely to change.
  - Took a stronger focus to build a relationship with customers whose future value was likely to increase.
- Behavioral segmentation model
  - Acxiom clustered Golden Casket's customers within value bands.
  - Thirteen behavioral clusters emerged. Acxiom found that six of these variables accurately defined customer behavior:
    - The number of games played
    - The number of certificates used
    - Brand
    - The total amount spent
    - The number of games played per week
    - Methods of play chosen
  - This model told Golden Casket which customers could be influenced to move to a more desirable cluster.
- Cross-sell model
  - Using a neural network to track historical behavior, each customer was scored with a percentage probability of playing another of the seven games. Table 10-11 shows the way it worked (all names are fictional).
- Since Jane Smith is 95 percent likely to play Saturday Gold Lotto, the strategy is to reinforce her behavior. Trying to cross-sell other

Table 10-11 Lotto Results

	Likelihood of Playing These Games			
	Saturday Gold Lotto	Wednesday Gold Lotto	Tuesday Oz Lotto	Thursday Powerball
Jane Smith	95.0%	2.0%	2.0%	1.0%
John Brown	23.0%	25.0%	27.0%	25.0%
Pat Johnson	65.0%	31.0%	3.0%	1.0%

brands to Jane would waste marketing dollars, create annoyance, and undermine her loyalty.

- John Brown is a good candidate to purchase all brands. His behavior is always reinforced to retain his loyalty.
- Pat Johnson prefers Saturday Gold Lotto, but Golden Casket should try to cross-sell her on Wednesday Gold Lotto at every opportunity.

How the Program Worked in Practice

The entire loyalty program was restructured and relaunched around the cross-sell model. When players purchased an entry, each receipt gave them a chance to win a free surprise game instantly at the point of purchase. Which free game they could win was determined using the cross-sell model (e.g., Jane Smith would win a free Saturday Gold Lotto game, whereas Pat Johnson would win a Wednesday Gold Lotto game).

The terminals at the 1150 retailers were linked to the central Golden Casket database. When any of the 710,000 active Winners Circle players purchased an entry, a personal message was printed at the top of the lottery receipt. If the cross-selling model indicated that the player was likely to play Powerball, the message would promote Powerball.

The personal message was also used to alert flag players to outstanding prizes. Before this system, Golden Casket had mailed more than 10,000 checks a week, at a cost of $520,000 per year for the mailing alone. With the new system, special messages printed on the receipts alerted winners to their prizes, which could be claimed at the retail agent.

A screen message on the agent's terminal also used the cross-sell model on each customer, prompting the agent to either cross-sell the appropriate game or reinforce the customers' Winners Circle buying habit. If the player was to be cross-sold Powerball, the agent would be prompted to mention the Powerball jackpot for that week.

The cross-selling recommendation was put on the call center screens as well. When a player called, a screen would prompt the call center operator as to what game to suggest. The model was also used to develop direct-mail cross-selling offers. One example was a letter and promotional premarked certificate that was mailed to 50,000 players identified by the models. Of those who were sent the offer, 21 percent played the game identified by the certificate, compared to 1 percent of the control group (10 percent of the file). Interestingly, the promotional certificate was available in the store to the control group. Prior to using the model, Golden Casket averaged response rates of 10 to 12 percent. The company now consistently achieves direct-mail response rates of over 30 percent by using combinations of the models.

The Golden Casket Web site was upgraded to allow Winners Circle players access to their personal information. Players can check for outstanding prizes, update their details, and opt in and out of various offers such as, "Email me every time the Powerball jackpot reaches $5 million." Additionally, when a Winners Circle player visits online, the cross-selling table is used to populate the banner ad and promotional fields.

Selecting Media Using the Model

Every television program, radio program, newspaper, and magazine in Australia is profiled by the Roy Morgan research survey. The survey provides Australian companies that buy mainstream media with the Mosaic geodemographic profile of customers of each media type and program.

Golden Casket used the behavioral models to select target markets by media zone. These target segments are geodemographically profiled against the Roy Morgan survey to create a ranking that gives a "best fit" to "worst fit" portrait to assist Golden Casket in media buying. Using this system, Golden Casket determined that radio station B105 in the 9:00 a.m to noon hours was the best geodemographic match for a Powerball ad. For every 1 percent increase in media-buying effectiveness, Golden Casket was able to save about $100,000. This new approach changed the way Golden Casket bought advertising. The company determined that in regional areas, less expensive off-peak television could be purchased without compromising reach goals for specific brands.

Results of the New System

Golden Casket is now more focused on managing customer relationships. Instead of casting a wide net, customer models have enabled

Golden Casket to focus on customers who are more likely to purchase its products. The Web is used to reduce costs via self-answered queries, where normally it would cost Golden Casket more than $7 to answer each call. Web visits are virtually free.

Using the models has tripled Golden Casket's incremental revenue from direct mail with cell sizes of 50,000. It is anticipated that going to smaller cell sizes and using email will continue to increase these response rates.

Golden Casket's original rewards loyalty program was complex and generic, with an annual fee of $2. Only 486,000 of the 723,000 active players participated in the program. Using Acxiom's computer models, the rewards program was restructured and the annual fee was increased to $3. Additional features, including weekly $10,000 bonus drawings and surprise games, were added, and check fees were abolished. There are now 710,000 players participating in the program, and the relaunch generated $1.1 million in incremental income, which was equivalent to gross profit, as no cost of goods sold resulted from the change.

Overall, customer modeling and database marketing have allowed Golden Casket to be more targeted in its communication, to strengthen player loyalty, to increase the efficiency and effectiveness of media buying, and to reduce costs in the business.

Life Matters

Scotiabank, based in Toronto, Canada, launched an integrated one-to-one marketing program called Life Matters in a series of "waves" targeted at specific customer groups. Each wave of this program, which was the brainchild of Jonathan Huth, vice president, relationship database marketing, included a bundled marketing package with varying financial product offers. Customers were selected on the basis of their product holdings, credit criteria, and demographic data in Scotiabank's data warehouse plus predictive models. The initial direct-mail message was followed by a personal call from a branch officer or call center representative. The campaigns were supported through all possible channels, including direct mail; mass advertising through TV, newspapers, radio, and online; point-of-sale materials at branches; outbound telemarketing; and personal contact by branch personnel.

The Canadian consumer marketplace for financial products was highly competitive. Aggressive marketing by single-product "mono-lines," particularly credit cards, had increased the amount of near-junk mail that consumers were receiving. Capturing and increasing the scope of business from existing customers (rather than trying to acquire new customers) was the goal of the new program. The objectives of the new program were to:

- Increase bookings and profits from database marketing campaigns.
- Reduce the cost of campaign creation and mailings, and increase response rates.
- Automate multisegment and multichannel campaigns, while having the flexibility to implement rapid changes in design and targeting.
- Enable the database marketing group to manage entire closed-loop campaigns, including tests and controls and measurement of results.
- Make effective use of the bank's data warehouse.
- Bundle relevant offers in a single but varying package, reducing clutter for the customer and thus becoming more customer-focused.

The bank began the Life Matters campaign with a test of 50,000 customers to prove the concept. Response rates of 25 percent led to acceptance of the idea. As a result, several additional bank business lines asked to be included in the second wave.

The second wave was aimed at an additional 565,000 bank customers, divided into 60 test and control cells. The mailings were done in two drops to take call center capability into consideration. The third wave reached over 800,000 customers, divided into 750 cells. The fourth wave was also aimed at 800,000 customers, but they were divided into only 270 cells. This last wave included more sophisticated modeling that integrated each individual customer's propensity to purchase each of the products or services being offered within the package and the expected profitability of each new sale to the bank.

To illustrate the technique, in the Life Matters 2 campaign, the offers were the following:

- Each customer was offered a preapproved line of credit based on that customer's creditworthiness. Since these customers were preapproved, all they had to do was to accept the offer without further credit adjudication. The offers had credit limits ranging from $5000 to $15,000.
- Customers were invited to switch their deposit accounts from another financial institution automatically, with fees waived for 3 months.
- New term deposits were offered with different rate incentives, based on the profitability of the targeted customer.
- The wave tested different mortgage offers to determine which would pull the best.

Customers to be included in the program were pulled from the bank's data warehouse of over 6 million retail customers. The candidates were selected on the basis of an estimate of their need for the products included in the offer. In Life Matters 2, for example, customers who did not own the products being offered were selected. In Life Matters 4, the prime criterion for selection was the potential profitability of the account.

How the Campaign Changed the Bank's Marketing Approach

Prior to implementing Life Matters, the bank's database marketing campaigns had primarily been focused on a single product. It was possible for a customer to be repeatedly contacted with several product-centered offers that were sometimes confusing and frustrating. The new system allowed the bank to communicate with customers in a more customer-focused manner, while at the same time reducing the costs associated with running many single-product campaigns. Bundling the offers allowed the database marketing group to balance customer focus with the objectives of various product lines and channel capacity constraints for lead follow-up.

As a result of the lessons learned through the successive waves, the bank was able to develop complex campaigns approximately 25 to 40 percent faster than by using the previous SAS-based approach. Annual marketing program cost savings of approximately Can$3.5 million were achieved through eliminating separate product campaign mail and branch contact costs.

The cost and time savings enabled the database marketing team to execute campaigns for other divisions, such as Wealth Management, Insurance, and Small Business.

In total, 120 percent more marketing campaigns were run than had been run in the previous 12-month period, resulting in almost 9 million customer contacts—an increase of 180 percent. Life Matters campaigns yielded response rates of over 20 percent and produced an average return on investment of over 100 percent.

Profitable Use of Customer Data

The Union Bank of Norway (UBN) had 1 million customers and $25 billion in assets. During the last 20 years, as the bank had grown and become more automated, it had become clear that bank employees were not interacting directly with customers as often as they had been, which meant that the bank was losing touch with its customers' needs. The bank was still conducting traditional direct marketing programs with some success, its highest response rate being about 10 percent.

Since it operated multiple computer platforms with data scattered among the 175 branches, the bank could not easily gather and use customer-specific information. Getting a full view of a group of customers took days. Bank management wanted to store and access customer-specific information in a responsive, easy-to-use format. The goal was to improve revenue and margins through cross-selling and increasing customer use of its most profitable products.

To solve these problems, the bank turned to NCR's Teradata Division, installing a Teradata data warehouse in 1995 to capture and store all information about customers, including transactions going back 4 years and about 40 data elements from customer survey responses. In 1999, UBN added the Teradata CRM solution, a relationship optimization and campaign management application, for its events-based marketing initiative.

The Teradata system became the foundation for UBN's loyalty program and event-based marketing initiative. It helped the bank determine whom to contact, as it prioritized customers, looking at each customer and evaluating whether that customer needed to be contacted.

Events were detected by a set of business rules that searched the database nightly or weekly to determine if there had been any significant changes in a customer's life. For example, if a customer made a large deposit in a low-interest account, the system alerted a banker to contact the customer and let the customer know that he or she was losing money.

Before implementing its event-driven marketing approach, the bank was concerned that customers might be sensitive to the "Big Brother" effect. Customer feedback from the pilot program showed that the fears were unjustified and proved the relevancy of both the offer and the quality of the interactions.

Result of the New System

By using the data warehouse for direct marketing, UBN increased cross sales, measured against controls. The bank computed a payback period on the investment of less than 12 months. Compared to a previous 2 to 5 percent response rate, traditional campaigns using information in the data warehouse produced conversion rates of up to 40 percent. Loyalty programs gave UBN response rates of up to 70 percent. A pilot program for event-based marketing yielded conversion rates of up to 60 percent.

The 60 percent sales conversion rate includes the customer history picture provided by the new database. Some of those who were contacted did not express an immediate interest. Their response was recorded in the database. Later, the customer ended up purchasing the additional products from self-generated decisions or as a result of an automated follow-up. The new conversion rate represented an 1100 percent improvement over the bank's previous average close rate for direct marketing campaigns.

Dealing with Churn in Cellular Service

Cellular communications firms have been losing 2.9 percent of their customers each month, or up to 35 percent per year. In addition, companies have to disconnect many customers for nonpayment of bills. Disconnecting the wrong customer can translate into significant revenue losses, while keeping delinquent customers also affects profitability.

A wireless service provider was formed by combining the customers of 11 different companies within a short space of time. Its first job was to create a unified database covering the more than 20 million customers that had been in 11 different databases. Rather than waiting years for a data warehouse, the provider created an immediate temporary marketing data mart that combined the billing data from each company. This data mart was accessed by SAS products.

The data mart allowed managers in 35 different markets to analyze the data, giving each manager the ability to handle customer trends on a local level. Local managers could immediately address churn, instituting local incentives to keep customers or to rework their existing contract.

Examples of the tactics used to reduce churn were initiatives for:

- Rewarding customers by donating to the Special Olympics
- Reduced rates for particular customers
- A special deal on a new phone
- Free movie rentals at Blockbuster Video
- Price plans developed after analyzing customer behavior
- Phone trade-in programs

Overall, the wireless service provider wanted to know why customers were leaving, broken down by

- Amount of time with the company
- Minute use
- Price plan
- Thirty other specific market-level and company-level trends

Armed with these objectives, the wireless service provider reorganized its IT department and hired a dozen SAS programmers to construct a decision support system. When the temporary database was built, it installed several SAS products on its Sun Enterprise servers, including Enterprise Miner and AppDev Studio.

Results of the First Year

As a result of the analysis, the company reduced its churn rate significantly compared to a number of control groups selected to match each of the the test groups receiving the promotions. Even a 1 percent reduction in churn rates produced several million dollars in additional revenue. Several valuable lessons were learned:

- Old equipment turned out to be a top reason for churn. As a result, the company strengthened its trade-in program and allowed customers to get a new phone every time they signed a new contract.
- The database enabled the company to determine which delinquent customers should be kept and which should be dropped based on modeling and measuring the future profitability of each.
- The company was now able to make educated predictions about customer behavior, saving the company millions of dollars per year. Decision making no longer relied on educated guesses as to what would draw and hold customers, but was based on hard facts and figures that provided a detailed map for marketing strategies to follow when creating campaigns.

In the process of creating the database, the wireless service provider achieved some valuable benchmarks:

- Reports could now be produced in days instead of weeks, and reports that were previously impossible could now be created.
- The company could now produce both companywide and market-level analysis of customer behavior.
- New fields had been added to its database. These new fields gave the company the power to make better predictive decisions.
- Through customer profiling, the company was able to tailor messages to different customer groups more effectively.

Getting Customers to Join a Club

YourSport (a fictitious name for a real company) is an enterprise built around active sports participants and fans. The sports include, among others:

- Football and rugby
- Tennis and cricket
- Motor sports
- Skiing, sailing, and swimming
- Bicycling and boxing

To publicize and generate enthusiasm for these sports, YourSport broadcast sports events and maintained a very active Web site with news about sports on several continents in several languages. The Web site included news about teams, chat rooms, fan clubs, videos, TV schedules, and the ability to shop for clothing and equipment used in the sports or by fans.

YourSport established a club that allowed its members to chat with their favorite sports stars and get in touch with their favorite YourSport commentators through message boards. From newsletters to free email, members could create their own sports Web sites and stay tuned to the latest on-air action through the YourSport TV schedule. The club, which had a nominal one-time membership fee, proved to be a major marketing success.

YourSport had had a fulfillment database for many years, but it had no customer marketing database. It knew what its sales were, but it knew little about its customers and their behavior. This could be learned from a marketing database. To build and maintain its customer marketing database, Scott Andrews of YourSport turned to Karen Coolbaugh at CSC Advanced Database Solutions. The information maintained on this database enabled Scott to do some highly professional analytical work to determine the value of the YourSport customer. Scott had access to the database via the Web using the CSC-provided software Brio. Using this software, he was able to make some profitable marketing decisions.

Scott found several useful ways to segment YourSport customers:

- Sports team members and nonmembers together equal all buyers.
- Club members and nonmembers together equal all buyers.

By segmenting customers in this way, Scott was able to draw some valuable conclusions:

- Team and club members were very strong contributors who converted to multibuyer status at high rates regardless of time on the buyer file.
- In their first year, team buyers contributed at a rate that was five times that of nonteam buyers. Within the same time frame, club buyers contributed at a rate that was eight times that of non-club members.
- In the second year, team buyers again contributed at a rate that was five times that of their nonteam counterparts. Club members contributed at a rate that was 11 times better than that of their nonclub counterparts.
- YourSport recouped most of the $12 maximum investment to acquire a new buyer, on average, within the first 9 months of a buyer's first purchase. On the average, a buyer who was on file for 2 years contributed approximately $39.
- After being on file for 1 year, club members contributed $71, and team buyers contributed $89.
- Within 2 years of their first purchase, 81 percent of club members had converted to multibuyer status. In this same time frame, only 41 percent of the average customers converted to multibuyer status.
- Team and club buyers contributed roughly the same amount during their second year as they did during their first.

The difference between club or team members and nonmembers, shown in Table 10-12, was striking. In terms of conversion rates from one-time buyers to multibuyers, Figures 10-2 and 10-3 show how the team and club members ranked.

Table 10-12 Segment Performance during the Second Year

	Conversion percent	Orders per customer	Profit per customer
Team	75.6%	2.46	$169.34
Nonteam	43.4%	0.68	$18.09
Club	80.5%	2.32	$127.63
Nonclub	39.1%	0.43	$7.30

Figure 10-2 Team Performance in Conversion to Multibuyers

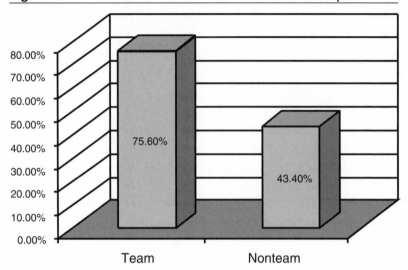

Resulting Marketing Decisions

The database permitted YourSport to determine the customer lifetime value of several customer segments using this same approach. With that information, the company was able to make strategic marketing decisions that were of great value to the enterprise. Included in these decisions were the following:

- Keep a maximum marginal investment in consumer lists of $12. Previously there had been no way to determine what that maximum would be.
- Set the maximum marginal investment in team-specific marketing efforts at $30.
- Since club members were so valuable, provide incentives to increase club membership, whereas previously, there had been no incentives.
- Send targeted emails to people who were not club members, encouraging them to join.
- Add membership rewards, such as travel benefits, to the club to encourage increased membership.

Figure 10-3   Club Performance in Conversion to Multibuyers

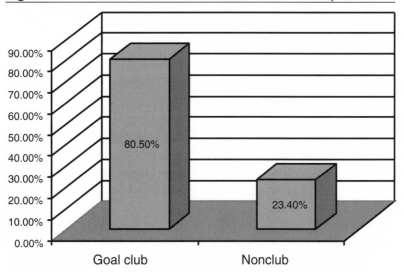

Additional Analytical Steps

Any good marketing initiative, such as the customer value study, always leads not only to marketing recommendations, but also to ideas for further analysis. This study suggested analysis of

- Purchasers by products bought in the first order
- Purchasers by brand of merchandise
- Multichannel buying behavior
- The value of incentive purchases
- LTV by region of the world and within U.S. markets
- Multicompany and multisport purchasers

The Value of the Database

Today YourSport is miles ahead of its position before CSC built its customer marketing database. It understands its customers better, and it has been able to use that knowledge to increase sales, cross sales, and retention. The database has paid for itself many times over.

What Works

- Using the 80 percent rule to simplify customer management
- Using risk/revenue analysis to concentrate on the key 44 percent of your customers
- Capturing and using email names at every step in your customer communications programs
- Determining the possible improvements in conversion rates before you waste money on any customer management program
- Creating a simple, understandable system for putting customers into segments (such as those used by iMarket, Golden Casket, and Scotiabank) and using these segments to guide your customer management program
- Where possible, using an event-driven approach to customer management such as that used by Union Bank of Norway
- Running your customer management programs based on the segment that customers are in, rather than on some overall marketing plan that does not take customer status into account

What Doesn't Work

- Building a warehouse for 100 percent of your customers
- Trying to manage 100 percent of your customers
- Trying to operate without a customer database
- Managing a communications program today without emails
- Launching a customer management program without first determining the benefits and costs
- Providing customer management benefits to all customers equally, rather than to specific segments

Quiz

1. Using the 80 percent rule, you should
   a. Concentrate on the top 80 percent of your customers.
   b. Clean up 80 percent of your files first.

    c. Get rid of the bottom 20 percent of your customers.

    d. Build a data warehouse.

    e. Do none of the above.

2. You should spend your marketing resources on those customers who (best answer)

    a. Are most likely to defect.

    b. Have the highest LTV.

    c. Are priority B.

    d. Are not priority C.

    e. Have the highest LTV and the lowest likelihood of defecting.

3. Which of the following was not a feature of the iMarket customer management program?

    a. Welcome letter

    b. Renewal fax

    c. Birthday cards

    d. RFM analysis

    e. Customer support survey

4. The 13 Golden Casket behavioral clusters were defined by all but which of the following?

    a. Total amount spent

    b. Methods of play

    c. Number of certificates used

    d. Brand

    e. Geographic region

5. What was the most important key to Golden Casket's success?

    a. The cross-sell model

    b. The Powerball

    c. The Winner's Circle

    d. Gold Lotto

    e. The Oz Lotto

6. Which were not among the results that Golden Casket achieved by using the new modeling system?

    a. The annual fee was raised.

    b. The company received $1.1 million in incremental revenue.

    c. The number of active players increased by 234,000.

    d. Many customers were driven to use the Web.

    e. Brand managers fought over the more profitable customers.

7. As a result of the Life Matters program all but which of the following happened?
   a. Thirty-five percent more marketing campaigns were run in a 9-month period.
   b. Customers were ranked by RFM with a maximum score of 125.
   c. Annual marketing program savings were $3.5 million.
   d. There were 10 million customer contacts in 9 months, an increase of 25 percent.
   e. There were 48,000 new accounts opened.

8. In the Bank of Norway case study, all but which of the following resulted?
   a. The bank added 2000 new total customers each month.
   b. There was a 60 percent conversion rate.
   c. The new database produced responses of 70 to 80 percent.
   d. There was an 1100 percent increase in the bank's conversion rate.
   e. The payback period for the database investment was 12 months.

9. The company rewarded its customers with
   a. Phone trade-in
   b. Donations to the Special Olympics
   c. Free movie rentals
   d. Price plans based on customer behavior
   e. All of the above

10. The company's benchmarks from the program included all but which of the following?
   a. Reports produced in a few weeks
   b. Market-level analysis possible
   c. Messages that could be tailored to customer segments
   d. New fields added to the database
   e. Fields that permitted it to make predictive decisions

CHAPTER 11

LETTING THEM COME
BEHIND THE COUNTER

*Tupperware used to be sold through neighborhood parties. They were
fun. You saw everyone in the neighborhood, and you got the opportunity
to buy some kitchen storage containers that you couldn't buy in stores.*

*There is an old story about a Tupperware salesman who was all
thumbs. He arrived at a party with a big box of Tupperware products
and a catalog, but he did not seem to know his business. He took each
item out of the box and could not remember its name or its price, or
even what it was used for. He was an embarrassment to the group.
After watching him flounder around for about 10 minutes, members
of the party began to help him. They took items out of his box, looked
them up in his catalog, and figured out the prices for him. Soon, everyone in the room was assisting this helpless man. By the time the party
was over, the man had sold more Tupperware than most salesmen sold
in a week. In fact, this was his standard method of operation. He always
appeared befuddled. He sold Tupperware by getting customers involved.*

That is what is happening today on the Web. Instead of the standard "We demonstrate, you watch," companies are learning to
let customers come behind the counter and figure things out for
themselves. In many cases, this is proving highly profitable.

There has always been a distance between suppliers and customers.
This distance is typified by the counter. The clerk stands on one side,
ready to answer questions and ring up sales. You stand on the other

side waiting for service. You are not supposed to invade the clerk's space. All of this is changing with the Web.

The Web permits customers to get instant access to lots of information that previously was available only through telephone calls or personal visits. Federal Express was one of the first to start this with its package tracking system. Today, anyone can enter a FedEx package number on the FedEx Web site and instantly find out what has happened to the package at each point in its journey. Before FedEx had this Web site, you could call a FedEx operator and get the same information—in fact, you can still do that today. But by going to the Web, you can get the information faster, you never get put on hold, and you can print out all the information on your PC printer. It is a wonderful system for the customer. How is it for FedEx? It is a huge cost saving. Toll-free calls to operators cost companies between $2 and $7 per call, including the cost of the call and the cost of the operator. Web visits cost absolutely nothing once the system is set up and running.

Super Customer Service

You hear people saying that no one is making money on the Web, but that's not quite true. Few companies are profiting from sales to consumers over the Web, but hundreds of companies are *saving money* and *building customer relationships* through customer service on the Web. These functions generate more profits than all direct Web consumer sales put together.

Marketing and customer service are usually separate departments within a company. They have separate goals and methods. However, that situation is changing because of the realization that good customer service leads to higher levels of retention and sales. There are several factors driving this change:

- Industry has discovered the value of loyal customers. They buy more, buy more often, are cheaper to serve, have higher retention rates, and are more profitable than newly acquired customers.
- Marketers have discovered that there are two methods that it can use to influence the level of customer loyalty: recruiting the right

kind of customers to begin with, and treating them very well once they are acquired.

• Excellent customer care is the most important method for improving customer loyalty. Customer service personnel are the front-line troops in the battle to win customers' loyalty.

• To provide good customer care, customer contact personnel have to be empowered with information and the authority to make decisions and to act on the customer's behalf.

In other words, marketing is no longer a matter of thinking up clever advertising and direct-mail pieces. Good marketing involves everyone in the company who has contact with customers. Marketing and customer service are coming together.

Customers Are Not All Alike

Some customer service advocates say, "We will give super service to all of our customers." This is a lofty sentiment, but a bad idea. Companies are learning that we must not treat all customers alike, because customers are not all alike. Some are loyal and put all their trust in us. Others are indifferent and spend most of their money elsewhere. Many customers not only are not profitable but cost us money and will never be profitable. Figure 11-1 repeats the graph of the customers of a southern bank that was shown in Chapter 1.

Why should we spend money trying to retain customers who are robbing the company of value and hurting the enterprise? What we really want to do is provide super service to the top two segments so that we can retain them. They are the lifeblood of the enterprise. We want to give them services that we could not possibly afford to provide to everyone. If we limited our services to those things that we could afford to give everyone, the services would be so meager that they would be meaningless to the recipients and useless for influencing loyalty.

So what are the rules for successful customer service programs?

• *Provide good information.* Customer service reps (CSRs) must have access to the customer marketing database. They must know what

Figure 11-1   Profitability

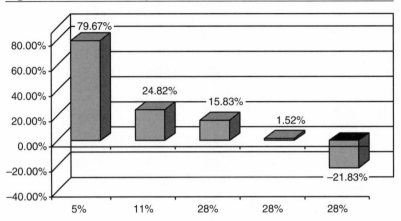

each customer has bought in the past and each customer's profitability. They must have a record of past complaints and compliments. They must know who the key people are in each firm and what those people's opinions about the CSR's company and its products are.

- *Empower customer service.* If customer service personnel are just message takers, people will not unburden themselves to them. Customer service personnel have to represent your firm. They must be able to do what the owner of the firm would do: make decisions that are in the interest of both the customer and the firm. They must be delegated the authority to act to solve problems.
- *Set up test and control groups.* Good customer service is not just nice to have. It can be highly profitable. However, you must prove to management that the money spent on customer service is creating customer loyalty and profits for the firm. The only way that can be done is to set up control groups so that you can measure the performance of the test groups correctly. Many executives will oppose the creation of control groups, saying, "We must treat all customers alike." Fight this old-fashioned way of thinking with all your might. Without control groups, you can never prove that what you are doing is having the desired effects and justifies your enlarged customer service budget.

Along Comes the Web

Customer service, however, is expensive. With thousands of calls per day at a cost of $2 to $7 per call, companies have seen a significant drain on their bottom line. Customer lifetime value analysis must be used to determine whether the helpfulness and relationship building is worth the cost. In some cases, companies have found that it was not paying its way. Most banks that have done profitability analyses have discovered that about half of their customers are unprofitable. A good part of the reason for the lack of profits can be traced to the expense of customer service. When Federal Express started the system that enabled customer reps to field questions on the exact status of every package shipped at any time, it was wonderful. But it came at a significant cost. If every customer called to learn the status of his or her shipments, all shipments would cost at least $2 more than they do. Using the Web has saved this money.

The Internet Saves the Day

The Internet is gradually replacing the customer service rep. Instead of paying for the cost of a toll-free call and the salary of a customer service rep who reads information off a computer screen, companies are learning that their customers can look at that same screen directly on the Internet and get the answers themselves. What's more, customers like it better. What is the saving produced by fielding a call on the Web instead of on the phone? Between $2 and $7 per call. Banks are discovering the saving from the Internet. Transactions on the phone with a live operator cost banks $2 or more. Those on the Web cost about a penny each.

The big savings, however, come from inviting customers to come into your company to read the same screens that your employees read. Customers become part of your company family. This is real relationship marketing.

Every business-to-business company in America (or in the world, for that matter) can profit by opening up its internal company data and making them available to customers on the Web. There are three reasons for this:

1. The Web site will probably pay for itself in savings on toll-free calls and operator time.
2. It may increase sales to new prospects (although that is not a sure thing).
3. It provides a way to recognize and build relationships with customers that will improve loyalty and retention.

Who is doing this? Customers use Dell Computer's Web site to check their order status 50,000 times per week. The same calls to Dell's customer service reps would cost Dell $200,000 per week. Dell also saves several million dollars per year by encouraging 200,000 customers per week to make their troubleshooting inquiries through the Web.

Customer Service on the Web

Amazon showed us the way: "Welcome back, Arthur. If you're not Arthur, click here." This is wonderful one-to-one marketing. Many companies have copied this method. They are finding that it works. It is what the old corner grocer used to do. He stood at the entrance to his store and said, "Hello, Mrs. Williams. How's your daughter taking to Radcliffe?"

Most large companies today are spending millions of dollars on customer service. Hundreds of CSRs are answering customers' questions and selling products. Many of the CSRs' functions can be performed by a good Web site. Look at the work of a CSR. She takes scores of incoming calls per day. She has a computer linked to the company's main server. As customers ask her questions, she manipulates her mouse and her keyboard to get the answers on her screen. Then she reads the answers to the customers over the phone. She gives information, and she takes orders. A typical call to a CSR costs $6.50. In most cases, a really good Web site can replace a high percentage of the CSRs' functions. The method is to give the customers the same access to the company server that the CSR has. Figure 11-2*a* shows what is happening now, and Figure 11-2*b* shows the new system.

Figure 11-2   Elimination of the CSR. (*a*) Current system. (*b*) New system.

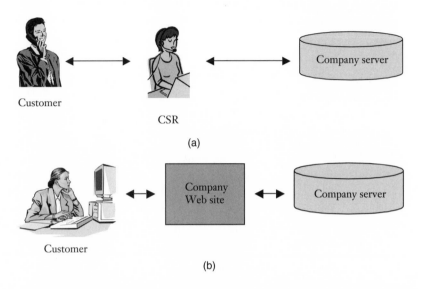

Customer

CSR

Company server

(a)

Customer

Company Web site

Company server

(b)

With the new system, we have eliminated the CSR and the telephone call. Instead, customers using the Web site see the same information that the CSRs see. They place the same orders, using the same credit cards. One company was spending almost $50 million per year on CSR functions. It was fielding 6 percent of its queries on the Web. A consultant estimated that if the company could raise the percentage of its CSR work that was going to the Web site to 30 percent over a 3-year period, assuming a 15 percent annual growth rate, it could save more than $20 million per year in 3 years. That is the promise of the Web. These are numbers that go right to the bottom line.

Profits like this can come about only if customers will use the Web instead of calling a CSR. How can you get them to do that?

- The Web site has to be as good as or better than the services provided by a CSR. Study what your CSRs are doing and saying. Design your Web site to do the same thing, but then go one step further. Provide customers with lookup functions that are more sophisticated than anything that a CSR could do.
- The Web site has to be publicized so that your customers know about it.

- The Web site has to be personalized. It has to have the same friendly personal relationship that a good CSR has. Amazon doesn't say, "Welcome back, Arthur" just because it is a neat thing to say. Amazon says it because it keeps Arthur coming back.
- The Web site has to have a live agent function. Studies show that 74 percent of Web shopping carts are abandoned at checkout. The reason is that at the last minute, people have questions that the Web site doesn't answer. You have to put a button on your Web site that provides a text chat with a live agent. CSRs can handle four text chats at once. This software is provided by several companies, including www.liveperson.com.

Once your Web site is as good as a CSR, you can measure your success by the percentage of your customer service queries made and orders taken on the Web rather than by a live agent.

The Web is not a panacea. It will support but never replace direct mail, catalogs, retail stores, malls, brand names, TV, newspapers, magazines, radio, and books. It can be a very important channel, but only if the company already has other profitable channels for sales that the Web will supplement. You can profit from the Web, but you have to look in the right place.

Premier Pages

Dell began putting its marketing and technical information on the Web in 1994. By 1996, customers could come to the Dell Web site, configure the computer they wanted, and place an order. However, the orders came to Dell as emails. Dell had to retype them into its ordering system! In 1998 the company introduced Premier Pages, which let business customers tailor what their employees could see and order. Today, the Dell system is all electronic. Seventy percent of Dell's sales are business to business.

In many cases, Dell negotiated volume prices for its best customers. The way it works is this: A deal is worked out between Dell and the purchasing officer at the target company. Dell agrees to provide the Web page and a volume-pricing deal. The purchasing officer agrees to give the special address of this Dell Web page to all employees who want to buy computer products. It takes Dell only 30 minutes to create a new Premier Page for a new business customer.

When an employee comes to the site, he registers as being an employee and purchases whatever he needs, providing the Dell site with the purchase order number. Every month the purchasing officer gets a report from Dell showing which of her employees have made purchases and what they have bought. She has complete information about what her firm is buying from Dell, who is buying it, and what each employee bought. These reports are very useful for a purchasing department. They also show the savings that the company has made through its volume deal with Dell. Dell has set up tens of thousands of these business-to-business pages. They give Dell a tremendous advantage in business sales. Today, all of Dell's competitors are copying the system and are trying to catch up.

The Dell system gives the business customer a lot of information. Dell has put 54,000 pages of service information on the Web, and this can be accessed by any customer at any time. The Premier Page lets the customer know where any given system is in the production process. Dell prepares for the order's arrival by sending shipment information automatically by email. Once the system arrives, the customer can troubleshoot and upgrade it online.

Getting companies to use the Dell Premier Page system is not always easy. When Dell tried to get Eastman Chemical to use a Dell Premier Page for ordering, Eastman at first refused, saying it was too much work. The company had its own internal ordering system and preferred to send Dell a fax of the order. In response, Dell revised the site for Eastman to make it conform to Eastman's system. Eastman now uses the Dell site for its computer orders.

There are many advantages to Dell from its Web ordering system. Dell's statistics show that without a Premier Page it takes five phone calls from prospects before the company gets an actual order. The first phone calls are for information and prices. But if the prospects use the Web site first, Dell finds that it can sell products on the first phone call. As a result, Dell's profits on Web sales are 30 percent higher than its profits on other sales.

Once the site is established, Dell uses the tracking information to increase sales. At one point, an IS director checked networking equipment on his Dell site. He did not buy. The next week, a Dell salesperson called this IS director (based on the Web statistics) to see if she could help the IS director with his networking purchases. The basis of satisfactory customer relationships is knowledge, and the use of that knowledge for helpful communications. Without the Web visit, how would the salesperson have known that she should call on the IS director to discuss networking equipment? This is effective use of the Web.

Letting the Supplier Come behind the Counter

We have been talking as if the Web facilitates marketing communications between customer and supplier, which it does. But there is another vital relationship that is also made possible by the Web. You can invite your suppliers to come behind the counter as well.

In *Strategic Database Marketing*, I described the super service that the Marriott Hotels Web site provides to professional meeting planners. A meeting planner who logs on to this site can find all the Marriott hotels in any given area, indexed by the services offered. When the planner picks out a hotel, she can see how many conference rooms are available and their capacity, and she can see a picture of the hotel and a map showing its location. Most of this information cannot easily be described on the telephone. When you see it on your PC in living color, you can print it out and carry it around. That is super customer service. In Chapter 12 I report that Lands' End discovered that customers who filled out a personal description of their bodies were 70 percent more likely to make a purchase than other Web visitors. Getting customers involved, as the Tupperware salesman did, is the route to customer loyalty and sales.

So, what should you do? What is your role in the new economy? Everyone who is reading this book has either customers or customers of clients who could be helped by letting them come behind the counter. What are the advantages?

- Customers become more loyal if they look up what they need themselves.
- The costs to the supplier are lower than the costs of the traditional ordering system. You eliminate the customer service reps, the phone calls, and the manual typing of orders.
- Errors in ordering are reduced, since a well-designed Web site provides a picture of the product being ordered and the correct part number.

How Difficult Is It to Set Up Such a System?

Let's start with what we know. Every company in America has put its inventories and its technical information on computers. This has happened in the last 20 years. These data are available to company employees using PCs or mainframe terminals. In most midsized or larger companies today, authorized employees can look up almost anything and see it on a computer screen.

The next step may cost some money, but it is definitely achievable. Get a programmer to make the data on the screens available to customers through the Web. Set up a microsite that major customers can access using a PIN and a password. Make the site user-friendly, following the three-click rule: Everything that anyone would want to see on the site should be available in three clicks of a mouse. To do this, you have to think like a customer: What would I, as a customer, want to see on this site? Then design the site with that in mind.

Work with your customers to design the site. Make getting information and ordering very easy. Set up their accounts so that they can get information free and parts or services, which they have to pay for, with one click (see Figure 11-3 for an example). Amazon is a master at this technique. Amazon lets its customers look up all their past purchases through the Web. I have bought so many books from Amazon that I sometimes cannot remember what I have bought. In three clicks, I can find out all the books and videos that I have ever bought from Amazon, including the prices I paid and the dates I bought them.

Figure 11-3   One-Click Ordering

Browse Ordering via 1-Click

- 1-Click Default Address
- 1-Click Settings
- 1-Click Technical Troubleshooting
- Reviewing & Changing 1-Click Orders
- Sending Gifts With 1-Click
- Shipment Consolidation
- Turning 1-Click On & Off
- Using 1-Click at Public Terminals

I looked up my most recent book, *Strategic Database Marketing,* 2nd edition, on the Amazon.com site. In addition to the price and a picture of the cover, there was a summary of the book, 43 sample pages that visitors could read and print, nine reviews of the book, and a Sales Rank Number: 5744. Amazon ranks the sales of all books daily, from 1 to 1,000,000 or more. In addition, Amazon reported that my book was selling very well to employees of NCR, the makers of Teradata computers. What bookstore could possibly provide such interesting and valuable information?

Set up reports so that you can know on a daily, weekly, and monthly basis which customers are visiting your sites, what they do there, and what they buy there. Design the reports so that your customers can see them as well, print them on their PC printers, or download them into their own reporting systems.

Once you have a system set up, how do you get customers to use it? After all, most of them are happy calling your operators on a toll-free line and wasting your money. Why would they change? Why would they go to the Web to get information or to order from you? People do what is in their own best interest, not what is in your best interest. You have to give them some kind of incentive. What are the ways of doing this?

- For business-to-business operations, work with the purchasing officer at each customer site. Offer these purchasing officers a deal that they cannot refuse: If they will persuade their employees to use the site, you will give the company a volume price break.

- Provide monthly reports to the purchasing officer telling her what her employees are buying.
- Put the purchasing officers on an advisory panel. Invite them to come to Hawaii with you once a year to discuss business. You figure it out. There is some good way to make it worth their while.
- If your site is for consumers, you have to come up with relevant incentives. The way to start is to figure what you get out of the system and share some of the proceeds with your customers.

When the site is ready, you will need to send an email to all your customers like the ones that Boeing uses:

> *To provide more value and better service to our customers, we have developed a way to use the sophisticated technology of the World Wide Web to give customers direct access to our extensive part information and ordering system. You can now order parts and view part information through a new World Wide Web site called the Boeing Part Analysis & Requirement Tracking (PART) Page*

How do you justify such a system to your management? The software costs are not trivial. Let's try some numbers. What would it cost to let your customers come behind the counter? Table 11-1 gives some sample one-time costs.

This assumes that your products, services, and technical data are already in electronic form. If they are, $400,000 should enable you to set up a Web microsite to which customers with an ID and password could come to see your products and place orders. The reporting software would provide Web reports to the customers. Promotion is the money needed to let customers know about the system so that they will

Table 11-1 One-Time Costs

Web access software	$400,000
Reporting software	$ 20,000
Promotion	$ 30,000
Total	$450,000

use it. If we amortize the cost of the new system over 3 years and add in the operating costs, the results look something like Table 11-2.

Let's suppose that you have a business-to-business company with several thousand customers but that you apply the costs of the new system only to your best 1000 customers. We will charge the total cost of the system against these best customers, even though many others will probably use it. Table 11-3 gives the base lifetime value of these 1000 customers before we introduce the new system.

On average, each of these 1000 best customers spends $28,000 per year with you. It costs $400 to acquire each of these customers, and you are spending $50 per year on marketing costs to maintain relationships with them. After 3 years, the LTV is over $16,000.

If the new system is successful, it will create two changes in customer behavior. Those who adopt the new system will be more loyal. The retention rate will rise from 70 percent to 75 percent. In addition,

Table 11-2 Yearly Costs

Costs	Month	Year
Site maintenance	$ 4,000	$ 48,000
Amortization of one-time cost	$12,500	$150,000
System management	$ 6,000	$ 72,000
Total	$22,500	$270,000

Table 11-3 Base LTV

	Year 1	Year 2	Year 3
Retention rate	70%	75%	80%
Customers	1,000	700	525
Annual spending	$28,000	$29,000	$30,000
Revenue	$28,000,000	$20,300,000	$15,750,000
Costs	70%	68%	67%
Operating costs	$19,600,000	$13,804,000	$10,552,500
Acquisition cost ($400)	$ 400,000		
Marketing cost ($50)	$ 50,000	$ 35,000	$ 26,250
Total costs	$20,050,000	$13,839,000	$10,578,750
Profit	$7,950,000	$6,461,000	$5,171,250
Discount rate	1.10	1.19	1.28
NPV of profit	$7,227,273	$5,429,412	$4,040,039
Cumulative NPV of profit	$7,227,273	$12,656,684	$16,696,724
Lifetime value	$7,227.27	$12,656.68	$16,696.72

the average spending rate will increase from $28,000 to $29,000. These are not unreasonable assumptions. The new lifetime value is shown in Table 11-4.

Assuming that you replace the lost customers as they disappear, the 3-year payoff rate for the new system for your 1000 best customers will look like Table 11-5. The 3-year result would be a net profit of almost a million dollars, after deducting the costs of the upgraded Web site.

Boeing Spare Parts

Idle airplanes cost airlines thousands of dollars per hour. How many times have you sat in an airplane waiting for engineers to replace some

Table 11-4 Improved LTV with New System

	Year 1	Year 2	Year 3
Retention rate	75%	80%	85%
Customers	1,000	750	600
Annual spending	$29,000	$30,000	$31,000
Revenue	$29,000,000	$22,500,000	$18,600,000
Costs	70%	68%	67%
Operating costs	$20,300,000	$15,300,000	$12,462,000
Acquisition cost ($400)	$ 400,000		
Marketing cost ($50)	$ 50,000	$ 37,500	$ 30,000
Web site costs	$ 270,000	$ 270,000	$ 270,000
Total costs	$21,020,000	$15,607,500	$12,762,000
Profit	$7,980,000	$6,892,500	$5,838,000
Discount rate	1.10	1.19	1.28
NPV of profit	$7,254,545	$5,792,017	$4,560,938
Cumulative NPV of profit	$7,254,545	$13,046,562	$17,607,500
Lifetime value	$7,254.55	$13,046.56	$17,607.50

Table 11-5 Gain from Changes

	Year 1	Year 2	Year 3
New LTV	$7,254.55	$13,046.56	$17,607.50
Old LTV	$7,227.27	$12,656.68	$16,696.72
Difference	$ 27.27	$ 389.88	$ 910.78
For 1000 customers	$27,273	$389,878	$910,776

malfunctioning part? Did you ever wonder where all the parts used at the hundreds of airfields that our planes fly out of in the United States come from? One missing $50 part can cost an airline thousands of dollars. But airlines cannot afford to keep every possible part at every possible airport from which their planes fly. The answer is to have quick access to spare parts from the manufacturer.

For many years, Boeing had a customer service parts-ordering system with operators standing by 24 hours a day. Each operator had a computer terminal that helped him to locate the needed parts for his frantic customers. It was not easy. There are 2000 suppliers of parts for Boeing airplanes. There is competition. There are Asian suppliers who make replacements for most of the parts in Boeing planes. Spare parts for Boeing airplanes are a $7 billion per year business, and Boeing wants to get as much of that business as it can. So, several years ago, Boeing decided to let its customers come behind the counter. It gave its customers the same access to spare parts that its employees have. Boeing's Airline Logistics Support organization is now an integral part of Boeing's customer support operation.

Airline customers can log on to the Boeing customer support Web site with a PIN and have access to 400,000 parts in Boeing warehouses in Seattle, Atlanta, Los Angeles, Singapore, London, Dubai, and Amsterdam. The airline customer can find where her needed part is located, place her order without human intervention, and, if necessary, send a driver over to pick up the part.

The Boeing Spares organization was the first to offer spares ordering on the World Wide Web. Now more than 600 customers access the Boeing PART Page (see Figure 11-4). Boeing provides its customers with routine, next-day shipment of spares. The Spares organization also offers the Global Airline Inventory Network, an exclusive service in which Boeing manages an airline's supply chain for expendable airframe spare parts. The network is designed to eliminate costly inventory inefficiencies.

Industry studies indicate that for every $1 of spare parts inventory, airlines spend an additional 35 cents on inventory holding and materials management costs. Designed to attack these inefficiencies and costs, the new Boeing system provides both airlines and their suppliers with a more efficient supply chain.

Figure 11-4   The Boeing Global Airline Inventory Network

Here's how the Boeing system works:

- Boeing takes responsibility for purchasing, inventory management, and logistics for their airline customers' expendable airframe parts.
- All airframe parts are forward-deployed by Boeing at or near the airline's point of use. That means that the parts are stored either in a Boeing partner's warehouse or actually at one of the airline customer's parts departments.
- Boeing and other suppliers own these airframe parts until they are actually used. An airline pays for parts only as it uses them. This significantly reduces the airline's inventory holding costs.
- A supply chain management system serves as the "command center" for the network, monitoring the parts use of customer airlines and allowing suppliers to better forecast demand and plan production accordingly.
- The existing Boeing spare parts distribution system, with seven regional distribution centers around the world, is the backbone of the network. In addition to Boeing's proprietary parts, these distribution centers stock many of the other 2000 suppliers' parts, creating a single parts-distribution channel.

This system helps airlines reduce costs and frees up significant amounts of capital that were formerly tied up in inventory. It enables suppliers to benefit from the efficiencies that come from better demand forecasting and using a single distribution channel.

A Word of Caution

The systems described in this chapter may not work for your situation. The payoffs from letting customers behind the counter can come only if

- The customers actually want to come behind the counter and will use your new Web site to do so.
- The customers gain something that is of value to them from using your new system.
- The costs of setting up the system are not too high in relation to the payback. Some companies have spent millions of dollars on such systems with no hope of payback. Boeing's system was very, very expensive. But the company was building market share in a $7 billion market.
- The system will have a measurable impact on your customers' retention and spending rates. How can you know that? You must run little tests to find out.
- You have tested everything on a small scale before you make big mistakes.

What Works

- For every piece of information that you have stored in your company computers, figure out if it would be of interest to some of your customers. If so, find a way to let them access this information directly on the Web without human intervention. Let them come behind the counter.
- Set up special Web sites for your best customers. Provide reports to your customers on what they are buying and who is buying it.
- Provide volume-pricing arrangements to induce your customers to use your new Web site for ordering.

- Before you do anything, use the tables in this chapter to determine whether your new system will be profitable. If it will be, use these tables to sell your concept to your management.

What Doesn't Work

- Setting up a Web site for customer access without talking to your customers first to determine whether they would use it.
- Setting up such a system without first working out the LTV charts that show what profit you could make from the system. Many, if not most, such systems will not be profitable.
- Spending too much on a software system without first testing the concepts on a small scale.

Quiz

1. What was the point of the Tupperware story?
   a. Befuddled salesmen are the best.
   b. Customers like to participate in the selling process.
   c. Tupperware is no longer successful with parties.
   d. You should run parties to sell products.
   e. None of the above.
2. Why provide customer service over the Web?
   a. It saves millions of dollars.
   b. Customers never get put on hold.
   c. You can provide data and pictures that are unavailable in any other way.
   d. You can build loyalty.
   e. All of the above.
3. Which of the following is not one of the rules for successful customer service?
   a. Provide good information.
   b. Empower the CSR agents.
   c. Set up test and control groups.

    d. Eliminate toll-free calls so that people must use the Web.

    e. None of the above; they are all rules for successful customer service.

4. Which of the following is not one of the rules for successful Web customer service?

    a. The Web site must be as good as or better than a CSR.

    b. The Web site must be publicized.

    c. The Web site must be personalized.

    d. You must have a live agent function.

    e. None of the above; they are all rules for successful Web customer service.

5. Which of the following is not a feature of the Dell Premier Pages system?

    a. Vendor-managed inventory

    b. Monthly reports

    c. IDs and passwords

    d. Volume-pricing discounts

    e. 30-minute setup time

6. What does "forward deployed" mean in the Boeing parts case?

    a. The parts are owned by Boeing customers.

    b. The parts are warehoused in customers' warehouses.

    c. The text does not make this clear.

    d. Boeing does not know where the parts are.

    e. None of the above.

7. Which of the following is not one of the advantages of letting customers come behind the counter?

    a. Customers become more loyal.

    b. Costs are lower.

    c. Customers like it better.

    d. Errors are reduced.

    e. More CSRs are needed.

8. Prepare a 3-year lifetime value table for a business-to-consumer supplier who has a retention rate of 45 percent, 55 percent, 65 percent; a cost ratio of 65 percent, 62 percent, 60 percent; an average sale of $60, $65, $70 per visit; visits per year of 2.1, 2.5, 2.8; an interest rate of 8 percent; a risk factor of 1.5; an acquisition cost of $46; and an original number of customers of 200,000.

9. Prepare a revised table showing a 4 percent increase in the retention rate, an increase in the number of visits per year of 0.4, and a $4 increase in the average spending per visit. Spend $8 per customer per year on marketing to achieve these results.

10. Using the previous two tables, prepare a table showing the gains or losses from the new marketing program in Question 9, assuming that the company continues to have 200,000 customers.

CHAPTER 12

CAN DATABASE MARKETING WORK FOR CATALOGERS?

Catalogs are the fastest-growing and most profitable direct marketing method in use today. The old Sears Roebuck and Montgomery Ward big books are gone forever. But what has replaced them are 16 billion small specialized catalogs that are mailed each year to millions of U.S. households. Why are catalogers succeeding today?

- *Lightning-fast fulfillment.* Remember "allow 6 to 8 weeks for delivery"? Who can stay in business today saying that? Many catalogers today even offer next-day service. That means that they have streamlined their warehouses and have UPS and FedEx trucks constantly backed up to their doors.
- *Massive exchange of names.* North America is about the only place in the world where you can rent the names of mail-order buyers. In almost every other country in the world, marketers hold customer names in an Al Gore "lock box." Helena, my wife, is an avid catalog shopper. She gets from six to ten catalogs a day, all year long. She loves them—she reads every page of every catalog as if they were novels. As soon as she places an order, the cataloger immediately rents her name to dozens of other catalogers, who rush to fill our mailbox. Without this universal name exchange, the U.S. catalog industry as we know it would soon die.
- *Universally available credit cards.* Not only do all catalogers depend on them, but all consumers have them. Just about every American family receives at least two credit card solicitations per week.

What does this mean for the catalogers? Financial success. The problem of getting paid for products has almost disappeared.

- *Sophisticated telesales.* Today's call center software is one of the most complex aspects of cataloging. Millions of agents staff centers on a 24/7 basis. Using Caller ID, the call center software recognizes previous customers and calls up their purchase history on the screen *before the call is answered.* The computer terminal screens enable the agent to find any product immediately, so that she can immediately begin to discuss colors, sizes, and prices effortlessly. If the caller is a previous customer, the agent doesn't have to get the name and address a second time.

- *No-hassle return policy.* Modern catalogers make it very easy to return merchandise—and *the best ones pay the return postage.* Customers may exchange or get a credit or a full refund *with no questions asked!* Such service was unheard of a decade ago, but it has become standard; 20 percent of all items ordered are returned.

Use of Database Marketing

With all these new developments, you would think that catalogers would be in the forefront of database marketing today. You would be wrong. While every cataloger creates a house file of customers so that it can mail them catalogs and exchange their names with other catalogers, few catalogers have a marketing database system. Recent studies show that catalogers with sales of more than $100 million per year spend an average of $18,000 on database marketing. That does not pay the salary of even a half a person to do database marketing. Those with sales of less than $100 million spend almost nothing in this field. Why not?

To explain this, let's define what we mean by database marketing. In modern DBM, a company keeps track of customer purchases and crafts special customer communications that are designed to build retention, referrals, loyalty, and cross sales. Why aren't catalogers doing this?

The explanation lies in the nature of modern catalog operations. Catalogers have developed a universally successful method of operating. In theory, catalogs could be personalized, with Arthur Hughes getting a catalog containing things that the sender assumes he would be interested in, and Helena Hughes getting a catalog from the same company with a different selection of products. Several catalogers have tried this. It is technically possible. However, the increase in sales was disappointing. Personalization of catalogs is expensive, and so few catalogers do it because the increased sales from personalization are not sufficient to cover the cost of personalization. Catalogers print 500,000 or more identical copies, trying to get the per-piece cost as low as possible. They mail these catalogs to their house file plus hundreds of thousands of rented names. This method keeps the marketing costs to a minimum.

How to Personalize

There is a form of personalization for catalogers, however. Most catalogers produce 10 to 15 different books per year. One cataloger, for instance, may produce some books featuring dress clothes, some with sports clothes, and some with children's clothes. If a customer buys children's clothes, she will get the children's clothes catalogs. This sounds like personalization. But herein lies a problem: The catalog's house file of previous buyers is often very small relative to the rented list of external names. Previous buyers are *always* the best responders. Why leave a previous buyer out of the sports clothing catalog mailing just because all she has bought before was children's clothes? It does not make economic sense. So previous buyers will get all the catalogs. Where does database marketing figure in that? If you cannot personalize your communications, you cannot really do database marketing, so few catalogers spend any money on database marketing. That is, they didn't until the advent of the Web.

Catalogs and the Web

My wife, Helena, buys all the clothes and gifts in our family. She is a catalog freak. She recently spent $35,000 on catalog items in 1 year. She does extensive research in the catalogs to find exactly what she wants. Once she has selected the items, she usually orders by phone, but occasionally she orders over the Web. Almost every one of the catalogs has both a toll-free number and a Web site. She rarely uses the Web sites. She uses them only as an ordering device, once she has found what she wants in the catalog.

This squares with Sears Canada's experience: 92 percent of Canadian customers buying from the Sears Canada Web site have the paper catalog in front of them. Why doesn't Helena use the Web sites as a shopping medium?

- She enjoys reading catalogs. They are a form of relaxation, like reading a magazine. She does not find sitting at a computer relaxing.
- She cannot count on the colors on our PC being as true as the colors in the catalogs
- It takes too long to find items on a Web site. She can find a sweater or dress that she wants in a catalog in a few seconds. On the Web, waiting for page after page to download is simply a waste of her time.
- She can sit on the sofa and flip through catalogs. She can take them to the kitchen or the bathroom. You can't do any of these things on the Web.
- Talking to an operator is much more satisfying than ordering on the Web. Helena likes talking to people. The operators seem to know when things are out of stock and can make helpful suggestions for substitutes. Most Web sites don't tell you that the item is out of stock and very rarely make alternative suggestions

So why does she use the Web at all? Because she hates to be put on hold when she calls an operator. It is the result of desperation, not a choice.

More and more customers are placing catalog orders on the Web. Most catalogers have already put all their catalog items on their Web sites, so that customers can look at them and place orders. But the Web is not replacing the paper catalogs. In fact, it seems to be increasing them. In 1995, 13.2 billion catalogs were mailed in the United States. By 2000, despite the growth in Web catalog sites, the number of paper catalogs distributed had grown to 16 billion. By 2001, about 11 percent of catalog sales were placed through the Web.

The Web Is an Ordering Medium

The Web is an excellent ordering medium. You never get put on hold. Each year more people learn to use the Web. Some catalogers estimate that by 2005 they may have 35 percent of their orders placed through the Web.

The Web, however, does not seem to be an effective sales medium. Very few of the orders that arrive at a catalog Web site come from people who were simply browsing the Web. What brings the visitors is the arrival of the paper catalog. Once they had built their catalog Web site, many catalogers tried to use advertising, mailed promotions, and affiliate programs to bring people to the Web site to shop. However, the increase in sales seldom paid for the cost of the promotions. The catalogers discovered that the paper catalog itself is the only really effective way to drive customers to their Web sites. So since they still need the catalog, why do catalogers bother to have a Web site at all? There are many valid reasons:

- *Reduced ordering costs.* It costs a cataloger $4 or more to take an order over the telephone. Orders placed through the Web have a variable cost of a few pennies. Saving $4 per order can make a big difference.
- *Email communications.* Catalogers have found that they can improve the response to a catalog by using email to notify customers of its imminent arrival. They can also use their database of previous purchases to flag certain items for customers' attention in an email with a <u>click here</u> inside it that jumps the customer to the item in the Web catalog. To use email communications, however, the cataloger must have people's email names.
- *Email name capture.* All catalog Web sites insist on receiving the customer's email name as part of the transaction. At the same time, they permit the customer to "opt out" to receiving emails concerning future product promotions. A vast majority of customers do not say "No" to this question, thereby providing permission for use of their email for commercial messages. At the same time, this permission also involves the placement of a cookie on the customer's computer.

- *Building a relationship with customers.* Before the Web, catalogers could not afford to make a lot of nonproductive phone calls or send direct mail to customers. They received orders and shipped them rapidly. With the Web, this is beginning to change. When the customer places an order on the Web, he receives an immediate thank you on the screen, followed by a simultaneous email confirmation. He can use the confirmation to cancel the order with a single click. (Why would a cataloger make it so easy to cancel an order? Because 20 percent of all catalog orders are returned. Having the order canceled before it is shipped saves money.) When the order is shipped, the customer gets another email: Your order was shipped today. Finally, when the order arrives, he gets another email: Did it arrive on time? Were you happy with it? <u>Click here</u> to respond. This type of communication builds relationships like those enjoyed by the old corner grocers who knew their customers and talked with them frequently. This type of relationship building increases loyalty and repeat sales. It is the first time catalogers have been able to make effective use of a database.
- *Creating one-click ordering.* Amazon.com started it (as it did many other things on the Web). You come to the amazon.com site and find a book, video, or CD that you are interested in. You click once, and it is shipped. There's no need for you to give your address, telephone number, credit card number, or other such information. It's like walking out of the corner grocer's store with a big turkey and saying, "Put it on my tab." People love this kind of personal life simplification and will return to a site that makes it possible.
- *Collecting demographic information.* While they are taking orders on the Web, catalogers collect demographic information from customers. Getting customers to update their profile on the Web is easy, and much less expensive than getting the same information during a telephone order session. They can learn the customer's age, income, family composition, preferences, and lifestyle.
- *Using demographic information for personalized communications.* Using this information, catalogers can send out personalized email messages. Since catalogs are always mass produced, the email becomes the only method of personalization.

- *Web personalization.* All good Web sites gain customers' permission to use cookies by giving them a chance to "opt out." More than 95 percent of customers agree to their use. By using cookies, a visitor returning to a catalog Web site sees "Welcome Back, Susan." Susan can see items that the cataloger thinks (or she has told them) she is interested in based on her past purchases and Web activity. What catalogers tried and failed to do in catalog personalization is now economically possible using the Web.
- *Control groups.* Control groups can be created in the database to test customers' reactions to innovations in the Web site. Such groups were almost impossible to use effectively with mass mailings of catalogs.
- *Online focus groups.* In Chapter 6 we describe how Universal Music used online focus groups to determine customers' reaction to the release of a new music CD. Catalogers can now use online focus groups to determine customers' reactions to new products.
- *Measuring multibuyer performance.* The Web offers the opportunity to track what customers are looking at, which is not possible with a paper catalog. However, few catalogers have yet taken advantage of this feature, since it requires not just sophisticated software, but creative marketers who can look at the data and draw profitable conclusions from what they see. The scarcest commodity in all of database marketing is the creative imagination needed to drive new marketing programs. Marketers are usually awash with data that they cannot figure out how to use profitably.

How Some Catalogers Are Using the Web

Once the landsend.com Web site was constructed, the company wanted to try additional methods besides the paper catalog that would induce shoppers to come to its site and buy. It introduced several new ideas that seemed to work.

- *Live customer service* that allowed customers to send messages and receive replies in real time (see Figure 12-1). The customer support agents could synchronize their screens with customers' so that they could see the same screen the customer was seeing at home. They could help shoppers with their choices and in selecting cross sales.

- *A virtual model* that customers could use to try on clothes (see Figure 12-2).
- *My Personal Shopper,* who helps you the way a good clerk in a department store would (see Figure 12-3).

How well did these things work? Conversion rates among those who used the virtual model were 26 percent higher than among those

Figure 12-1 Lands' End Live. © Lands' End, Inc. Used with permission.

Having problems?
Need questions answered?
Click the button to talk to us.

Figure 12-2 My Virtual Model. © Lands' End, Inc. Used with permission.

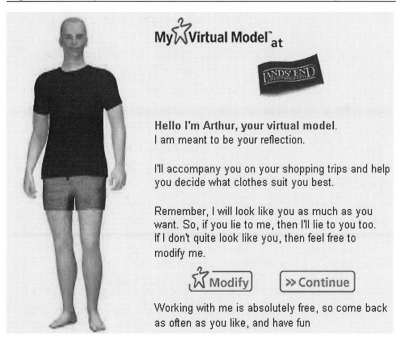

Figure   12-3 My Personal Shopper. © Lands' End, Inc. Used with permission.

My PERSONAL SHOPPER
Like having a personal wardrobe consultant!

My Personal Shopper lets you access an expert shopper who suggests products that best suit your unique taste, style and preferences.

[men's items]   [women's items]

who didn't. Conversion rates among those who used the personal shopper were 80 percent higher than the average for other customers.

Other catalogers have also developed innovative methods to bring customers to their site.

- *Use of affiliates.* Ashford.com, a jeweler, promotes its site through 12,000 affiliates who are linked to Ashford in return for a 7 percent share of the net revenue. This program brings in 15 percent of Ashford's sales. Ashford also uses Web advertising and Web newsletters to previous customers.

- *Web newsletters* from catalogers may seem like a bonanza because they are so inexpensive to send. However, they are also annoying. Forrester Research found that more than half of consumers say they receive too many commercial emails. Most long-term Net users delete all promotional emails without reading them. However, the value of a Web newsletter can be easily determined by creating a control group and determining whether the total sales, number of sales, average order size, departments shopped, and so on are greater for those getting the newsletter than they are for the control group. If there is no difference, drop the newsletter like a hot potato.

Problems for Catalogers Shifting to the Web

Many catalogers have fulfillment systems that use a legacy system that is not compatible with the modern servers that are used today for the

Web and for customer service. A considerable amount of software rewriting is necessary. Only the larger catalogers can afford such an effort.

One company that succeeded in this effort was the Sharper Image (www.sharperimage.com). The company put all its customers on a single database so that it could determine their purchases through each of the three channels: retail stores (60 percent), catalog phone orders (23 percent), and Web orders (17 percent). The top customers were identified by lifetime value and recency of purchase. Gold customers got special offers, preferred mailings, and gifts during the holidays. They also got sneak-preview emails on new items.

The Sharper Image's email list grew to over 500,000. It sent out between two and four emails per customer per month. It also sent out emails to new prospects, letting them know that a new catalog was coming out and offering a merchandise certificate. The emails did not reduce the number of paper catalogs sent out; they increased it. The number of catalogs sent out by the Sharper Image grew by 20 percent every year, with 62 million being sent out by 2000. Both catalogs and special mailers worked for this company.

The Web Creates Multibuyers

A survey by the National Retail Federation showed that catalog customers who buy on the Web buy 20 percent more than customers who respond to a catalog only by mail or phone. Web shoppers also spend 33 percent more in retail stores than retail shoppers who do not use the Web. A survey of 48,000 shoppers in all channels by Shop.org found that shoppers who bought via all three channels—retail store, catalog, and the Web—represented 34 percent of all Web shoppers. In-store shoppers who also bought from the same retailer online spent an average of $600 more per year than typical in-store shoppers.

Macys.com saw its Web site as a stand-alone store carrying items that were not available in its catalog. Customers visiting the Web site registered their age, gender, family status, and the product lines of greatest interest to them. Macy's learned whether the customer planned to buy a home, take a vacation, have a baby, or get married anytime soon.

Macy's click-through rates on emails featuring items on the Web site averaged 10 percent, with 2 to 3 percent of those clicking making a purchase. When customers make a purchase at the macys.com site, a pop-up window asks them to rate their Web experience. The company found that many customers left the site quickly if they did not find what they wanted in the search window. As a result, when a search failed, Macy's visitors got a window showing the address, phone number, and directions to the nearest Macy's store.

Office Depot introduced Web ordering for its catalog as Office Depot Online. It has been profitable since day one. The company soon discovered that catalog customers who ordered through the Web spent 33 percent more than other catalog shoppers. In 2001, Office Depot Online sales grew by 30 percent to $1.5 billion, representing 14 percent of all Office Depot sales. Office Depot, like Dell, set up Web pages for special customers such as Bank of America. By 2001, 85 percent of Bank of America's office supplies were provided by Office Depot through the Web. These Web pages permitted Office Depot to make special volume price adjustments for large customers, which it could not easily arrange without the Web to keep track of the hundreds of thousands of individual orders.

Use of Collaborative Filtering

The Internet has opened up a range of new opportunities for personalization that may lead many catalogers to reconsider their attitude toward database marketing. Amazon has shown us the way. Amazon uses emails and its Web site to suggest books and movies to customers that they might be interested in, using collaborative filtering to come up with the suggestions.

Collaborative filtering is provided by www.Netperceptions.com, among others. It consists of software that makes use of a client's database of customers and their previous purchases. The goal of the software is to determine what a person's lifestyle and preferences are and then to find other customers within the database who have similar tastes. Whatever the cataloger had sold to those similar customers might appeal to you, so the cataloger suggests it to you. One of the most convincing uses of collaborative filtering was an experiment tried with Great Universal Stores (GUS), the largest cataloger in the United Kingdom. Before collaborative filtering, GUS customer service reps were getting a 20 percent cross-selling rate on orders placed from the paper catalog. That means that in one call out of five, the rep was able to sell the customer an item from the catalog that the customer had not intended to buy.

Netperceptions.com introduced collaborative filtering into the GUS call center software, using the huge GUS customer database. The suggested next best product showed up on the customer service rep's screen as soon as the rep typed in the first purchase requested by the caller. The company's previous success at cross-selling was due to the customer service rep's native intelligence. If a woman ordered a dress, the rep might suggest matching shoes, a belt, or a handbag. The suggestions from the collaborative software were described by the GUS reps as "spooky." The software might suggest selling towels to the woman who ordered the dress. Towels? What was the relationship of towels to the dress? There was none—except that the software had found similar women in the GUS database and had found that many of them also bought towels. The amazing thing about the software was that it worked. After getting used to it for 6 weeks, GUS customer service reps were getting a 40 percent cross-selling rate—double what they had been getting before. Now *that* is database marketing, folks. Collaborative filtering is used by more than 200 American companies. It requires a large database and super fast software. It is not for the mom-and-pop catalog operation, or for the timid.

In the past 2 years, I have probably spent more than a thousand dollars with Amazon, some of which was the result of Amazon's collaborative filtering suggestions. One email that I received a year ago has stuck in my mind. It said:

> *Two years ago you bought* Dark Sun *by Richard Rhodes. You may be interested to learn that Richard Rhodes has just had a new book published called* Why They Kill. *To learn more about this book, or to order it,* click here.

Well, I clicked, I bought it, and I loved it. This new book had nothing to do with the previous book except the author. This is database marketing.

What Catalogers Have to Guard against When They Use the Web

- *Web search for products is slow.* Flipping through a catalog is easy. You can find what you want and order it. You can't flip through a Web site. To find a cardigan sweater in Appleseed's catalog took about 45 seconds. To find the same sweater *from scratch* on Appleseed's Web site took 3 minutes. To find the sweater on the Web site using the catalog number took about 1 minute. Fast search is possible, but only if very clever marketers team up with very clever Web programmers.
- *The colors on the Web are not true.* There is no way that catalogers can know what users' monitors are doing to the pictures of their products. There is no known cure for this disease.
- *Out-of-stock information is seldom accurate.* When you call a telemarketer, her software tells her and she tells you that the item you want is out of stock. Web sites seldom do. As a result, you place the order and find out by email a few days later that the item is out of stock. After a few experiences like this, you stick with a live operator. This is really inexcusable. To get customer acceptance, Web sites have to be as good as or better than a live operator. They have to know what is out of stock in real time and be able make instant recommendations on substitutes.

Lifetime Value Changes for Catalogers

Let's see what would happen to a cataloger if it were to adopt the database initiatives proposed in this chapter. To understand the change, let's start with a traditional successful cataloger. This company has already put its catalog on the Web. It sends out 2,000,000 books every 6 months, at an in-the-mail cost of $2 per book. The company gets an overall response rate of 4 percent. Included in the mailing are 500,000 new names. These produce responses from 20,000 first-time buyers. We are going to trace the lifetime value of these 20,000 first-time buyers over four rounds (2 years). The average order size on the first buy is $120, of which the product and fulfillment costs are 40 percent. In the second-round mailing 6 months later to these 20,000 first-time buyers, the purchase rate is 40 percent and the average order size is $130. This rises over the next year to $150, and the purchase rate rises to 50 percent. Of the original 20,000 first-time buyers in round 1, there are 1800 who are still buying 2 years later. Meanwhile, of course, the company has proceeded with additional prospect mailings that are producing identical charts every 6 months. The lifetime value of the original 20,000 first-time buyers after the fourth round is $67.68, as shown in Table 12-1.

Let us now assume that the cataloger has adopted many of the recommendations made in this chapter. The company has spent $1,200,000 on software for its Web site that does several significant things:

- Asks for customer profiles, capturing email names and customer preferences and demographics. This reaches 20 percent on the first round and an additional 20 percent on each additional round.

Table 12-1 LTV of Catalog First-Time Buyers

	Round 1	Round 2	Round 3	Round 4
Customers	20,000	8,000	3,600	1,800
Purchase rate	100%	40%	45%	50%
Average purchase	$120	$130	$140	$150
Revenue	$2,400,000	$1,040,000	$504,000	$270,000
Cost percent	40%	40%	40%	40%
Costs	$960,000	$416,000	$201,600	$108,000
Number mailed	500,000	20,000	20,000	20,000
Mailed cost	$2.00	$2.00	$2.00	$2.00
Mail costs	$1,000,000	$40,000	$40,000	$40,000
Total costs	$1,960,000	$456,000	$241,600	$148,000
Profit	$440,000	$584,000	$262,400	$122,000
Discount rate	1.00	1.04	1.08	1.12
NPV of profit	$440,000	$561,954	$242,963	$108,699
Cumulative NPV of profit	$440,000	$1,001,954	$1,244,917	$1,353,616
Lifetime value	$22.00	$50.10	$62.25	$67.68

- Provides one-click ordering for all customers who complete the profile, along with personalized emails and Web site opening pages.
- Sends an email thank you for each order, an email when the order is shipped, and an email asking if the order was satisfactory.
- Provides personalized emails announcing the arrival of each book, with click here for items that it is assumed the customer is interested in.
- Uses collaborative filtering to make suggestions on next best product, leading to a cross-selling rate of 40 percent.
- Offers an advanced search feature that permits customers to find products faster.
- Has live shopper support for people who want to have a text chat with a customer service rep while they are on the site, or who want to call on another line to talk to a live agent.

The $1,200,000 software, amortized across 3 years, will represent a cost of $200,000 for each group of first-time buyers acquired ($1,200,000/3 = $400,000/2 per year = $200,000).

The result of these changes can be seen in the Table 12-2.

The purchase rate for the second-time buyers has risen from 40 percent to 50 percent. The average order size has increased. The costs have

Table 12-2 Improved LTV with Web Site Software

	Round 1	Round 2	Round 3	Round 4
Customers	20,000	10,000	5,500	3,300
Purchase rate	100%	50%	55%	60%
Average purchase	$120	$140	$155	$170
Revenue	$2,400,000	$1,400,000	$852,500	$561,000
Cost percent	40%	38%	37%	36%
Costs	$960,000	$532,000	$315,425	$201,960
Number mailed	500,000	20,000	20,000	20,000
Mailed cost	$2.00	$2.00	$2.00	$2.00
Mail costs	$1,000,000	$40,000	$40,000	$40,000
Software cost	$200,000	$0	$0	$0
Total costs	$2,160,000	$572,000	$355,425	$241,960
Profit	$240,000	$828,000	$497,075	$319,040
Discount rate	1.00	1.04	1.08	1.12
NPV of profit	$240,000	$796,743	$460,255	$284,256
Cumulative NPV of profit	$240,000	$1,036,743	$1,496,998	$1,781,254
Lifetime value	$12.00	$51.84	$74.85	$89.06

Table 12-3 Gains from Software Improvements

	Round 1	Round 2	Round 3	Round 4
New LTV	$12.00	$51.84	$74.85	$89.06
Old LTV	$22.00	$50.10	$62.25	$67.68
Difference	($10.00)	$ 1.74	$12.60	$21.38
Times 80,000 ($800,000)		$139,156	$1,008,323	$1,710,552

gone down as a result of increased use of the Web rather than telephone calls. Against that, there is a software cost for each group of first-time buyers of $200,000. Lifetime value has gone up to $89.06, from $67.68.

Overall, the changes will increase profit by a total of $1.7 million over 2 years, as shown in Table 12-3. Note that these profits of $1.7 million include all costs, including the heavy losses in round 1 that resulted from the initial software costs.

Each cataloger will have to work out its own figures based on its own situation. In the end, however, the results will probably be close to those shown here. When it is done right, database marketing works. Customer communications work. People respond when people they know and have done business with write to them and pay attention to them. Statistics from other catalogers discussed in this chapter show that when you adopt the improvements listed in this chapter

- The repurchase rate will go up.
- The average order size will go up.
- The cost of order fulfillment will come down.
- Cross sales will go up.

Building B2B Catalog Sales

A business-to-business cataloger with sales in excess of $14 million had never built a marketing database. It turned to Sejal Shah at CSC Advanced Database Solutions to come up with a plan. Here is what he found:

- The cataloger had about 55,000 current customers who spent an average of $250 per year.
- It mailed about 300,000 catalogs every quarter at $1 each and had an annual response rate of 6.2 percent.

- Its margin on product was about 53 percent, out of which it had to take the cost of the catalogs and about 10 percent for fulfillment.

Sejal recommended two methods for building sales with a database:

1. Building a customer database and using it to determine the profiles of the most profitable customers, then using those profiles to mail catalogs to companies whose profiles matched the profiles of these profitable customers
2. Using emails to communicate with customers, leading to increased cross sales, larger order size, increased frequency of orders, and increased retention

Creating Customer Profiles

The method that Sejal proposed was this:

- Once the database was built, append D&B data and use analytical software to determine the profile of the most profitable customers. Each customer profile would include these data:
  - SIC codes
  - Total purchases in the past 12 months
  - Key product groups purchased
  - Total employees and total sales
- Using this analysis, marketers at the cataloger could develop a market penetration report for each profile. The penetration report would look something like Table 12-4.

Table 12-4 Market Penetration

Profile group	Company customers	U.S. universe	Market penetration
A	10,221	109,334	9.35%
B	8,874	99,447	8.92%
C	3,341	45,331	7.37%
D	2,116	69,004	3.07%
E	1,984	83,556	2.37%
F	445	4,801	9.27%
Total	26,981	411,473	6.56%

This report clearly identified those companies that were the most likely prospects for further sales. Using these profiles, the company could acquire the names of prospects that matched the SIC codes and other data in the profiles.

Using these numbers as a base, what results could the cataloger expect from the prospect mailings? Certainly not the 6.2 percent received on the existing catalogs. Those were sales to existing customers, many of whom had been purchasing from this cataloger for years. Sejal estimated that with the new mailings, the cataloger would get about one-third of the sales rates that it got from the regular catalog mailing. As a result, he predicted that the cataloger would get a response in the first year from about 2 percent of those who received a catalog.

How many catalogs should be mailed? Sejal proposed three scenarios: a conservative, a bold, and an aggressive one. In the conservative scenario, the cataloger would mail to about 150,000 new names each quarter, or 600,000 during the year. The bold total would be 1 million per year, and the aggressive would be 1.6 million in total.

Putting everything together, Table 12-5 shows what Sejal projected for the results of the first year's increased mailings. As a result of the new database and mailing strategy, the cataloger would gain between $3 and $7 million in sales, spend $200,000 for the database and software, and still make a substantial profit. Many companies expect to lose

Table 12-5 First-Year Results

	Conservative	Bold	Aggressive
New mailing	600,000	1,000,000	1,600,000
Response rate	2.20%	2.00%	1.80%
New customers	13,200	20,000	28,800
Average order	$250	$250	$250
Revenue	$3,300,000	$5,000,000	$7,200,000
Name rental ($100/M)	$60,000	$100,000	$160,000
Catalogs @ $1	$600,000	$1,000,000	$1,600,000
Fulfillment @ 10%	$330,000	$500,000	$720,000
Database	$200,000	$200,000	$200,000
One-time DB costs	$140,000	$140,000	$140,000
Cost of goods (47%)	$1,551,000	$2,350,000	$3,384,000
Total costs	$2,881,000	$4,290,000	$6,204,000
Net profit	$419,000	$710,000	$996,000
Investment	$1,000,000	$1,440,000	$2,100,000
Return on investment	1.42	1.49	1.47

money in their first year of database marketing and recoup it later. This study shows that for this company, it was not necessary to predict a loss. Furthermore, this chart includes only new sales. Sejal assumed that the cataloger would also continue to get the existing annual sales of about $14 million.

One-Time Setup Costs

In addition to the annual database costs, there were one-time setup costs, shown in Table 12-6.

Email Marketing

Sejal projected that in the second year, the cataloger could gain from email marketing to its existing customers. The use of email marketing was possible only when the cataloger had a substantial number of customer records that included email names and permission to use them. Since the cataloger did not have many email names to start with, Sejal suggested that it become aggressive about capturing email names on all future sales, thus rapidly building up a base of customer email names.

What could be done with email marketing? Sejal suggested several techniques:

- Regular promotions of existing products, particularly before and after the catalog arrives
- Promotions of sale items
- Last-minute specials
- Retention messages (thank you for your business, customer surveys, etc.)
- Follow-up messages (thank you for your order; your order will be shipped on . . .)

Table 12-6 One-Time Setup Costs

Needs assessment	$ 30,000
Design and development	$ 100,000
Training	$ 10,000
Total	$ 140,000

- Viral marketing ("New product specs are available. Send them to a coworker.")
- Email newsletters with product information

What results might the cataloger get from email marketing? The experience of other catalogers suggests a lift in sales of between 5 and 20 percent using well-targeted and appreciated emails. For this cataloger, Sejal conservatively projected only 5 percent. He used that figure to estimate the increased sales and profits from emails (Table 12-7).

By adding the email profits to the prospecting profits, Sejal was able to predict the cataloger's profits for the second year, as shown in Table 12-8. The second year's response rate was projected to increase

Table 12-7 Profit from Email Marketing, Year 2

	Conservative	Bold	Aggressive
Old customers	10,000	10,000	10,000
New customers	18,600	30,000	46,400
Total	28,600	40,000	56,400
Sales @ $250	$7,150,000	$10,000,000	$14,100,000
5% increase	$357,500	$500,000	$705,000
Profit @ 35%	$125,125	$175,000	$246,750

Table 12-8 Second-Year Results

	Conservative	Bold	Aggressive
New mailing	600,000	1,000,000	1,600,000
Response rate	3.10%	3.00%	2.90%
Customers	18,600	30,000	46,400
Average order	$250	$250	$250
Revenue	$4,650,000	$7,500,000	$11,600,000
Name rental ($100/M)	$ 60,000	$ 100,000	$ 160,000
Catalogs @ $1	$ 600,000	$1,000,000	$1,600,000
Fulfillment @ 10%	$ 465,000	$ 750,000	$1,160,000
Database	$ 350,000	$ 350,000	$ 350,000
Cost of goods (47%)	$2,185,500	$3,525,000	$5,452,000
Total costs	$3,660,500	$5,725,000	$8,722,000
New mail profit	$ 989,500	$1,775,000	$2,878,000
Email profit	$ 125,125	$ 175,000	$ 246,750
Total profit	$1,114,625	$1,950,000	$3,124,750
Investment	$1,010,000	$1,450,000	$2,110,000
Return on investment	2.10	2.34	2.48

from 2 percent to 3 percent for a number of reasons. The first year's mailing would show which SICs were pulling and which were not, so the cataloger should get much better at selecting names. In addition, many of the customers mailed to in the first year would be getting their second year's worth of catalogs. Since the long-term projection of catalog response for this cataloger was 6 percent, these second-year customers should respond at a rate closer to that, bringing the average up to 3 percent or higher. The only surprise in the second year is the increased cost of the database. The software used in the first year did not include a provision for email marketing. Sejal recommended a software upgrade that moved the database cost up to $350,000 per year.

What this case study shows is how to go about calculating the benefits from database marketing. Too many people think that it is a nice concept, but have no idea of how to prove it.

Summary

Catalogers never made much use of database marketing until the advent of the Web, because the nature of modern cataloging made it uneconomical to provide personalized communications. Now that the Web has arrived, catalogers should rapidly begin to use database marketing to build relationships with customers and to increase loyalty and cross sales. The methods are out there and are within the reach of all but the smallest catalogers. The increases in sales and profits can be substantial.

What Works

- One-click ordering
- Personalization of the Web site with cookies
- Cross sales accompanied by personalization and collaborative filtering
- Using the Web site to capture customer profiles, email names, and preferences
- Saving order fulfillment costs through increased use of the Web

- Email communications to drive traffic to the catalog and the Web
- Using customer-created profiles to capture email names and demographic information
- Using profiles to create personalized communications and Web sites
- Using control groups to measure the response to customer communications
- Online focus groups using captured customer email names
- Measuring multibuyer performance and using it to drive marketing strategy
- Live customer service on a catalog Web site
- Virtual models created by the customer

What Doesn't Work

- Expecting to drive traffic to a catalog Web site without a paper catalog
- Fancy flash pages that take too long to download
- Web sites that lack the information known to telephone sales reps
- Web newsletters, which may be overused
- Slow product search on Web catalog sites

Quiz

1. Catalogs are succeeding today for all but which of the following reasons?
   a. Personalized catalogs
   b. Lightning-fast fulfillment
   c. Universal credit cards
   d. Sophisticated telesales
   e. No-hassle returns
2. Why don't many catalogers today do database marketing?
   a. It provides no sales lift.
   b. They have never heard of it.
   c. The economics of catalog production.

    d. All of the above.

    e. None of the above.

3. Give three reasons why catalogers have profitable Web sites today.

4. What did Office Depot find was the valuable feature of customers who shopped both at the retail stores and on the Web?

5. When GUS adopted collaborative filtering, what marketing method did it change and by how much?

    a. Catalog distribution was down 8 percent.

    b. Cross sales were up 100 percent.

    c. Web visits were up 15 percent.

    d. Call abandonment was down 10 percent.

    e. None of the above.

6. List four things that catalogers need to add to their Web sites if they are going to succeed on the Web.

7. What did Macy's do when it found that customers were leaving its site when they didn't find what they wanted?

8. What is the advantage to Lands' End of having a personal shopper? Conversion rates were up:

    a. 10 percent

    b. 20 percent

    c. 30 percent

    d. 40 percent

    e. None of the above

9. As the Sharper Image email campaign grew in size, what happened to its catalog distribution?

    a. It went down 5 percent

    b. It went down 10 percent

    c. It went down 20 percent

    d. It went down 25 percent

    e. None of the above

10. What is the advantage of a Virtual Model to Lands' End? Conversion rates were up by

    a. 16 percent

    b. 26 percent

    c. 36 percent

    d. 46 percent

    e. 56 percent

CHAPTER 13

FINDING LOYAL CUSTOMERS

For years, retailers have argued that having regularly advertised, deeply discounted prices brings price-oriented customers into their stores but that, over time, these customers convert to regular, profitable customers.

Research done by the Retail Strategy Center Inc. based in Greenville, South Carolina, shows that this widely held belief is a myth=? . A handful of these customers do convert into "good" regular customers, but the majority actually defect within twelve months of their first shopping visit. I have yet to find a retailer anywhere in the world whose investment in this type of shopper has yielded an attractive return on investment.

Brian Woolf, *Customer Specific Marketing*

Most companies are set up for customer acquisition. Few are set up for customer retention. Yet, as you can tell from reading this book, retention is almost always more profitable than acquisition. Most companies lose money on the first sale to a customer. The profits they make are derived from the second and subsequent sales. Does that mean that companies can ignore acquisition? No. It means that acquisition should be conducted with long-term retention in mind.

Frederick Reichheld, in his book *The Loyalty Effect*, which I cannot praise too highly, points out that the method a company uses to acquire customers often determines whether the company will be successful in the long run. Deep discounts, for example, do not create loyalty. They cheapen the image of the brand, cost you valuable margin, and focus the customer's attention on the wrong thing: the price of the product instead of its quality and the service you offer.

Finally, we cannot assume that every acquired customer is good for the firm. Fleet Bank discovered that half the customers it was acquiring destroyed value and would never be profitable for the bank.

There are dozens of acquisition methods, several of which are covered in case studies in this chapter. In general we can summarize them as follows:

- *Mass marketing* through TV, radio, and print ads. With general-use products and packaged goods, mass marketing is far preferable to direct marketing for customer acquisition. Of course, to acquire customers through mass marketing, you have to have a method of capturing customers' names, addresses, and email names when they buy in retail stores. Without this step, you have sold product, but you have not acquired a customer.
- *Creating profiles* of your existing customers, then renting names of prospects who resemble your profitable customers.
- *Exchanging customer names* with other businesses. The catalog industry uses this idea extensively. It works very well. This is contrary to the idea that is prevalent in the rest of the world, particularly Europe and Japan, that customer names are a corporate asset that could be ruined if the company were to allow them to become known to any outsider. Renting customer names has become a profit center in many companies and, as such, is a positive good to the direct marketing industry.
- *Providing a method by which customers can register with you* when they buy a product. This is done for computers and software and for many electrical products. Millions of people willingly register. The best method in use today for getting people to register is through a Web microsite that you set up specifically for this purpose. The site should be listed on the product packaging or on the product itself. Providing a reward helps.
- *Determining which clusters your consumer customers come from* and seeking additional customers in other households located in those clusters.

- *Doing penetration analysis* by zip code or SIC code and finding out where you are strong and where you are weak. Armed with this knowledge, you can better direct your acquisition strategy. It is easier to sell in areas where your name is a household word than in areas where you are unknown.
- *Giving customers an incentive to provide you with referrals.* As we will show you, referred customers are better than the average customer and are worth cultivating.

Penetration Analysis

Table 13-1 gives a simplified example of a penetration study for a company that sells to several industries.

The company has 29,000 customers, roughly divided into four sectors. As you can see, most of the company's sales come from light manufacturing. The companies with the highest lifetime value are in heavy manufacturing. But the high-technology sector is particularly interesting. The U.S. universe comes from Dun & Bradstreet data. It shows the number of companies in the SIC codes that Weldon sells to. As you can see, Weldon's penetration in the high-technology sector is very high: 42 percent. This means that Weldon is a household word in this industry. It will be much easier for Weldon to pick up an additional customer in this sector than in any of the other three because it is so well known there. This shows the power of penetration analysis.

Table 13-1 Penetration Analysis

	Weldon customers	U.S. universe	Penetration ratio	Lifetime value	Target potential	Rank
Metal production	254	2,433	10.44%	$145,067	$15,144.68	3
Light manufacturing	15,442	162,009	9.53%	$5,914	$563.70	4
Heavy manufacturing	44	1,288	3.42%	$988,145	$33,756.51	2
High technology	612	1,453	42.12%	$127,675	$53,776.39	1
Total	29,198	167,183	17.46%			

Target potential is derived by simply multiplying the penetration ratio by the lifetime value. This is a simple approach, but it has value.

Here is another approach to customer acquisition for a business-to-business situation.

Finding Leads for Equipment Financing

Equipment financing is not really like any other type of business. The amounts involved can be huge. The terms, the length of the lease, and the items financed are seldom standard (as they are in automobile or home mortgage financing). It is hard to predict companies' need for financing, as decisions on equipment purchases are seldom made on a predictable schedule. As a result, finding leads is tough. Which companies are going to need financing, and when?

The situation is complicated by the fact that the industry is highly competitive. In addition to banks, there are finance companies that specialize in equipment financing. There is very little customer loyalty, as decisions are made primarily on rates rather than on provider affinity, service, or brand. To further complicate the picture, the equipment financing sales force, like all sales forces, is highly skeptical of central assistance. The salespeople tend to be independent and are more comfortable developing their own sales processes than participating in a group effort. To grow its equipment financing business, KeyBank's direct marketing group had to come up with a system that served up leads to its Key Equipment Financing sales force in a way that was both productive and acceptable to the staff.

Key's direct marketing group developed a unique way of solving this problem with the help of a team from SIGMA Marketing Group. The solution involved a combination of direct mail, telemarketing, and leasing managers in a system driven by a model using Dun & Bradstreet data.

In analyzing the situation, both groups saw that Key's 30 leasing managers were spending entirely too much time trying to find leads. The life of a leasing manager was very demanding, with constant travel and much time spent chasing possible leads that might not materialize. Once they had a solid lead, the leasing managers found that closing the sale could be a fairly straightforward process. SIGMA recommended setting up a lead-discovery process that would produce qualified leads for the leasing managers so that they could focus on closing sales and not waste time on lead development.

There were four parts to the system:

1. Create a relevant and highly targeted prospecting list that the leasing managers would find credible.
2. Develop a compelling direct-mail communication on behalf of each leasing manager that would permit effective telemarketing follow-up.
3. Have outbound telemarketing associates work closely with the leasing managers so that the leads and appointments generated would be relevant and worthwhile.
4. Create a lead-generation database to track and identify the business generated by the leasing managers using this program in terms of both pending and closed deals.

Creating a Universe of Prospects

Using Key's data, SIGMA created a CHAID (chi-square Automatic Interaction Detector, a statistical technique) model to identify the characteristics of Key's current leasing customers. This model identified the best predictors of a company's likelihood to be a leasing customer. They were (in order)

- Company sales volume
- Year company started
- Company number of employees
- Dun's Major Industry

Ten segments were created. The top two segments, with ownership indices of 269 or greater, were

1. Ownership rate of 30.5 percent, with Dun's Major Industry classification of Mining, Communications/Utilities, Business

Services, or missing and year company started being pre-1960 or missing.

2. Ownership rate of 20.2 percent, with Dun's Major Industry classifications of Mining, Communications/Utilities, Business Services, or missing; year company started being 1960 to the present; and sales volume greater than $5 million.

A sign-up form was developed for each leasing manager that captured not only all their contact information, but also those attributes that they wanted a lead to have, such as geography, sales size, and industry. Each leasing manager furnished a sample of his or her signature for use in the outgoing communications.

The information from these two sources was combined into a list order for Dun & Bradstreet. The D&B list was divided geographically by leasing manager, and the leasing managers were asked to make any additions, edits, or deletions to the list that they wanted.

Armed with a good, edited list, Key and SIGMA worked to develop compelling and relevant direct-mail communications that could be mailed on behalf of each leasing manager. The leasing managers were able to schedule the mailings by geography and quantity over 2-week intervals, staggered so that they would not have more leads than they could handle at any one time.

To set up appointments, one outbound phone associate was dedicated to each group of three leasing managers. The associate held phone conversations with each leasing manager on a regular basis to understand the specific nuances of what each leasing manager valued in a lead (e.g., the prospect's role, budget, or timing). Some of the leasing managers even wanted the associates to set up their appointments for them and provided the associate with their calendars. The leasing managers could use email or a toll-free number to talk to their associate while they were in the field on visits. When the associate generated a lead or set up an appointment, the associate would call and email the facts and details of the lead (e.g., who, what, when, and desired amount) to the leasing manager. Upon receiving the message, the leasing manager would often call the associate back to obtain further information about the prospect (e.g., personality, potential barriers to acceptance, and who the decision maker was).

Of course, many prospects were not ready to do business at the time the calls were made. The associate would then ask when they might need equipment leasing in the future and would note the answer in the calling database. Software in the calling database automatically brought the prospect's name back to the associate's attention when the time for a follow-up call had arrived. As the callers gained valuable information from the initial phone contacts, the information was added to the calling database. As a result, the lead rates steadily increased over time as the aggregated knowledge from the calling database grew.

Finally, a series of daily and weekly reports was created to measure mail, calling, and lead activity overall. Additional reports were created to track mail, calls, and leads at the leasing manager level so that best practices could be identified and shared with the rest of the group.

Measuring Success

How do you know if a program like this is really working? It may look good on paper and it may seem to be generating leads and appointments, but is it really better than the old system of letting leasing managers forage for themselves? How can you prove that the money spent is really worthwhile? There is a really simple way to determine whether a program like this is successful: Are the leasing managers using it? At first, only 7 of the 30 leasing managers signed on to use the system. As the success of the program became clear, more and more leasing managers signed on. At the end of 6 months, 20 of the leasing managers were actively using the system. It became the central focus of the Key Equipment Financing lead-generation program. Within 4 months, the lease accounts generated by the program as a percentage of total accounts grew from 1 percent to 1.5 percent—an increase of 50 percent. At the same time, the program also boosted the loan accounts generated by the program from 2 percent to 4 percent—a gain of 100 percent in 4 months.

Managing Leads on the Web

One company provided content management solutions to more than 1200 companies worldwide. In its marketing programs, the firm produced online events, conducted telemarketing, and sent out direct mail and email. Despite the advanced technology of its products, it did not have very good systems for lead management. A review of its situation disclosed that the company had

- No lead-management system or method of lead-quality measurement
- No system for lead reporting, distribution, or tracking
- No e-marketing campaigns
- No integration of outsourced telemarketing with other lead activities
- An average of two online events per month that produced about 300 leads per quarter
- An average cost per lead that exceeded $500—more than double that of other programs

To solve these problems, the company created a new, home-grown lead-management solution. The core component was a central database that cleaned and standardized information on leads for distribution to the corporate sales force automation tool, SalesLogix. The system provided a closed-loop tracking mechanism that assigned a unique ID to each lead. The system included

- An online event registration system that captured not only the contact information, but also data about the lead and its possible need for the company's products.
- A global campaign information database that was used by marketing managers to input campaign details through a Web interface. The information was sent to the SalesLogix system to track the lead distribution resulting from the campaigns.
- The lead-submission process was changed from sending random emails, Excel spreadsheets, or voice messages manually to the use of an online Web form. This Web form allowed standardization of the information that was gathered about contacts.

- Marketing activities conducted outside the Web, including telemarketing activities, were transferred to the new system.

The three main functions of the new system were

1. *Importing.* The system used the email address as a key. When this was not available, it constructed a match key from the first and last names of the contact and the company name. A log was kept of all data imported to or exported from the database.
2. *Processing.* Country names, state names, area codes, phone numbers, zip codes, region codes, and activity dates were standardized. Competitors' names were removed from the database. Standard SIC codes were appended. Leads were assigned to the appropriate salesperson. Incomplete records were flagged, and blank fields were populated, either by software or manually. Separate tables were set up for individual contacts, activity information, event details, and data sources.
3. *Reporting.* Leads were furnished to the SalesLogix system daily. Daily, weekly, and monthly reports showed the growth of the database in the past, as well as the current volume of leads in the database. The system also created a weekly partner report to show the leads generated by partners.

Results

The new system decreased the cost per lead to about $50. It did so through

- Establishing a 100 percent tracking mechanism for every lead that was generated worldwide
- Setting up lead-quality metrics that filtered out 25 percent of the raw leads
- Increasing lead volume from 300 to 9600 per quarter
- Increasing online events from 2 per month to 12 per month
- Introducing biweekly e-marketing campaigns for customer and partner communications

- Bringing telemarketing in-house and integrating it with the lead-flow process
- Setting up a global lead-distribution and lead-reporting system that operated through the Web

Building a Relationship with Prospects

BMW developed a unique program for building a relationship with prospects even before the prospect made a firm decision to purchase a car. The process was called "Extending the Dialogue." BMW produces luxury cars that have a fierce customer brand loyalty. At the time that BMW started this program, the entire luxury car marketplace was sharply down—sales were 9 percent below the previous year's sales. In addition, BMW's key competitors, Mercedes Benz and Lexus, were expanding their product lines with strong product offerings.

The start of the new BMW program was a real-time prospect scoring system that identified BMW's "best prospects." The program was set up to communicate with these targeted prospects over a 6-week period.

Before the program could begin, Kay Madati, director of relationship marketing, the genius behind the program for BMW, asked msdbm of Los Angeles for help in overcoming a number of significant obstacles:

- Twelve different data systems had to be combined into a common marketing database.
- BMW had to get multiple departments to cooperate with one another and to share their data freely with a central source.
- BMW had to create an environment in which there was unselfish sharing of response and sales information among competing vendors.
- The company had to get a highly successful and independent dealer organization to share its information with BMW.
- It had to get prospects to describe their purchase intentions.
- It had to recognize that high-end consumers do not respond well to direct marketing efforts because they receive them from many companies.

- It had to deal with the fact that many consumers' computer equipment had slow Internet connections and Web browsers (like AOL) that could not receive HTML emails.
- BMW had not yet computed the lifetime value of its customers.
- At first, BMW could not deliver personalized content about the products that the customers owned or were interested in.
- BMW lacked a scoring system to determine who would be a great or a valuable prospect.
- In the past, BMW had not used accurate methods of evaluating success, such as control groups.
- BMW had to shift from being an entirely product-oriented company to being a customer-oriented company.

How the System Worked

The system that msdbm designed for BMW worked this way:

- First, BMW and msdbm profiled and analyzed current owners to determine who would make the best prospects, relying on both customer-supplied and appended data from 13 different sources.
- They decided to concentrate marketing dollars on these best prospects, using a 6-week communication program that involved both direct mail and email.
- They created lifetime value tables for the owners of new and used cars.
- They got a strong manager to work with the various vendors, internal departments, and dealers to encourage them to share information.
- They developed a process and methodology for a true relationship-building system using not only the Internet but also data from BMW's legacy systems, changing and updating all systems so that they could receive and use responses from the prospects.
- They surveyed participants to receive feedback on the program, refine the process, and improve the delivery system.
- They set up a control group to determine the effectiveness of the program.

- They provided a Web-based reporting system to track the results.
- The system was set up to manage 5 million prospects and customers in the database.
- They provided feedback on all the information to everyone in real time through the Web.

The Scoring System

Before prospects were put into the system, they had to be scored to identify those who were more likely to purchase, by model, and those who were less likely to purchase. The scoring system set up by msdbm automatically

- Performed regression and correlation analysis using customer-supplied and Experian data on current BMW owners to identify unique independent variables.
- Developed score ranges for variables based on frequency distribution, standard deviation, and historical experience.
- Scored samples of prospects and compared results.
- Developed lifetime value tables and assigned a value to each customer and participant.
- Delivered personalized content and information to each responder, whether the responder was a previous customer or a prospect.
- Used variables to score prospects; these variables included purchase time frame, make of current vehicle, age, income-to-price ratio, year of current car, source of prospect lead, and debt-to-income ratio.

BMW and msdbm set up a 6-week communication program that was targeted to people who had expressed an interest in BMW by responding to one of the current marketing programs, such as direct-mail or Internet requests. These prospects had come from rented mailing lists, in-house lists, and responses to advertising. Although this was a prospect-based program, current BMW customers who were interested in purchasing another BMW and who had responded to existing BMW programs were included.

The media used were print on demand, email, and Internet-based. The content was designed to be what the prospect was interested in receiving. There were a number of successive follow-ups that combined dealer calls, emails, personalized on-demand printing, and invitations to events.

Results of the Program

The effectiveness of the program was gauged by comparing the conversion rate of consumers enrolled in Extending the Dialogue to that of a control group. Conversions by participants in the program were 20 percent higher than in the control group. In detail, the program had these results:

- Communications were sent out to prospects and customers in a much more organized and timely way.
- The system beat the control group by 150 percent in terms of closing the sale.
- Sales of BMWs were up 25 percent for the year, while sales of all other luxury imports were down 7 percent.
- Overall sales increased by $25,000,000.
- Both management and dealers felt that they had a better understanding of the BMW customer, which allowed BMW to better target its promotions.
- BMW prospects appeared to have been receptive to this program, encouraging BMW to roll it out on a larger scale.

Telling Them What They Want to Hear

The *Weekly Standard* is a conservative weekly political journal. The magazine conducts extensive direct-mail campaigns using rented lists, most of which are political fund-raising and subscription lists. For help in increasing its subscriber base, it turned to Brian Brilliant at BMD in Alexandria, Virginia.

The source of a list often demonstrates the mindset of the people on that list. To leverage the limited data on potential customers, BMD's strategy was to insert a variable headline at the top of the letter that would relate in a marketing sense to the list from which the recipient came. For example, if John Doe's name came from a military list, then he would get a headline such as: "John Doe, we have some *shocking news* about American's decaying military." Seven headlines were created to match up with the rented lists. As you might expect, there were some lists that didn't fit any specific profile. They received a generic headline. The headlines that were not selected for each prospect were then used in the first paragraph as part of a variable message describing the variety of subject matter that readers might find in the publication.

How well would such an approach work? To find out, Brian created a control group for each list. The control group did not get a customized headline, but instead got a generic headline about the magazine. Comparing the controls to the customized headlines, the custom letters had, on average, a 24.8 percent better response rate and a 62.3 percent better pay-up rate. The agency attributed most of the boost in initial response rate to the "openability" of the package because of the personalized message. And it attributed the lift in pay-up rate to the fact that subscribers were told up front that the magazine contained content that would interest them. The method worked.

Cluster Coding

For the past 15 years, Claritas has done a brilliant job of dividing the U.S. population into 62 clusters with catchy names like Shotguns & Pickups and Pools & Patios. These clusters roughly reflect household income and living style. For some products (although not for most), the cluster someone lives in has something to do with the products that person tends to buy. People in some clusters drink imported beer. People in others drink only domestic. Folks in some clusters read the *New York Times*. Folks in others read the *New York Post*. People in still others do not take a newspaper at all. If your product can be shown to be particularly attractive to people in certain clusters, you can use this in your retention program. In a previous book, I described how the *Globe and Mail* in Toronto made highly profitable use of cluster coding to determine who read its newspaper and who didn't. With that knowledge, it was able to concentrate its telemarketing on the correct postal walks, saving millions of dollars per year in acquisition costs.

Should you use cluster coding? First of all, remember that cluster coding works only with consumer products. Second, consider whether your product appeals particularly to a certain class of people. If you think that it does, spend the money to have cluster coding affixed to 20,000 of your customers, ranked by revenue, and see if the clusters show you anything worthwhile. Any good service bureau can have cluster codes affixed to your file for about $120 per thousand, so your 20,000 will cost you a minimum of about $4000. In most cases, the clusters won't show you anything at all. If they do, you can use them to make some money. Let's assume that you have been sending direct mail to about 1.2 million customers per month, for which you spend about $650,000. Table 13-2 shows what your results might look like.

It is costing you about $30 to acquire a customer. This is your control. Now let's try to beat that. We are going to select prospects for mailing mainly from the correct clusters, with some others added to make sure you are right. Your mailing next month could look like Table 13-3.

Table 13-2 Results before Using Cluster Selection

	Nonselected direct mail	Cost	Sales	Rate	Cost per sale
Clusters with over 20% penetration	219,499	$111,944	7,463	3.4%	$15.00
Clusters with 5% to 19% penetration	452,991	$231,025	9,513	2.1%	$24.29
Clusters with less than 5% penetration	601,223	$306,624	4,810	0.8%	$63.75
Total customers	1,273,713	$649,594	21,786		$29.82

Table 13-3 Results after Using Cluster Selection

	Selected direct mail	Cost	Sales	Rate	Cost per sale
Clusters with over 20% penetration	950,000	$484,500	32,300	3.4%	$15.00
Clusters with 5 to 19% penetration	200,000	$102,000	4,200	2.1%	$24.29
Clusters with less than 5% penetration	50,000	$25,500	400	0.8%	$63.75
Total customers	1,200,000	$612,000	36,900		$16.59
Cluster coding	1,200,000	$144,000			
Total costs	1,200,000	$756,000	36,900		$20.49

You are still mailing 1.2 million pieces, and you are spending about $100,000 more than before, as your costs include $144,000 for selecting prospects by cluster. Even so, your cost per sale is down by $9, and you have gained 15,000 more customers on the same 1.2 million mailing. This shows the value of cluster coding, if it works for you.

Why did you do any mailing to clusters where your penetration was less than 20 percent? That is a good question. Self-preservation is the answer. As database marketers, we always have to justify what we do to management, which questions everything. "Why did you spend this $144,000?" your managers will ask. "Because I knew from previous tests that cluster coding would work," you answer. "Then why did you mail to prospects in the lower-performing clusters?" they will ask. You reply, "Because you would never have believed me if I hadn't tested some of these lower-performing clusters. Now you do."

Prospect LTV

When you do acquisition, you want to know the LTV of the prospects that you are trying to acquire. But how can you know anything about them, since they have never bought anything from you?

Many companies have been quite successful at this kind of analysis. First, you develop the LTV of your existing customers. Segment them by demographics, and develop the LTV of each group. Next, you append the same demographics to your list of prospects. Experian, Donnelly, Acxiom, and other companies will be delighted to append demographics (age, income, presence of children, home value, ethnicity, years at present address—some 200 different pieces of data) to your prospect file. They will even find prospects for you that have the demographics that you are looking for. Then you make the assumption that prospects that look just like your best customers will behave like your best customers and will have a similar LTV.

Armed with this prospect file, your next step is to test your marketing skills. Can you develop the right approach through mass marketing ads, letters, phone calls, or emails to win a significant number of these prospects as customers? The final step will be to determine whether

Table 13-4 Selling to Segments

	Customer 3-year LTV	Matching prospects mailed	Mailing cost	Sales to prospects	Prospect response rate	Cost per sale
Group A	$865	400,211	$244,129	6,804	1.70%	$35.88
Group B	$522	200,011	$122,007	5,800	2.90%	$21.03
Group C	$217	50,034	$ 30,521	1,601	3.20%	$19.06
Group D	$ 14	50,055	$ 30,534	1,802	3.60%	$16.94
Total		700,311	$427,190	16,007	2.29%	$26.69

these prospect look-alikes really do act like the customers that they were modeled after. When your tests are completed, do a direct-mail or email marketing promotion. You can create a table for prospects that looks like Table 13-4.

To create this table, you divided your customer base into four segments based on lifetime value. You determined the demographics of these four segments: income, age, presence of children, home value, and other criteria. Using these criteria, you rented prospect names that matched the profile of each segment, and you did a mailing to them. Your results were interesting. The prospects that matched your best customers with the highest lifetime value had the lowest response rate. Why should that be? It is not at all unusual. Banks, for example, find that their best customers are the least responsive. Rich people get more mail than poor people. They throw it away. In some cases, poor people are more likely to respond. You have to decide whether you want responses (acquired customers) or valuable long-term customers.

Group D is very interesting. It is costing you $17 to acquire customers who are worth $14. That does not make much sense. However, that is what most companies are doing because they have not read this book and they have not done the analysis. There is also another reason why most companies are acquiring worthless customers: They are set up for acquisition. They have a sales vice president who is compensated on the basis of the number of customers acquired. He does not get blamed if these customers are worthless. "It's marketing's job to make money with these customers. I just find 'em and rope 'em in, and I do a great job of it," he says. Is this true in your company? Of course it is, unless you have determined the lifetime value of your customers, divided them into segments, and figured out which segments are winners and which are losers.

That's what this book is all about—doing a thorough job of creating a marketing database, and profiling it to find out important facts. Then you use those facts to draw valuable and important conclusions.

Suppose Table 13-4 is a correct picture of the situation in your company. Your sales force is working hard, succeeding in bringing in a lot of worthless customers, and getting bonuses for it. What can you do about it? You have to do your homework, determine the lifetime value of the various customer segments, and then put your findings on the desk of top management. Convince management that the company may be acquiring the wrong people as customers. You will have a battle on your hands. It may get rough, but if you have done the job right and you stick to your guns, someone will recognize it. Then you have to work to change the situation. After all, the purpose of an enterprise is to make a profit, not just to acquire customers. We all know that, but we don't act on it.

In a previous book, I described the situation I found at a client that sold credit insurance for credit cards. A profiling exercise was conducted that divided the U.S. population into seven sectors. Analysis showed that only three of the seven sectors ever bought credit insurance. Armed with this information, the company went to several banks (its customers) and suggested to them that they stop telemarketing to these unresponsive segments, since the sales did not justify the expense. What did each bank's vice president of insurance respond? "Nuts. Call them all." You see, these vice presidents were compensated on the basis of the number of customers acquired, not the cost per acquisition or the profits from the insurance. So the insurance company went on calling everybody.

Selling Timeshares

Timeshares have become very popular in the past 10 years. More than a million families own a week at some resort where they can go for a vacation. RCI, a part of Cendant, makes a market in these timeshares; owners can deposit their timeshare week with RCI and, in return, receive a week at some other resort somewhere else in the world. Because of RCI, some families rarely return to the timeshare that they originally purchased.

The method whereby these timeshare owners are originally acquired has become quite scientific and interesting. Most developers of timeshares sell tours as an acquisition method. A tour is a weekend vacation that is offered to a family at below market rates—at prices as low as $50 for a 3-day family vacation at a hotel that is near a timeshare property. While they are at the hotel, as part of their payment for the weekend vacation, families are asked or required to take a tour of the timeshare and hear a pitch on the value of owning a timeshare. Most tour operators report that about 10 percent of the families that take a tour end up buying a timeshare, at prices ranging from $10,000 to $25,000 for 1 week.

The process of acquiring timeshare owners, therefore, has become a process of selling tours. If you can get people to take a tour, you can be confident that one in ten will make a purchase. The methods for tour selling have become very scientific. Direct mail is used to offer households within 90 minutes' driving distance of a timeshare resort a weekend at a nearby hotel at a fixed below-market price. The response rate to such direct-mail solicitations is about $\frac{3}{10}$ of 1 percent. Telemarketing then takes over to sign the respondents up for a tour. Here, again, scientific methods are used. Those who refuse a tour in June will be called again about touring in July, or August, or some other month. "Call until they tour or die" is the basic philosophy. And it works. Timeshares are one of the most profitable industries in the United States.

Some interesting lessons have been learned in the course of acquiring timeshare customers. These lessons can be useful in other industries. For example:

• Vacation packages can be sold with a hook (a requirement that the family listen to a pitch about the timeshare) or no hook (no pitch requirement). Statistics show that no-hook recipients are more likely to buy a timeshare than hook recipients. Why should this be so? A hook family has steeled itself in advance against the timeshare pitch: "OK, we will take their vacation, but we are certainly not going to plunk down money for a timeshare." The no-hook family's thinking is entirely different. Without the hook, the family members arrive thinking, "Isn't this great! A weekend in Orlando for only $69, and no responsibilities other than to have fun." While they are there, they say to themselves, "Well, these nice people have given us this great vacation. We might as well see what they have to offer. Maybe we would like to own a place here in Orlando."

- Tour direct mail that offers a specific date on the outside of the envelope has a better response rate than offers that say, "Come to Orlando this summer for a week on us," with no specific date mentioned. Why should this be so? If families think that if they don't accept this date, they will miss out on the vacation altogether, they are probably more motivated to act immediately than those who think, "Well, let's see if we can find a week when it is convenient for all of us to go together to Orlando." After a couple of days, they have forgotten the offer entirely. Direct mail must have some urgency about it, or it doesn't work well.
- Ugly one-color offers pull better than beautiful four-color offers. Why? This is one of the great mysteries of direct mail. Sometimes you don't know the reason, you just know the results.

Doing email right

Recently a Fortune 1000 retailer worked with Quris to create a comprehensive email program for their customers. The company had not used emails extensively before. The goal was to show a general increase in store activity and total net revenue through emails to opt-in email customers. They wanted to prove that they could influence customer behavior through emails. In the process of this experiment, they created one of the most comprehensive and valuable exercises in the whole direct marketing industry.

To test their program, they set up a test population of just under 220,000 customers who had previously provided the company with their emails, and permission to use them.

Barriers to success

- **Two Step Process.** The company does not sell products through the mail or through their website. Customers have to come in to the stores to buy. So, to find out if the email was doing any good, they had to measure store activity by the folks that got the emails. A lot of store transaction data had to be analyzed.

- **Setting up a Control Group.** Some people asked the company to send them emails about new product releases. To prove the value of the emails, they had to withhold emails from about 16,000 people who had asked for them.
- **Data Formats and Location.** As is common with large corporations, data was in different formats and in different places.
- **Channel Overlap.** There were many channels touching the customers. The same customers who got emails, also saw print ads, direct mail, websites and TV news about their products. How could the impact of email be determined, while controlling for the influence of other channels?
- **Electronic Coupons** were new to the company's customer. Technology and procedures for both distribution and redemption had to be developed, and customer acceptance/familiarity developed.

In doing their planning they learned that:

- Email programs have different goals from direct mail. While both are directed at increasing store activity, direct mail is offer-based while email has an information, entertainment and long-term relationship-building purpose. Both channels are directed at increasing store activity, but direct mail is more overtly offer-based and coupon redemption related. Email has broader objectives, focusing on ongoing customer contact aimed at building a relationship.
- Email recipients had to receive consistent communications. To track the email success it was necessary to measure the store activity of the targeted customers before and after the emails.
- Direct mail has unknown recipients until the campaign list criteria are specified. Email requires opt-in to receive the communication, but the recipient does not necessarily even have to be a customer. The company found that the recency of the opt-in had a significant impact on the customer's behavior. Those whose opt-in was over a year old had an overall response (at least one email open) during the

program of 20%. Email opt-ins newer than one year old had a response of over 85%.

• What customers received was a newsletter about the products. Quris also set up an interactive Web page where customers could become subscribers to the newsletter. Members could also sign up for the newsletter at the stores, through partner agreements and through sweepstakes.

Setting up the test and control groups

The sample of just under 220,000 was divided into nine different groups for testing purposes. A control group of nearly 16,000 opt-in email customers was assigned at random before the program began. This group got no email messages.

Customers with op-in's over a year old (nearly 90,000) got a reconnect message to which they could opt-out. Then the total test universe of over 170,000 was divided into four basic groups of about 43,000 each. Cells 1 and 2 got a constant message every two weeks. Cells 3 and 4 two got messages based on their prior month store visits. Cells 2 and 4 received eCoupons, while Cells 1 and 3 did not.

The coupons tested three offers:

• Get one product, get one free anytime
• Get one product, get one free in a 5 day period
• Get one product, get one free Monday through Thursday

A particular difficulty involved how to measure customer activity. Was it total expenditures, total number of transactions, frequency of transactions, etc. The company emerged from this test with valid quantitative measures to demonstrate the lift from email on an ongoing basis.

The company determines ROI based on incremental total net revenue (TNR)—Quris augmented this traditional analyses by isolating the source of the lift: i.e., did email drive new customers to the store? Or the same customers more frequently? Or the same customers to spend more? Also, Quris looked at the purchase propensities (e.g., comparing different types of transactions).

Results

- The lift for the entire test population compared to the control sample was 28%. In other words, sending emails twice a month increased sales by 28% over sending nothing.
- The total lift for customers who received electronic coupons was higher than for those with no coupons. The coupons worked.
- Previously active company customers had a higher lift in ROI than less active customers.
- The emails were successful in reactivating inactive members.
- It appeared that those who got regular messages responded better than those who got messages based on behavior.

This is a very interesting and valuable study. Quris and the company used all the techniques available to do a really thorough job of exploring the relationship between emails and customer behavior. There are too few companies that have rigorously used control groups to prove that what they were doing was working. This analysis validated the email channel to the company's senior management. As of 2003, the company sends out 8 newsletters and over 1.5 million emails per month.

Creating Referrals

Many companies have had success with referrals. The idea is to get your existing customers to recommend that people that they are related to, work with, or know also become customers. In other words, your customers become advocates. They tell their friends what a wonderful company or product you have, and they get these friends to try your product. Once someone has become a customer as a result of a referral, something wonderful happens. These referrals who become new customers display, as a group, higher retention levels and higher spending levels than the average customer who is recruited by other means. You can prove this for yourself.

First, you have to set up a formal referral program. Tell your customers about it, and make it easy for them to generate referrals by contacting a customer service rep or by going on the Web. Once you have a new name, address, and email name, it is your job to get that person to become a customer. However, you put the person's ID number into the referring customer's database record, and you put the referrer's ID into the referred customer's record. They are now tied together. You can now measure their retention and spending rates and their lifetime value.

Let's say that you have done this, and you discover that your typical customer has a 3-year LTV of $70, whereas your average referral has a 3-year LTV of $100. What can you do with that information? You can use it to create a special referral incentive program. America Online has done this. At various times, it has rewarded customers with $25 or $50 for recommending someone who also becomes a customer. This is a wonderful example of successful database marketing. There are two parts to the AOL story. In the first place, AOL has to spend a lot of money to acquire customers. It places ads on TV, sends out CDs in the mail, puts CDs in tens of thousands of stores in POS displays, and recruits customers through partnership arrangements. This must be expensive. I would imagine that it costs AOL at least $100 to acquire a new customer. Once acquired, however, these customers pay AOL $23 per month forever. What is the marginal cost of servicing a new customer? Not very much. Once you have the system and software in place, it is not that expensive to add a new customer—perhaps $5 per customer per month. At that rate, AOL is doing very well if it is spending $100 to acquire customers who produce $18 in net revenue per month.

Of course, some of these new customers do not stay. They cancel after a few months. This is true of all customers and all types of companies. That is where the referrals come in. Referrals are much less likely to cancel than people who are recruited by other means. Why? Because they know someone who is on AOL—the person who referred them. They may have joined to send that person email. They will some day have to face the question, "Well, how do you like AOL?" They don't want to have to say, "Well, I tried it, but I couldn't get it to work" or "I didn't like it" or "It was a waste of my money." They are not going to want to say these things to their friends. So they are more likely to remain as customers than people who have no such connections. For this reason, AOL can afford to give away a little money to acquire such people, and so can you.

Table 13-5 Regular-Customer LTV

	Year 1	Year 2	Year 3
Customers	100,000	60,000	39,000
Retention rate	60%	65%	70%
Spending rate	$275	$285	$295
Revenue	$27,500,000	$17,100,000	$11,505,000
Cost rate	60%	55%	54%
Costs	$16,500,000	$ 9,405,000	$6,212,700
Acquisition/retention cost ($120/$20)	$12,000,000	$ 1,200,000	$ 780,000
Total costs	$28,500,000	$10,605,000	$6,992,700
Profit	($1,000,000)	$6,495,000	$4,512,300
Discount rate	1.00	1.07	1.15
NPV of profit	($1,000,000)	$6,058,769	$3,926,525
Cumulative NPV of profit	($1,000,000)	$5,058,769	$8,985,294
Lifetime value	($10)	$50.59	$89.85

Do your homework and find out how much you are spending to acquire customers. Keep track of who is referring whom. Find out how much more valuable referrals are than regular customers. Then set up a program to share that profit and to reward your customers for referring other people who become customers. Table 13-5 shows how regular customers might look on a LTV chart.

Your regular customers cost you $120 to acquire and $20 to maintain once they are acquired. Your retention rate begins at 60 percent. These customers are worth $90 in the third year. Now let's look at referred customers (see Table 13-6). Let's say you can generate 10,000 referrals. As you can see, these referred customers have a much higher retention rate. As a result, even after we reward our regular customers with $50 per referred customer, these customers have a third-year LTV of $206 instead of $90. They are really profitable customers. You will discover the same thing. Figure it out, and design a referral program.

Summary

- From the Key Equipment case, we learned how to
  - Create relevant and highly targeted prospecting lists that the lead managers would believe to be credible.

Table 13-6 Referred-Customer LTV

	Year 1	Year 2	Year 3
Customers	10,000	8,000	6,560
Retention rate	80%	82%	85%
Spending rate	$275	$285	$295
Revenue	$2,750,000	$2,280,000	$1,935,200
Cost rate	60%	55%	54%
Costs	$1,650,000	$1,254,000	$1,045,008
Referral fee/retention fee ($50/$20)	$ 500,000	$ 160,000	$ 131,200
Total costs	$2,150,000	$1,414,000	$1,176,208
Profit	$600,000	$866,000	$758,992
Discount rate	1.00	1.07	1.15
NPV of profit	$600,000	$807,836	$660,462
Cumulative of NPV profit	$600,000	$1,407,836	$2,068,298
Lifetime value	$60	$140.78	$206.83

- Develop direct-mail communications from each lead manager that permit effective telemarketing follow-up.
- Have outbound telemarketing associates work closely with the lead managers.
- Create a lead-generation database that tracks and identifies the business generated by the lead managers from this program.
- From the SalesLogix case study, we learned how to develop
  - An online event registration system.
  - A global campaign information database into which marketing managers input campaign details through a Web interface.
- From the BMW study, we learned how to
  - Set up a 6-week communication program aimed at targeted prospects.
  - Use variables to score prospects.
  - Deliver personalized content and information to each responder.
- From the *Weekly Standard*, we learned to modify messages to prospects based on what we have learned about those prospects.
- From the timeshare study, we learned a two-step process: Sell them a tour, and let them buy the timeshare while they are on the tour.

So what have we learned overall from these studies?

- Long-term customer loyalty should be a prime consideration during customer acquisition. It rarely is. You can test this in your company by determining the LTV of your customers by segment.
- Mass marketing may be the best method of acquiring some customers.

What Works

- Profiling and modeling customers and looking for prospects that match the profile of profitable customers.
- Providing communications from a person who will be contacting the prospect.
- Providing personalized communications that reflect information that we have about the prospect.
- Using telemarketers to support field sales personnel.
- Using a two-step process to zero in on those who are most likely to buy.
- Giving prospects a direct and simple offer with a deadline. Too many choices reduce response.
- Using the Web as a means for keeping everyone in the company up to date on the acquisition process.

What Doesn't Work

- Acquiring customers by giving discounts. It works in the short term, but the customers do not stay with you.
- Assuming that every acquired customer is valuable. Many of them can be unprofitable.
- Concentrating on acquisition to the exclusion of retention.
- Hanging on to customer names and not exchanging them with others.

Quiz

1. In the prospect penetration case study, what can you use the target potential index for?
   a. Determining which customers are worthless
   b. Determining your retention budget
   c. Deciding which prospects you should aim at acquiring
   d. Nothing, since it is a worthless idea
   e. Scrap paper

2. What factor was not used to select prospects in the Key Equipment case?
   a. Major industry
   b. Products purchased
   c. Number of employees
   d. Year company started
   e. Sales volume

3. In the SalesLogix case, which of the following was not listed as being a problem to begin with?
   a. There were no e-marketing campaigns.
   b. The company lacked high-technology products.
   c. There was no lead-management system.
   d. Telemarketing was not integrated.
   e. The cost per lead was $500.

4. Which of the following was not one of the results of the SalesLogix case?
   a. Lead volume grew to 9600 per quarter.
   b. Online events grew to 12 per month.
   c. Telemarketing was outsourced to a better bureau.
   d. The system filtered out 25 percent of raw leads.
   e. There was 100 percent lead tracking.

5. In the BMW study, which one of the following was not done?
   a. Using Experian data in regressions.
   b. Delivering personalized content to prospects.
   c. Assigning LTV to each customer and participant.
   d. Using variables to score prospects.
   e. None of the above; all these things were done.

6. List four product categories that cluster coding probably works for and four that it probably doesn't work for.

7. Which of the following is probably not true of most companies?
   a. The company pays bonuses for customers, not for long-term customers.
   b. The company does not know whether new customers will be long-term or not.
   c. The company has not computed the LTV of customers or prospects.
   d. The company is highly customer-centric.
   e. Marketing and sales are going in different directions.

8. Why did the *Weekly Standard* custom approach work?
   a. Customers are dumb.
   b. Customers like to have their views agreed with.
   c. It was a fluke. Most such copy fails.
   d. The numbers are probably fake.
   e. None of the above.

9. In the timeshare case, if no-hook tours perform better, why does anyone sell hook tours?
   a. The data are wrong. Hook tours are better.
   b. Hook tours are traditional.
   c. It takes time to change an established system.
   d. It is hard to persuade people that what they are doing is wrong.
   e. Answers b, c, and d.

10. What are three things that msdbm did for BMW that helped to solve the problem?

CHAPTER 14

PROFILE MARKETING

For some time, creating customer profiles by appending data from outside sources to a database of customers and prospects has been a thriving business. The basis for this industry is the U.S. Bureau of the Census, which gathers data from every household in America every 10 years, the last time being in 2000. For most people, the census collects only a minimum amount of data: name, address, age, gender, and ethnicity. However, for 2 households out of 14, the census uses the "long form," which asks many questions about income, value of home, type of plumbing, occupation, and so on—over 200 pieces of data in all. These data are arranged for sale to businesses that are interested. Before providing this information to the business community, the Census Bureau scrambles the data by averaging the answers from the 2 households that filled out the long form and attributing these data to all 14 households in the group. Because of this, you cannot find out Arthur Hughes's actual income or home value from the census data. What you get appended to Arthur Hughes's record is the average of the data given by the 2 households out of 14 in the area in which Arthur lives.

This isn't a bad estimate because as America has evolved, most people live in subdivisions in which the houses are all of similar value. As a result, the incomes of the residents of each group of 14 houses are likely to be similar, as are their ages, number of children, and so on. Only a small percentage of Americans today live in diverse neighborhoods in which poor and rich or old and young live side by side.

To the census information, some large data companies, such as Equifax or Trans Union, add financial data derived from credit flows so that they can estimate a household's actual income and spending habits. State driver's license and vehicle registration information is used to determine a person's actual age and the type of car he or she drives. Catalogers' data files are used to determine responsiveness to direct-mail offers. Most communities have developed new mover files—databases of people who have just moved in. The U.S. Postal Service provides the National Change of Address (NCOA) system, which corrects addresses of households and businesses. By putting all this information together, it is possible to create a pretty accurate profile of any household or individual if you know the household address.

Profiles are used to create customer and prospect marketing segments. You can divide your database into such groups as

- Teenagers
- Young marrieds
- Families with small children
- Single women
- Families with college-age children
- Empty nesters
- Seniors
- College students

Once you have done this, you can check the national average for each category against your own customer database. You can get a picture of the type of person who buys your product and the type who does not. When you know this, you can greatly reduce your marketing costs by trying to reach only the most likely households instead of every household.

What can profiles tell you? Here are some sample profiling results in which a company compared its customers to the national average. To begin with, Figure 14-1 gives a profile by age range. It shows that this company's customers are clustered in the 35–54 age range, with the percentage of customers in this age range being much higher than the national average. Seniors are certainly not avid consumers of this company's products.

Figure 14-1   Profile by Age Range

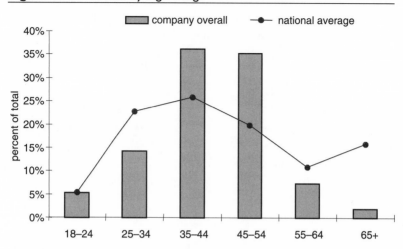

Figure 14-2   Actual Age Range of Customers

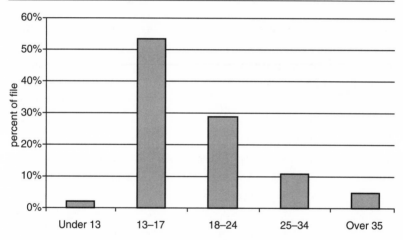

These numbers were derived from appended data that reflect the age of the head of the household. The company also asked its customers what their actual age was. The results were quite different, as shown in Figure 14-2. Here the company's customers actually were quite young—between 13 and 24. While Figure 14-1 gave the age of the head of the household, most of the company's customers were children in the

Figure 14-3   Income Ranges

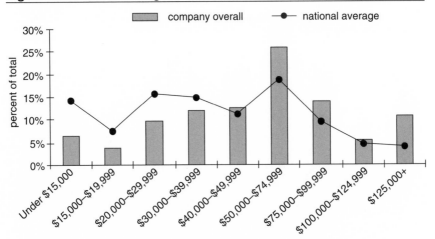

household. Conclusion: If you want to know the real facts, ask your customers directly. Appended data do not tell the whole story.

What is the income range of your customers? Figure 14-3 gives the results from the same company, using appended head of household data. What can we learn from this graph? The consumers of this company's products live in households in which the income is close to the national average. Poor people do not buy the products. Those with incomes over $50,000 clearly do.

In terms of gender, the company's products appeal more to women than to men, as Figure 14-4 shows. Nationwide, women make up about 51 percent of the population. But 62 percent of the consumers of this company's products are women.

How Modeling Can Help

Modeling is complicated and expensive. It usually requires the appending of external data, such as age, income, and presence of children. It requires expensive software manipulated by skilled analysts. The minimum cost for a model is usually $25,000, and some companies have spent well over

Figure 14-4   Profile by Gender

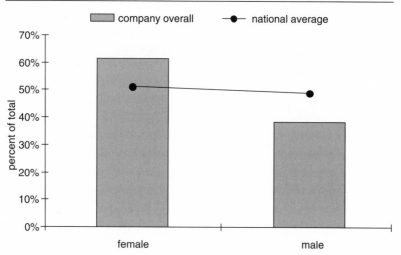

$200,000 for a complex model. So why does anyone do modeling? Because, for large projects, it may pay off and give you results that are better than those you could get without the model.

Summit Marketing Group in St. Louis did marketing for a major property and casualty insurance company. The P&C insurance market is very competitive. Hundreds of different companies offer automobile insurance, and customers continually shop for the best deal. The pressure to squeeze profits from every marketing dollar is intense. To help solve the problem, Summit developed an optimization model that was designed to maximize profits for each marketing campaign.

To acquire new automobile insurance customers, the P&C company sent mailings to approximately 1.2 million households in a 10-state area each month. The mailing list was drawn from a database of 9 million households that included response and sales history, demographics, and credit scores. To maximize profits, Summit focused on return on promotion (ROP). ROP is a discounted cashflow technique that is used to measure the net present value of a marketing investment. It is theoretically similar to ROI. ROP considers response probabilities, conversion rates, risk probabilities, acquisition costs, and other marketing decision factors. The goal of the model is to determine which factors are most important in creating the largest return on promotion, and to use these factors in selecting the 1.2 million names to receive the mailing each month. Since the company mailed every month, Summit had the previous months' history to use as a base. The objective was to use the model to get better and better at selecting the names to be mailed to, in order to continually improve profits.

The modeling process produced some surprising results:

- The best candidates were not necessarily the best responders. The best candidates probably already had insurance somewhere else and were unwilling to shift.
- The best responders were often the least creditworthy, since they have trouble getting insurance.
- Since the model mixes lifetime value, creditworthiness, and probability of response, the top response deciles are not necessarily the most profitable. The goal was profit, not response.

Table 14-1 shows the results of one month's mailing, comparing the previous month's selection methods with those used in the current month. The control group is what they were previously doing each month. The optimized group is the new way of doing exactly the same thing with better results.

Notice that the control group had higher revenue per sale ($1630) than the optimized group did ($1360). The optimized group compensated for this by having a higher response rate and a higher sales rate.

Table 14-1 Return on Promotion

	Control group	Optimized group	Percent changed	Number changed
Total mailed	1,264,571	1,264,571	0%	0
Cost of mailing	$547,559	$547,559	0%	0
Number of responses	13,366	16,090	20%	2724
Response rate	1.06%	1.27%	20%	0.22%
Number of sales	1,599	2,323	45%	724
Sales rate	12.0%	14.4%	21%	2.47%
Total revenue	$2,605,603	$3,158,151	21%	$553,208
Revenue per sale	$1,630	$1,360	−17%	($270)
Profit	$95,896	$187,851	96%	$91,955
Return on promotion	18%	34%	96%	16.8%

This allowed total revenue to increase by over $500,000 and profits to increase by over $90,000 for *one month's mailing*. This translates into $6 million in added revenue and $1 million in added profit on an annual basis. If the model cost $200,000 to run, it was still a worthwhile investment for the insurance company.

Getting Customers to Enter Their Own Profiles

The best data come from your customers themselves. Many of them will be glad to give you information for free. In the past, sending survey forms to customers by direct mail and receiving direct-mail responses was a very expensive process. Only a small percentage of customers (usually less than 7 percent) would respond to such a survey. When they mailed in their survey forms, the data from these forms had to be entered into a database by hand. The cost per completed survey was substantial, as Table 14-2 shows. To justify this expenditure, you had better have a very profitable marketing project.

All this has changed with the advent of the Internet. Today companies make survey forms an important part of their Web site. They encourage people to come to the site and complete a survey form. The costs are dramatically different. Assume that you already have a person's email address. You ask that person to complete a survey by email, directing him to your Web site. When he gets there, he does all the work.

Table 14-2 Cost per Survey by Mail

	Amounts
Requests sent	200,000
Cost per request	$0.60
Cost	$120,000
Response rate	7.0%
Responses	14,000
Return postage	$0.80
Data entry cost	$0.35
Response cost	$16,100
Total cost	$136,100
Cost per survey	$9.72

Table 14-3 Cost per Survey by Email

	Amounts
Requests sent	200,000
Cost per email	$0.04
Cost	$8,000
Response rate	7.0%
Responses	14,000
Data entry	$0.00
Data entry cost	$0
Total cost	$8,000
Cost per survey	$0.57

There is no data entry cost. A Web response customer profile will cost you about $0.57, as shown in Table 14-3.

Why would customers want to give you this information? You have to come up with some good reasons, or they won't do it. One way to get them to do it is to call these surveys preference profiles instead. The benefit to the customer is that you will use these preference profiles to provide customized service just for her. Figure 14-5 gives an example of a preference profile.

Figure 14-6 shows how Macy's asks for profiles. Why should you register with Macy's? Figure 14-7 tells you why.

While visitors to your Web site are filling out these surveys, you can ask them their age, income, marital status, and so on. The information you get will be far more accurate than appended data.

Figure 14-5   Disney Survey

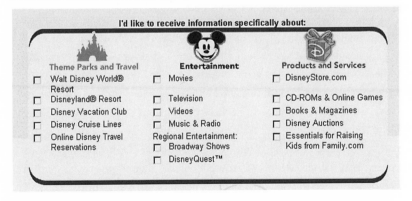

Figure 14-6   Macy's Survey

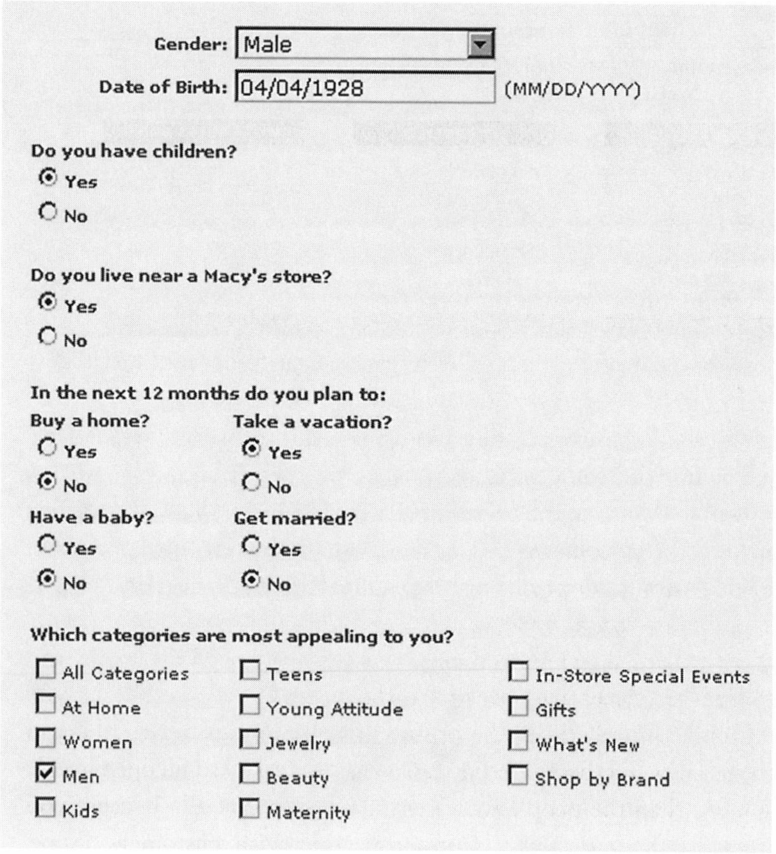

Gender: | Male ▼ |

Date of Birth: | 04/04/1928 | (MM/DD/YYYY)

Do you have children?
⦿ Yes
○ No

Do you live near a Macy's store?
⦿ Yes
○ No

In the next 12 months do you plan to:

Buy a home?	Take a vacation?
○ Yes	⦿ Yes
⦿ No	○ No
Have a baby?	**Get married?**
○ Yes	○ Yes
⦿ No	⦿ No

Which categories are most appealing to you?

☐ All Categories	☐ Teens	☐ In-Store Special Events
☐ At Home	☐ Young Attitude	☐ Gifts
☐ Women	☐ Jewelry	☐ What's New
☑ Men	☐ Beauty	☐ Shop by Brand
☐ Kids	☐ Maternity	

Effect on the Customer

Having customers fill out preferences profiles does more for you than just provide information. It will change the behavior of your prospects and customers. Once they have invested their time in filling out your profile and have thought about the types of services they would like to receive from you, they will think differently about your company. They will be more responsive to your next offer, whether it is a direct-mail, email, print, TV, or radio offer. You have moved them one step closer to being profitable customers. You can prove that to your satisfaction by comparing two groups of similar customers. To one group, you send

Figure 14-7   Reasons to Fill Out the Macy's Survey

My Info

Registering with macys.com enables you to use all our convenient site features and check out quickly.

ORDER STATUS	MY PROFILE	MY ADDRESS BOOK
Track the status of your current orders, and see a history of your purchases at macys.com.	Tell us a little bit about yourself, and we'll serve you better in the future with personal shopping assistance.	Create and store shipping addresses for easy access any time you're signed in at macys.com.

MY WALLET	MY MACY'S CLOSET	MY WISH LIST
Securely save your billing address information for faster Checkout.	Mix, match and save wardrobe items and ensembles. View My Macy's Closet demo	Let others know exactly what you're wishing for, and your wishes may come true.

an email offer to complete their profile. To the other group, you do not. Table 14-4 shows an example of the results.

If you look at this table, it is clear that those who completed your profile turned out to be much better spenders than those who did not. This does not necessarily prove that the profiles were worth it. Maybe the people who filled out the profile were better customers to begin with. But why did the nonresponders who were asked to fill out a profile buy more than the people who were not solicited at all? Because you communicated with them! Communicating with customers always improves relations and sales—sometimes not as much as you would hope, but always more than noncommunication. So if you want to determine the true result of your profiling operation, don't just look at the

Table 14-4 Results of a Survey

	Test	Control
Customers	200,000	200,000
Not completed	186,000	200,000
Annual sales	$4,836,000	$3,200,000
Sales per person	$26	$16
Completed	14,000	
Annual sales	$1,512,000	
Sales per person	$108	

Figure 14-8   *New York Times* Survey

Today's Headlines
Simplify your life with Today's Headlines customized to your specifications. In one concise e-mail you can choose the number of headlines you want to receive from any or all of the major sections of NYTimes.com. Customize Today's Headlines now by selecting your preferences below (see sample).

Section	Headlines	Section	Headlines	Section	Headlines
☐ National	1 ▾	☐ Technology	1 ▾	☐ Arts	1 ▾
☐ International	1 ▾	☐ Politics	1 ▾	☐ NY Region	1 ▾
☐ Business	1 ▾	☐ Sports	1 ▾	☐ Op-Ed	1 ▾

Select edition: ⦿ Early   ◯ Late   ◯ Both

performance of the responders. Use a control group to see if the non-responders also do better. They will. Figure 14-8 shows the kind of information that the *New York Times* gets from its readers on the Web.

The Web Quiz

One of the most innovative and practical methods of customer profiling through Web response is the Web quiz. People are encouraged to go to a Web site to take a quiz. In most cases, the quiz concerns your product. When they take the quiz, they get a score that tells them whether they need your product and which of your products meets their needs.

Iomega, the maker of Zip storage disks, turned to Bob McKim of msdbm of Los Angeles to design a Web quiz that would attract business customers. Msdbm has perfected this technique. The company used direct mail and email to prompt IT directors to come to Iomega's Web site to take a quiz (see Figure 14-9). The quiz asked the easy questions about data storage given in the following list. As you look through these questions and think about your answers, you will see that you are easily drawn into the Iomega way of thinking. Each question has a yes or no answer.

1. At least once a quarter we make copies of all our data and store them off site.

Figure 14-9   Web Quiz

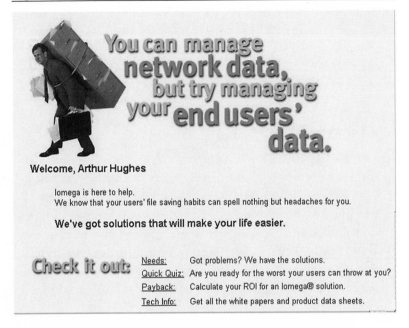

2. My organization keeps at least three copies of our data and always
   backs up to the oldest version.
3. My end users travel safely by carrying a disk copy of all their
   important data.
4. My end users always carry a disk copy with them when they're on
   the road so that they can share large amounts of data.
5. My end users back up all their data at least once a week.
6. My end users all have a continuous backup product to protect
   data between backups.
7. My end users employ a file version retention program to track
   file changes.
8. My end users have actually practiced restoring data from backup
   disks—just in case.
9. We use disk passwords to keep private data secure.
10. All our data disks are accurately labeled so we know what's on
    them and when they were created.

When the last yes or no has been checked, the user hits the Submit button and sees the score (see Figure 14-10). Clicking on the Needs button brings up a further analysis of the user's needs for Iomega products, as shown in Figure 14-11. After a series of questions, another screen provides a "Here's What I'm Struggling With" button that brings the user to a customized list of solutions that involve Iomega products.

Getting Users to Register

So far, the users are having fun on your Web site. You have their name and their email name, which is wonderful because you can use them to follow up. To get complete information on the users, however, Iomega wanted their company data. It gave people an incentive to provide this by making an offer. Bob McKim advised Iomega to offer respondents a drawing for an Iomega HipDip Digital Audio Player. To enter the drawing, users had to provide their address, their position in their company, information about the number of PCs in the organization, and their authority over purchases.

Results

This kind of Web response can be very profitable. Overall, the direct mail produced a response rate of 1.42 percent and a registration rate of

Figure 14-10 Results of the Quiz

Figure 14-11   The Fix for Your Problems

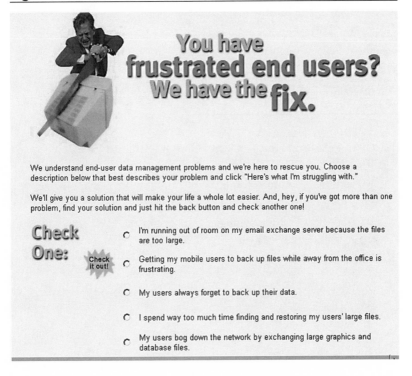

You have frustrated end users? We have the fix.

We understand end-user data management problems and we're here to rescue you. Choose a description below that best describes your problem and click "Here's what I'm struggling with."

We'll give you a solution that will make your life a whole lot easier. And, hey, if you've got more than one problem, find your solution and just hit the back button and check another one!

Check One: Check it out!

○ I'm running out of room on my email exchange server because the files are too large.

○ Getting my mobile users to back up files while away from the office is frustrating.

○ My users always forget to back up their data.

○ I spend way too much time finding and restoring my users' large files.

○ My users bog down the network by exchanging large graphics and database files.

1.01 percent. These registrants provided their names and company information and took the survey. The email promotion produced a response rate of 3.49 percent with a registration rate of 1.95 percent. It is significant that the email promotion was so much more productive. Figuring in the cost of the mailing, the results are shown in Table 14-5.

Email promotion proved to be 11 times as cost-effective as direct mail. Why would that be? There seem to be several reasons:

- The product was a computer product, so potential users all had computers.
- The audience was IT directors, who were used to email and were on the Web every day.
- The click-through process from an email takes only a second. Trying to enter a URL from a direct-mail piece takes at

Table 14-5 Cost of a Survey

	Direct mail	Email
Unit cost	$0.71	$0.12
Cost for 50,000	$35,500	$6,000
Response rate	1.42%	3.49%
Number of responses	710	1,745
Registration rate	1.01%	1.95%
Number registered	505	975
Cost per lead	$70.30	$6.15

least a minute—60 times as long. Compare these two sentences:

> To take the 1-minute Iomega Quiz and enter to win a prize, click here.

> To take the 1-minute Iomega Quiz, go on the Web and enter www.msdbmdata/iomega/.

Which is easier?

What Works

- Appending data to your customer file to learn your customers' demographics and create a profile
- Using the profile to find prospects that match the profile of your best customers
- Asking customers to complete their own profile
- Using a customer's profile to customize and personalize that customer's Web experience
- Using a quiz on the Web to find out about what customers want, and then offering it to them
- Comparing your customer profiles to the national average
- Using a model to improve your response rate on promotions

What Doesn't Work

- Getting people to fill out long, boring profile forms
- Assuming that the head of the household is the customer

Quiz

1. Go on the Web and find a company that asks you to complete your personal profile. See what is good and bad about the way this company goes about it.

2. Figure out how you could use customer profiles in your business. How can you collect the data? How will you give your customers an incentive to provide information?

3. In the P&C case study, what was the cost per piece of the mailing?
    a. $0.33
    b. $0.43
    c. $0.53
    d. $0.63
    e. None of the above

4. In the P&C case study, why didn't the P&C company select those with the highest revenue per sale?
    a. This is a trick question: It did.
    b. The optimized group had higher total sales.
    c. The optimized group had higher response rates.
    d. Both b and c.

5. Why are the best responders not necessarily the best people to target in a mailing?

6. After a mailing to 100,000 customers, six of them telephoned to say that they did not like the text of the mailing. On what basis would you repeat the same mailing, despite these phone calls?

7. If you ask 400,000 people to complete a profile and only 2 percent respond by doing so, on what basis could you say that the exercise was worthwhile?

8. Could you use a Web quiz in your business? Who would take the quiz? What would be in it for them?

CHAPTER 15

A FAREWELL TO THE READER

Thank you for making this journey with me. We have had some laughs, and, I hope, we have learned something that will be useful for our jobs. What have we learned?

Database Marketing Works

After two decades, database marketing is alive and well. It is being used by thousands of companies throughout America, and to a certain extent throughout the developed world. It is highly accountable and can be measured. You can prove that what you are doing is working, making customers happy and making profits for your company. Here are some of the lessons that have emerged from 14 chapters of theory and 40 case studies:

- *Database marketing is not the same thing as CRM.* You can call it CRM, but that is rather like calling a terrorist a freedom fighter. CRM is aimed at making the right offer to the right person at the right time, based on massive amounts of data accumulated in a warehouse. No warehouse can hold the amount of data on the behavior of an individual that is needed if CRM is to deliver profits. The warehouse would need to know what the customer is thinking, what his values are, what he did yesterday, and what he wants to do right now. CRM is a nice idea that does not work in practice and wastes millions of dollars on an impossible quest. What does work is database marketing, which is essentially aimed at divining the behavior of customer segments and designing marketing programs for those segments. This process is economically possible and can be highly successful.

- *Database marketing is incremental.* Database marketing is a channel for exchanging information with customers. For database marketing to work, there have to be other channels that are delivering the basic sales: mass marketing, retail stores, catalogs, interactive Web sites, salespeople, distributors, agents, outbound telemarketing, or direct mail. What database marketing does is make incremental improvements in customer retention rates, response rates, referrals, cross sales, frequency of sales, and average order sizes. Database marketing builds relationships with customers that bind them to your company and your brand. Done right, it makes customers happy and gives them a feeling of identification with you, your products, your company, and your employees. It helps prevent defections.

- *The Internet has enabled database marketing to deliver on its promises.* The idea was always to use the database to communicate with customers and make them happy. But direct-mail and telephone communications are so expensive, in relation to the good that they do, that they can be used only sparingly. Email to customers is almost free. It is instant. It can be highly personalized, delivering up-to-the-minute information. It is the best thing to hit database marketing in the last 20 years.

- *The Web is not a selling medium; it is an ordering medium.* An entire industry based on Web advertising and sales was created, wasted hundreds of billions of dollars, and then died within 5 years. What did we learn from this? The Web is a passive medium, not an active one like TV, radio, telemarketing, direct mail, or retail stores. It is not a very powerful advertising medium. People will buy products and services over the Web, but they first have to be stimulated by something else: catalogs, direct mail, or mass marketing. As an ordering medium, the Web can be superb. It cuts the cost of a customer contact by more than $3. It can be tied to a database so that each customer sees something different, customized for her, when she clicks on a site. But she is unlikely to click on that site without some outside stimulus.

- *People like communications.* The heart of database marketing is not the database but the customized and personalized communications with customers that are created using the database. Communications work. They keep customers from defecting. They make people happy (and angry as well). They help to sell goods and to increase loyalty, referrals, cross sales, order frequency, and order size. Without an active and creative communications program, the database is worthless.

- *Everything in database marketing can and should be measured.* Whenever you design a new strategy, program, or communication, you must set aside a control group that *does not get* the Gold card, communication, newsletter, offer, discount, premium, or special service that is being extended to your test group. This is the only way for you to know and prove to management that your expenditures for database marketing are producing a positive return on investment. If you are not constantly testing new ideas, setting aside control groups, and measuring, you are not doing database marketing.

- *Lifetime value is the key measurement technique for database marketing.* You must learn how to compute customer lifetime value and use it in evaluating and designing your marketing strategy. LTV is a forward-looking concept that includes spending rate, discount rate, retention rate, referral rate, product costs, and marketing expenditures. It is the only way to know how much you should spend on acquisition and retention. It is an essential step to use in getting your marketing budget approved each year.

- *Database marketing is not about discounts.* Discounts are used in mass marketing campaigns, and they work. They don't work in database marketing. Why not? Because the basic idea in database marketing is to build a close personal relationship with each customer that is based on quality, service, friendship, loyalty, and communications. You would not give a neighbor $5 for helping you carry a chest of drawers up your stairs. It would be an insult. Instead, you offer your neighbor a cup of coffee or a beer and 15 minutes of chat around the kitchen table. That is the kind of relationship that database marketing creates. Discounts send the wrong message: We are cheap guys whose basic product is overpriced. We want to buy your loyalty. We don't care about you. We care about your money.

- *Customers should not all be treated alike.* Some of your customers are Gold. They deliver huge amounts of sales and profits. Many customers of many companies are actually unprofitable. Why should you work to retain the loyalty and sales of an unprofitable customer? What should you do? First, create customer segments and learn who your Gold customers are. Create special programs and services just for them in order to retain them. Study the segment just below Gold. Create programs that will get them to move up. Study your bottom segment—the worthless people. Figure out how to either reprice the services you are giving them so that they are profitable or get rid of them altogether. If you treat all customers alike, your service budget will be stretched so thin that you will be unable to use it to modify customer behavior.

- *Most successful database marketers outsource the construction of their database.* Why? Because it is cheaper and faster, and the product is better. To take a ridiculous example, it would be possible to go to auto parts suppliers and assemble a company truck from spare parts. Since no one in your company has ever done this before, it would take a year or more and be quite expensive, and the result certainly would not perform as well as a production model bought from GM, Ford, or Chrysler. But it would have the advantage that, as a result, your staff would now know how to build a truck from spare parts. The problem with this approach is that most companies are not in the truck manufacturing business. They are in some other line of work. Building a truck would be a costly diversion from their core business. And, during that year, the company could not use the truck to make deliveries.

  The same principle applies to building a marketing database from spare parts. No one in most companies (including the IT department) has done this before. It takes a long time, since there is a learning curve associated with each process. It takes time to study the available software packages (there are scores of them) and to install and learn to use the ones chosen. When the database is finished, it will not work as well as one that was built by an experienced service bureau that has already built dozens of them and has a trained technical staff whose only job is building and maintaining marketing databases. Finally, you cannot get any benefit from the home-grown database during the year or more that is needed to build it. You get the benefit only after it is up and running.

Once your database is up and running, it can be migrated to in-house maintenance at any time. In fact, however, if the database is built correctly, your marketers will be so happy with the results of using it that they will forget about wanting to maintain it. When you are driving a new BMW down the interstate at 75 mph, who wants to stop and become a garage mechanic?

- *Caller ID and cookies have become essential database marketing tools.* Caller ID is used by customer service reps to recognize customers, call them by name, and see their history with the company on the screen before they even answer the phone. This type of recognition builds relationships and loyalty. Cookies are used the same way on the Web. Web sites are configured differently for each repeat visitor, based on that visitor's expressed preferences on the previous visit. Cookies build relationships and loyalty.

- *Many customers will gladly give you their profiles over the Web.* What is a nuisance on paper or over the phone becomes a fun exercise over the Web. The marketer can use the profiles to learn more about customers and provide them with what they want (as opposed to what the company wants to sell them). Profiles open up an entirely new and productive channel for customer contact.

- *Marketing databases today are stored in a relational format* on a server accessed by marketers over the Web. Many different marketers can access the company customer database simultaneously, using IDs and passwords so that they see only the data that they need. Because of the Web, the database can be used by remote offices, salespeople on the road, and even overseas branches of the company. Another advantage of the Web as an access tool for marketers is that all the marketer needs to have is a browser. She does not need to have any database software on her PC.

- *Becoming customer-centric is seldom an achievable goal.* For the last decade, marketers have talked about shifting their company from being product- and brand-centric to being customer-centric. "Don't sell products. Find out what customers want to buy and sell them that." This is a wonderful idea, but few companies are doing it. If we were really to become customer-centric, we would segment our customers and create a manager for each segment. We would give these managers greater authority than that given to brand or product managers. In most cases, this does not work. The compensation system within a company is very difficult to arrange. If the Silver Segment manager does a good job, many of his customers will become Gold, and he will lose them. How do you give him an incentive to do that? Before you mouth platitudes about becoming customer-centric, think it through. See if you can make it work on paper. It won't. Forget it, and do a good job of database marketing within your current organization.

Summary

Database marketing is a method of getting incremental increases in retention and sales when sales are conducted primarily through other channels, but it is also much more than that. It is a way of making people happy. People like to buy products and services. They like to establish personal relationships with their suppliers. They like to be recognized, thanked, and chatted with. They like to receive wanted communications. You can do all this with database marketing using the Web, phone, and direct mail. You cannot do these things with mass marketing. Merchants used to recognize customers and communicate directly with them in small retail stores, but most of the companies using database marketing today are not proprietors of small retail stores. What successful database marketing does is to bring back the close personal relationships that used to exist between customers and local stores and that have been lost as our country and economy have grown. In doing database marketing well today, you are making the world a happier, more satisfying, and better place to live. And you will be making an honest living doing it.

HOW TO KEEP UP WITH DATABASE MARKETING

I n the months ahead, you will need to stay abreast of the new developments in our industry. Here are some ways of doing this.

Attend Conferences

National Center for Database Marketing, two conferences per year, www.the-dma.org.
Direct Marketing to Business, www.dbmshow.com.
Other DMA conferences: Net marketing, brand, and others, www.the-dma.org.

Read Magazines

DM News, www.dmnews.com.
Target Marketing, www2.targetonline.com.
Direct magazine, www.primediabusiness.com.
iMarketing magazine, www.imarketingnews.com.

Visit Web Sites

www.dbmarketing.com

www.computerstrategy.com
www.1to1.com
www.gartner.com

Read Books

The Complete Database Marketer, by Arthur Middleton Hughes (New York: McGraw-Hill, 1996).
Strategic Database Marketing, by Arthur Middleton Hughes (New York: McGraw-Hill, 2000).
The Loyalty Effect, by Frederick Reichheld (Boston: Harvard Business Press, 2001).
Loyalty Marketing, the Second Act, by Brian Woolf (Greenville, SC: Teal Books, 2002).
Customer Specific Marketing, by Brian Woolf (Greenville, SC: Teal Books, 1998).
Data Mining Cookbook, by Olivia Rud (New York: Wiley, 2000).

Exchange Information

I am going to make a request of you as a reader. If you are using any of the techniques in this book in your work and you have a wonderful example of success, could you contact me at dbmarkets@aol.com and let me know about it? I would like to publish your success in an article and perhaps a later book. When we share our experiences in this way, database marketing becomes more and more successful as a technique, and I get to write more books.

Get Help

Many companies will help you to build your database or send emails. One that I can highly recommend that you consult is www.computer-strategy.com.

ANSWERS TO QUIZZES

Chapter 1

1. (c) Treating all customers alike
2. (a) Customer communications
3. (e) 0.4 percent
4. (d) Marketing strategy
5. (a) Those customers in priority A and priority B
6. (b) The resources available to devote to the best customers will be too small.
7. (d) On the computer holding the database
8. (c) It made innovative use of the Web.
9. (d) Those who do not get any of the test communications
10. (e) Not a good way to recruit new customers who last

Chapter 2

1. (e) Increased employee loyalty is essential to increased customer retention.
2. (c) The marketing costs
3. (a) CRM software is not available today.
4. This paragraph cannot be converted into English. It is incomprehensible.

5. (*d*) 50 percent
6. (*b*) Build a data warehouse
7. (*b*) Net present value
8. (*c*) The basic product sales are produced by other channels.
9. (*d*) Because the compensation system cannot be changed
10. (*c*) Mass marketing

Chapter 3

1. (*b*) The public feared that the government was going to go after the Web next.
2. (*c*) The Web is a passive medium.
3. (*b*) Because of the economics of the supermarket industry
4. (*a*) There are none. It is a wonderful idea.
5. (*b*) The e-Citi customers could not use Citibank branches.
6. (*c*) Many competitors copied its ideas and stole its customers.
7. (*c*) Keep customer communications to a minimum.
8. (*b*) Don't try to compete with telephone customer service.
9. (*e*) Customer service
10. (*e*) Consumer product sales

Chapter 4

1. $D = (1 + i * \text{rf})^n = (1 + 0.06 * 1.4)^2 = 1.175$
2. $\$45,447,221/1.175 = \$38,678,486$
3.

	Year 1	Year 2	Year 3
Customers	312,886	219,445	188,994
Retention rate			

4. (*a*) Make it go up
5. (*d*) Both *a* and *b*
6. (*b*) Movement in the lifetime value in future years

7. (d) The one with the highest value to the company, which is determined by multiplying the probability of purchase and the profitability if purchased
8. (a) Revise your marketing program.
9. (a) Work to retain segment B and increase the LTV of segment A.

Chapter 5

1.

	Year 1	Year 2	Year 3
Customers	400,000	248,000	173,600
Retention rate	62%	70%	74%
Spending rate	$320	$340	$350
Revenue	$128,000,000	$84,320,000	$60,760,000
Cost rate	65%	63%	62%
Costs	$ 83,200,000	$53,121,600	$37,671,200
Acquisition cost ($140)	$ 56,000,000		
Total costs	$139,200,000	$53,121,600	$37,671,200
Profit	−$11,200,000	$31,198,400	$23,088,800
Discount rate	1	1.22	1.35
NPV of profit	−$11,200,000	$25,572,459	$17,102,815
Cumulative NPV of profit	−$11,200,000	$14,372,459	$31,475,274
Lifetime value	−$28	$35.93	$78.69

2.

	Year 1	Year 2	Year 3
Customers	400,000	264,000	195,360
Retention rate	66%	74%	78%
Spending rate	$332	$352	$362
Revenue	$132,800,000	$92,928,000	$70,720,320
Cost percent	65%	63%	62%
Costs	$ 86,320,000	$58,544,640	$43,846,598
Acquisition cost ($140)	$ 56,000,000		
Marketing cost ($6)	$ 2,400,000	$ 1,584,000	$ 1,172,160
Total costs	$144,720,000	$60,128,640	$45,018,758
Profit	−$11,920,000	$32,799,360	$25,701,562
Discount rate	1	1.22	1.35
NPV of profit	−$11,920,000	$26,884,721	$19,038,194
Cumulative NPV of profit	−$11,920,000	$14,964,721	$34,002,915
Lifetime value	−$30	$37.41	$85.01

3.

	Year 1	Year 2	Year 3
Old LTV	−$28.00	$35.93	$78.69
New LTV	−$29.80	$37.41	$85.01
Difference	−$1.80	$1.48	$6.32
400,000 customers	−$720,000	$592,262	$2,527,641

4.

Mailing	100,000	$0.05	$5,000.00
Response	1,200	1.20%	
Response revenue		$78.69	$94,425.82
Less mailing		$5,000	$89,425.82
Per name			$0.89
Offer price			$0.45
Sales	4	$1.79	
Commission		25%	$1.34

5. Answers will vary. You have to do the work.
6. Any five of the six following answers are correct:
   a. Low margin.
   b. Coupon redemption is very slow.
   c. To make a profit, you need repeat sales (low margin). You can't redeem a coupon for every sale, or you would go broke. Therefore, you never find out about the subsequent sales.
   d. There is no way to figure out if you are succeeding.
   e. Discounts don't produce loyalty.
   f. Manufacturers won't buy the names.
7. Answers will vary.
8. Answers will vary.
9. Answers will vary.
10. Answers will vary.

Chapter 6

1. (*c*) Cooperation between IT and Marketing
2.

Mailed	Cost	Total
100,000	$0.05	$5000.00
Response	**Response rate**	**Cost for each**
1160	1.16%	$4.31

3. (*b*) Mutual fund offer. It is easier to get people to do more of what they are doing than it is to get them to do something else.
4. (*d*) Emails are so inexpensive you can concentrate on maximizing profits.
5. Answers will vary.
6.

	Cost each	Contacts	Cost	Order rate	Cost per sale	Sales	ROI
Telemarketing	$5.00	100	$500.00	8	$62.50	$1600	25.6%
Email	$0.06	100	$6.00	3	$2.00	$600	300%

7. Name, email name, permission to use the email name, zip code. You should also try to get at least one other fact, such as customer preference for contact, income, age, or family composition.
8. (*d*) The control group
9. Sales = $150,000; ROI = 8.32; cost = $18,750
10. (*d*) The subject line

Chapter 7

1. (*a*) People are curious about the offering.
2. (*a*) A high-tech flash page
3.

	Rate	Number	Dollars
Mails	$0.11	100,000	$11,000
Click-through	0.67%	670	$16.42
Registrations	48%	322	$34.20

4. (*b*) You can accurately predict response rates.
5. (*e*) None of the above; it proved all of them.
6. (*e*) To reduce churn
7. (*e*) Video clips
8. (*b*) Fax
9. (*c*) Email
10. (*a*) Phone

Chapter 8

1. (*d*) Segments cost less but produce similar results.
2. (*b*) Preferences
3. (*b*) Credit card matching
4. (*a*) Web customer response
5. (*c*) Ignoring them
6. (*b*) Cross shopping was reduced by 35 percent (it increased by 35 percent).
7.

	Number promoted	Sales rate	Lift	Lift in sales
Teens	100,000	8.80%	1.80%	1,800
Control	20,000	7.00%		
20s and 30s	100,000	6.60%	0.80%	800
Control	20,000	5.80%		
40s and 50s	90,000	7.20%	1.20%	1,080
Control	20,000	6.00%		
Seniors	60,000	5.10%	0.80%	480
Control	20,000	4.30%		
Total	430,000			4,160

8. (*e*) 6
9. (*a*) Something that you can relate to and design programs for
10. (*d*) After each promotion.

Chapter 9

1. (*b*) Existing customers were modeled.
2. (*c*) Prizm cluster codes
3. (*c*) SIC analysis
4. (*e*) 50 percent
5. (*a*) Vendors do the selling for their customers.
6. (*d*) A rate calculated using the agent's previous sales
7. (*a*) The Web
8. (*e*) All of the above
9. (*a*) The supplier
10. (*c*) Business customers usually pay long after shipment.

Chapter 10

1. (*b*) Clean up 80 percent of your files first.
2. (*d*) Are not in priority C
3. (*c*) Birthday cards
4. (*e*) Geographic region
5. (*a*) The cross-sell model
6. (*e*) Brand managers fought over the more profitable customers.
7. (*b*) Customers were ranked by RFM with a maximum score of 125.
8. (*a*) The bank added 2000 new total customers each month.
9. (*e*) All of the above
10. (*a*) Reports produced in a few weeks

Chapter 11

1. (*b*) Customers like to participate in the selling process.
2. (*e*) All of the above.
3. (*d*) Eliminate toll-free calls so that people must use the Web.
4. (*e*) None of the above; they are all rules for successful Web customer service.
5. (*a*) Vendor-managed inventory
6. (*b*) The parts are warehoused in customers' warehouses.
7. (*e*) More CSRs are needed.
8.

	Year 1	Year 2	Year 3
Customers	200,000	90,000	49,500
Retention rate	45%	55%	65%
Basket size	$60	$65	$70
Visits per year	2.10	2.50	2.80
Revenue	$25,200,000	$14,625,000	$9,702,000
Cost percent	65%	62%	60%
Costs	$16,380,000	$9,067,500	$5,821,200
Acquisition cost ($46)	$ 9,200,000		
Total costs	$25,580,000	$9,067,500	$5,821,200
Profit	−$380,000	$5,557,500	$3,880,800
Discount rate	1	1.25	1.4
NPV of profit	−$380,000	$4,446,000	$2,772,000
Cumulative NPV of profit	−$380,000	$4,066,000	$6,838,000
Lifetime value	−$1.90	$20.33	$34.19

9.

	Year 1	Year 2	Year 3
Customers	200,000	98,000	57,820
Retention rate	49%	59%	69%
Basket size	$64	$69	$74
Visits per year	2.50	2.90	3.20
Revenue	$32,000,000	$19,609,800	$13,691,776
Cost rate	65%	62%	60%
Costs	$20,800,000	$12,158,076	$8,215,066
Acquisition cost ($46)	$ 9,200,000		
Retention cost ($8)	$ 1,600,000	$ 784,000	$ 462,560
Total costs	$31,600,000	$12,942,076	$8,677,626
Profit	$400,000	$6,667,724	$5,014,150
Discount rate	1	1.25	1.4
NPV of profit	$400,000	$5,334,179	$3,581,536
Cumulative NPV of profit	$400,000	$5,734,179	$9,315,715
Lifetime value	$2.00	$28.67	$46.58

10.

	Year 1	Year 2	Year 3
Old LTV	-$1.90	$20.33	$34.19
New LTV	$2.00	$28.67	$46.58
Difference	$3.90	$8.34	$12.39
200,000 customers	$780,000	$1,668,179	$2,477,715

Chapter 12

1. (*a*) Personalized catalogs
2. (*a*) It provides no sales lift.
3. To reach high end customers; to reduce ordering costs; to open up another channel
4. They spent 33 percent more than regular customers.
5. Cross sales were up 100 percent.
6. They need to add:
   a. Customer profiles capturing emails and customer preferences and demographics. This reaches 20 percent on the first round and an additional 20 percent on each additional round.
   b. One-click ordering for all customers completing their profile, plus personalized emails and Web site opening pages.

    c. Email thank you for all orders, emails when the order is shipped, email asking people if the order was satisfactory.

    d. Personalized emails announcing the arrival of each catalog, with <u>click here</u> for items that it is assumed the customer is interested in.

    e. Collaborative filtering to make suggestions on next best product, leading to a cross-sale rate of 40 percent.

    f. Advanced search feature that permits customers to find products faster.

    g. Live shopper support for people who want to have a text chat with a customer service rep while they are on the site, or who want to call on another line to talk to a live agent.

7. It provided a window showing the address, phone number, and directions to the nearest Macy's store.

8. (*e*) None of the above; they were 80 percent higher.

9. (*e*) None of the above; catalog distribution increased by 20 percent per year.

10. (*b*) 26 percent

Chapter 13

1. (*c*) Deciding which prospects you should aim at acquiring

2. (*b*) Products purchased

3. (*b*) The company lacked high-technology products.

4. (*c*) Telemarketing was outsourced to a better bureau.

5. (*e*) None of the above; all these things were done.

6. Works: newspapers, mall location, luxury car sales, financial services

    Doesn't work: business-to-business, nonprofit, packaged goods, nonluxury cars

7. (*c*) The company has computed the LTV of customers or prospects.

8. (*b*) Customers like to have their views agreed with.

9. (*e*) Answers *b*, *c*, and *d*.

10. It:

    a. Performed regression and correlation analysis based on customer-supplied and Experian data on current BMW owners to identify unique independent variables.

    b. Developed score ranges for variables based on frequency distribution, standard deviation, and historic experience.

    c. Scored samples of prospects and compared results.

    d. Developed lifetime value tables and assigned a value to each customer and participant.

    e. Delivered personalized content and information to each responder, whether that responder was a previous customer or a prospect.

    f. Used variables to score prospects; these variables included purchase time frame, make of current vehicle, age, income-to-price ratio, year of current car, source of prospect lead, and debt-to-income ratio.

Chapter 14

1. Answers will vary.

2. Answers will vary.

3. (*b*) $547,559/1,264,571 = $0.43

4. (*d*) Both *b* and *c*.

5. Because they may be the least creditworthy

6. If the mailing was profitable, you should not have your marketing program derailed by six malcontents out of 100,000.

7. If the revenue from the information and sales to the 2 percent is profitable after deducting the cost of the profile, the response rate is unimportant.

8. Answers will vary.

INDEX

About the Author

Arthur M. Hughes is vice president for business development of CSC Advanced Database Solutions (www.cscads.com), which builds and maintains databases for major U.S. corporations. A pioneer in the use of databases to reach customers and impact their decision making, Hughes wrote the classic marketers' guidebooks Strategic Database Marketing and The Complete Database Marketer. He can be reached at ahughes@cscads.com